TONGA LIVELIHOODS IN RURAL ZIMBABWE

Based on extensive original fieldwork, this book examines the complex and diverse livelihoods of Zimbabwe's Tonga people as they have developed over time, including in the wake of the country's post-2000 political and economic crises.

Despite being endowed with natural resources, the northwest region of Zimbabwe inhabited by the Tonga people is one of the most marginalised and underdeveloped parts of the country, neglected by both colonial and postcolonial governments. The Tonga-speaking people are a minority ethnic group that settled on either side of the Zambezi River around 1,100 AD and remain deeply dependent on the river for their socio-economic livelihoods. This book reflects on the challenges faced by the Tonga people, from poor infrastructure, health and education facilities, to the issues caused by soil infertility and extremely low rainfall, which have been exacerbated by climate change. Many Tonga people were displaced by the construction of the Kariba Dam in the 1950s, and their access to the region's natural resources has been restricted by successive governments. Showcasing the research of Zimbabwean scholars in particular, this book not only reflects on the vulnerabilities faced by the Tonga, but it also looks beyond these, to the livelihood practices that are thriving despite these challenges, and the ways in which livelihoods intertwine with Tonga culture and society more broadly.

Overall, this book highlights the resilience of the Tonga people in the face of years of politico-economic crisis and will be an important contribution to research on livelihoods, ethnic minorities and rural development in Africa.

Kirk Helliker is a research professor in the Department of Sociology at Rhodes University in South Africa, where he heads the Unit of Zimbabwean Studies, which he founded. He published widely on Zimbabwean history, politics and society, and has supervised a significant number of PhD and MA students.

Joshua Matanzima is a PhD candidate in Anthropology, at La Trobe University, Australia. His research interests include anthropology of landscapes, human–wildlife conflicts, mining-induced displacements and borderland economics with special emphasis on the Zambezi Valley. He is co-editor of *Livelihoods of Ethnic Minorities in Rural Zimbabwe*.

ROUTLEDGE CONTEMPORARY AFRICA

The Failure of the International Criminal Court in Africa
Decolonising Global Justice
Everisto Benyera

African Identities and International Politics
Frank Aragbonfoh Abumere

Quality Assessment and Enhancement in Higher Education in Africa
Edited by Peter Neema-Abooki

Media Ownership in Africa in the Digital Age
Challenges, Continuity and Change
Edited by Winston Mano and Loubna El Mkaouar

Policing and the Rule of Law in Sub-Saharan Africa
Edited by Oluwagbenga Michael Akinlabi

Tonga Livelihoods in Rural Zimbabwe
Edited by Kirk Helliker and Joshua Matanzima

Women Writers of the *New* African Diaspora
Transnational Negotiations and Female Agency
Pauline Ada Uwakweh

For more information about this series, please visit: www.routledge.com/Routledge-Contemporary-Africa/book-series/RCAFR

TONGA LIVELIHOODS IN RURAL ZIMBABWE

Edited by Kirk Helliker and Joshua Matanzima

Routledge
Taylor & Francis Group
LONDON AND NEW YORK

First published 2023
by Routledge
4 Park Square, Milton Park, Abingdon, Oxon OX14 4RN

and by Routledge
605 Third Avenue, New York, NY 10158

Routledge is an imprint of the Taylor & Francis Group, an informa business

British Library Cataloguing-in-Publication Data
A catalogue record for this book is available from the British Library

ISBN: 978-1-032-24432-7 (hbk)
ISBN: 978-1-032-24435-8 (pbk)
ISBN: 978-1-003-27858-0 (ebk)

DOI: 10.4324/9781003278580

Typeset in Bembo
by Newgen Publishing UK

CONTENTS

CONTRIBUTORS

Codelia Govha Dhodho completed her PhD in History recently at Rhodes University (South Africa) and is currently a lecturer at Catholic University of Zimbabwe in Bulawayo, Zimbabwe, teaching History and Development Studies. Her research focuses on the social history of the Tonga of Binga District.

Vimbainashe Garaiza is a PhD student in Development Studies at Great Zimbabwe University. Her PhD topic is sustainable livelihoods and the role of small-scale fishing in Siabuwa in Binga, Zimbabwe. Her major research interests are sustainable livelihoods, fish farming, rural community development, cultural studies, ethnicity and identities.

Simbarashe Gukurume is a lecturer at Sol Plaatje University in South Africa working at the intersection of Sociology and Social Anthropology. His research interests include youth, informality, livelihoods and displacement, focusing on forms of agency, socialities and convivialities that emerge and are forged in times of protracted crises.

Ivan Marowa holds a PhD in African history from the University of Bayreuth, Germany. He is a senior lecturer in the Department of History Heritage and Knowledge Systems at the University of Zimbabwe. He has published on landscape and Zimbabwe's liberation struggle, human–wildlife conflict, rural livelihoods and collective memories.

Jennifer Muderedzi has a PhD and currently lives in Norway. Her career includes community and interprofessional-based education, as well as rehabilitation and psychosocial occupational therapy, in the United Kingdom and Zimbabwe. She is also a former academic at College of Health Sciences, University of Zimbabwe. She is a freelance researcher.

Teverayi Muguti is a PhD student in the History Department at Stellenbosch University in South Africa. His thesis is titled, "A History of Border Security Policy in Zimbabwe: The Case of the Zimbabwe-Zambia Border, c. 1963 to 2017". His research interests include African border studies and human–animal history in Zimbabwe.

Quegas Mutale has an MSc degree in Disaster Management and a BSc in Local Governance Studies. His research interests include human livelihoods, disaster resilience, indigenous knowledge systems and disaster risk reduction and management. He has seven years' experience in rural development and resides in Zimbabwe as an independent researcher.

Pottar Muzamba just completed his Master of Science degree in Disasters and Livelihoods Management with Women University in Africa, Zimbabwe. Previously he was a project officer with Binga Rural District Council for ten years (1996–2006); he presently works for Basilwizi Trust in Binga District as Project Officer-Education and Culture.

Taruvinga Muzingili holds a BSc Honours degree in Social Work. He works for Premier Service Medical Investment as a monitoring and evaluation specialist in Zimbabwe and is also an independent researcher. His research interests include child protection and environmental social work.

Christopher Mweembe is pursuing a PhD in International and Rural Development at the University of Reading in the United Kingdom. He is the Director of Basilwizi Trust, a community-based organisation facilitating sustainable development in the Zambezi Valley. His research interests include precarity, social protection and displacements.

Shumirai Nyota is a lecturer in African Languages at the Great Zimbabwe University and a research fellow at the University of South Africa. Her research interests include semantics, sociolinguistics, indigenous knowledge systems, endangered languages, marginalised languages and sustainable development.

Felix Tombindo is a social researcher with a background in Sociology and Anthropology. Currently, he is a doctoral candidate in African Studies and Anthropology at the University of Birmingham in the United Kingdom. He has ongoing research interests in livelihoods, agrarian studies, migration and development.

Lizzy Zinyemba is a social worker who is currently pursuing her doctoral studies, at the University of Zimbabwe, on the Tonga of Zimbabwe. She is also a lecturer at Bindura University of Science Education in Bindura, Zimbabwe.

ACKNOWLEDGEMENTS

This book is the sixth in an ongoing series of books published under the auspices of the Unit of Zimbabwean Studies, Department of Sociology at Rhodes University (South Africa). The first book published was titled *The Political Economy of Livelihoods in Contemporary Zimbabwe* (2018). Two others appeared in 2021: *Fast Track Land Occupations in Zimbabwe – In the Context of the Zvimurenga* and *Everyday Crisis-Living in Contemporary Zimbabwe*. The latest two volumes were published in 2022: *Capital Penetration and the Peasantry in Southern and Eastern Africa: Neoliberal Restructuring* and *Livelihoods of Ethnic Minorities in Rural Zimbabwe*.

The Unit was formed in 2015 and seeks to contribute to the development of emerging, early-career and mid-career Zimbabwean (and other) scholars.

Kirk Helliker
Research Professor
Head, Unit of Zimbabwean Studies

1

CONTEXTUALISING TONGA LIVES AND LIVELIHOODS IN ZIMBABWE

Joshua Matanzima and Kirk Helliker

Introduction

This book examines the lives and livelihoods of Tonga people in north-western Zimbabwe. Tonga people are found on both sides of the Zambezi River, to the north in Zambia and to the south in Zimbabwe. As mainly riverine people historically, they were forcefully displaced and resettled away from the Zambezi because of the construction of the Kariba Dam project in the late 1950s. Currently, Tonga people in Zimbabwe are found in the dry and arid districts of Binga, Nyaminyami and Gokwe. Binga has the largest concentration of Tonga-speaking people, with about 70% of the Tonga population residing there. As an ethnic minority in post-colonial Zimbabwe, the Tonga have experienced significant marginalisation which has only served to exacerbate the many livelihood challenges they once faced under colonialism subsequent to their forced removal from the Zambezi.

Broadly speaking, there is a dearth of scholarly literature on the Tonga of Zimbabwe, certainly in comparison to the prevailing literature on the Tonga in Zambia. This book contributes to countering this imbalance in the literature by highlighting the fieldwork-based case studies of the Tonga being undertaken currently by a number of Zimbabwean scholars. Indeed, this book represents the first collection of case studies about the Tonga in Zimbabwe specifically. The volume seeks to show the diversity and heterogeneity of Tonga livelihoods in both past and present Zimbabwe.

In this first chapter, we first offer a historical narrative of the Tonga and specifically the Tonga in Zimbabwe, starting with the pre-colonial times and ending with the post-colonial period. We then offer a thematic overview of the prevailing literature on the Tonga of Zimbabwe and demonstrate the importance of this volume to the scholarly literature, before closing off with an overview of each of the ensuing 11 chapters.

DOI: 10.4324/9781003278580-1

History of the Tonga

The Tonga comprise the third largest African language-ethnicity grouping in Zimbabwe (after the Shona and Ndebele), and yet they are little known to their fellow Zimbabweans, in part because they have always lived far from the main centres of population in the inhospitable north-western part of the country (Matthews 2007). The word "Tonga" derives from the Shona term *KuTonga* and was first used, it is believed, when they had their initial contact with the Shona in the Zambezi Valley at some unknown time. It refers to the Valley Tonga because they had no paramount Chief (Matanzima 2018). *KuTonga* means "to rule", with the Tonga regarded as people who rule themselves.

The identity and culture of the Tonga people in Zimbabwe is fluid, with this fluidity shaped by complex and diverse socio-political and economic circumstances over space and time. Over an extended period, Tonga people have experienced colonialism, involuntary resettlements, anti-colonial war and post-colonial restructuring, all of which have had implications for Tonga identity formation and experiences of belonging. Because of this, any notion of "being Tonga" should not be interpreted as entailing a static condition nor a homogeneous status, given the dynamic and variegated character of Tonga lives in colonial and post-colonial Zimbabwe.

Though the Tonga people are found generally in the north-western part of Zimbabwe, it is hence important to underscore that they have different histories and identities. Differences are at times contingent on spatial location, both past and present: some Tonga are located near towns, while others are in deep rural spaces; some are close to the Zambezi River, while others reside away from the River; and some live close to either Ndebele or Shona communities, while others do not. Currently, in the case of Binga District, where the Tonga ethnicity predominates, Ndebele people reside in some parts of it. In Nyaminyami and Gokwe districts, the Tonga people live together with Shona-speaking people of the Shangwe dialect. Furthermore, though they speak the *CiTonga* language, many Tonga also speak the language of their neighbours and intermarriages have occurred with the Shona and the Ndebele. The Tonga people of Gokwe and Nyaminyami speak *ChiShona* and those in some areas of Binga speak *IsiNdebele*.

Tonga interactions with these other ethnicities have historically and significantly configured their identity and language, with *CiTonga* incorporating Shona and Ndebele words in some instances. As well, historically and today, they have often been dominated by their Ndebele and Shona neighbours. As well, amongst white settlers and the Shona and Ndebele ethnicities, the Tonga became the subject of crude animalistic stereotypes including being depicted as "people with tails", "two-toed people", "witches" and "picturesque" as if part of nature. This fed into a long-term process of dehumanisation and marginalisation of the Tonga as backward and uncivilised, in both colonial and post-colonial times (Manyena 2013; Tischler 2013; Matanzima 2018; Matanzima 2022b; McGregor 2009).

Language, Origins and Pre-Colonial History

The origins of the Tonga remain unclear, though scholars generally believe that they originated from outside the Zambezi Valley (Colson 1960). Historically, they were a matrilineal society (Colson 1960; Scudder 1962; McGregor 2009), but recent research suggests that Tonga society is gradually transforming from matrilineal to patrilineal (Reynolds 2019). In this respect, some families no longer give the property of a deceased man to his sister's son as per matrilineal arrangements of the past; rather, sons and daughters of a deceased man now inherit their father's property. The Tonga's increased contact with patrilineal ethnicities (such as Ndebele and Shona) could be one of the factors bringing about this change.

The Tonga people of Zimbabwe were and are related to the Tonga people of Zambia, with the latter often referred to as the Gwembe Tonga (as the Zambezi Valley is sometimes called the Gwembe Valley). Before colonialism, the Zambezi Valley (on both sides of the Zambezi River) seems to have formed a single social-cultural unit. Although differences did exist, there were no major divergences between Tonga people on either side of the river. Hence, "historically it makes little sense to consider the ... Tonga of Zimbabwe apart from their Zambia brethren, with whom they have shared much precolonial experience" (Matthews 2007: 14). Based on these claims of historical similarity, it is not uncommon for Zimbabwean scholars of Tonga history to draw extensively upon the work by Colson and Scudder of the Tonga people of Zambia (Colson 1960, 1971; Scudder 1960, 1962, 2005; Scudder and Colson 2002).

Before colonialism, the Tonga people were a stateless society (Colson 1960; Matthews 2007). Certainly, there is no evidence of a large Tonga state or empire ever existing, although there are signs that certain Tonga groups adapted to the exigencies of trade and defence in the 19th century (and in some places earlier) by strengthening and secularising leadership positions (Matthews 2007). In this context, people were often referred to in a way consistent with their leaders' names. The concept and practice of chiefdoms in the Zambezi Valley was only introduced later by the colonialists. Particular geographical features (such as Zambezi River tributaries and local mountains) were used to demarcate chiefdoms. The Zambezi itself of course also became a boundary between two colonies, now Zimbabwe and Zambia.

In the mid-19th century, these "river-people" were part of the unstable, raided and tribute-paying frontier of two major state systems. To the north was the heartland of Kololo rule and subsequently the Lozi state, centred on the wide, open flood plains of the Zambezi. To the south was the Ndebele state centred on Bulawayo, which had replaced the authority of older Rozvi states in the early decades of the 19th century (McGregor 2009). These centralised polities often attacked each other along the Zambezi River, which made the Valley a conflict-ridden and turbulent region. The centralised polities also constantly raided the Tonga and seized their livestock, women and young men (Colson 1950), with the latter incorporated into the army regiments of these centralised societies. Because of this, some Tonga people became subsumed under the Ndebele or Lozi-Kololo at the time.

Under Colonialism before Kariba Dam

Before the creation of Lake Kariba in the 1950s, the Tonga's home was "the almost inaccessible middle Zambezi Valley between the rugged Batoka Gorge below Victoria Falls and the confluence of the Umniati (Sanyati) and Zambezi, some 200 miles downstream" (Matthews 2007: 13). The Zambezi Valley was bounded by the plateaus of Northern and Southern Rhodesia (i.e. Zambia and Zimbabwe, respectively). The Zambezi River was the boundary between the two territories, but it was a political boundary rather than a geographical or ecological barrier (Colson 1960) as people crossed it for different everyday socio-economic and religio-political reasons. As a result, even with the growing colonial influence, "[p]hysical conditions on either side of the river were much the same, and the people on either bank shared the same culture and were closely related" (Colson 1960: 5).

The Zambezi Valley was wider on the south bank than on the north bank. However, the Tonga population became more highly concentrated on the north bank when compared to the south bank (see below). The total population of the Zambezi Valley, as estimated for the mid-1950s, was 86,000, comprising about 55,000 on the northern side and 31,000 on the southern side (Reynolds 2019). The settlement and the distribution of homesteads of the Tonga in the Valley were heavily determined by the geography of the Valley itself. Elizabeth Colson thus gives an in-depth eyewitness description of the Tonga settlement in the Valley in the following words:

> The Zambezi plain was densely though unevenly populated. The villages lied within a mile or two of the river, for beyond this range the shortage of water throughout the dry season restricted settlement. Where the hills reached the Zambezi or where alluviums were restricted for some reason, a few small scattered villages may occupy a considerable stretch and constitute a neighbourhood. Where good soil is abundant, a series of large villages were found, frequently set so closely together that no discernible boundary separates one from another. This too, constituted a neighbourhood community which usually centres on the mouth of a tributary.
>
> *Colson 1960:* 7

Importantly, there were also Tonga people residing on the plateaus adjacent to the Zambezi Valley on both the south and north banks of the River. Those residing in these Uplands settled wherever fertile soil and permanent water was found, but these areas carried only sparse populations. Usually, upland Tonga communities were separated from one another by spurs of hills and some kilometres of bush (Colson 1960). Nevertheless, much of what we know today is about the Tonga people who lived along or close to the Zambezi River. These gained much attention in both Zambian and Zimbabwean scholarship because of their unique riverine lifestyle and their displacement from the Zambezi Valley in the late 1950s. When people hear about the Tonga, they assume that all Tonga lived in the Valley and were displaced, yet that is not the case for those long-established on the plateaus.

The Tonga people who resided along the River regarded themselves as a "River-People" (Saidi and Matanzima 2021; Matanzima and Saidi 2020; McGregor 2009). They identified themselves with the River as they had lived along it for likely over 500 years. The "River-People" marker distinguished them from the Tonga people of the Uplands or Hills, "though they [the former] often shared language and cultural traits with Tonga and Leya communities stretching up onto the plateaux both north and south" (McGregor 2009: 25).

The Zambezi Valley in which most Tonga people lived had a notoriously hot climate and the presence of tsetse fly which discouraged indigenous outsiders from migrating into the Valley (Matthews 2007). White colonial administrators also did not establish administration centres in the Valley because of its weather conditions, and reputation for malaria and sleeping sickness. Many white men who attempted settling in the Valley died. Even missionaries never established missions in the Valley on the south bank (Matanzima 2018). However, the Tonga River-People had become immune to the various diseases in the Valley because of their long-term habitation there.

This is not to suggest that the colonial conquest had no influence at all in the Valley, as certainly there was at least an indirect influence. For instance, the introduction of hut tax under colonialism significantly affected Tonga society, as many young men had to leave the Valley in search of employment in the railways and mines, including in and around Bulawayo (Colson 1960). Women remained in the Valley rearing children and farming along the River. Furthermore, the introduction of taxation reconfigured the distribution of the Tonga on both sides of the River. On the south bank (Southern Rhodesia), tax was higher than on the north bank (Northern Rhodesia), with the two banks under different colonial administrations. This pushed many Tonga people to move to and reside on the north bank (Ncube 1986), which in part explains the higher population density amongst the Tonga on the north bank. Furthermore, the north-bank Tonga owned cattle, while those on the south bank did not, as colonialists on the north bank introduced tsetse fly spraying in the Valley and those on the south bank did not (Scudder 1962).

The British colonialists also introduced political hierarchies in the Zambezi Valley and thereby disrupted a pronounced Tonga egalitarianism that was centuries old. Though the British did not settle and establish administration centres in the Valley, they did embed colonial administration into it by way of introducing chiefs and headmen (Colson 1960). These political structures were unfamiliar to Tonga people, and the latter passively resisted their existence and authority. In fact, despite the presence of colonial political structures, the Tonga continued as much as possible to pursue their own well-established egalitarian arrangements and practices.

At the same time, the colonial intrusion led to the solidification of fixed boundaries across and between villages as well as the introduction of new ways of dealing with criminal cases that were centred around the Chief's court.

In the lower Zambezi region, around what is now known as the Kariba gorge area, the Tonga lived close to the Shangwe and Korekore sub-Shona dialects spoken in the Sampakaruma and Nyamhunga chiefdoms, respectively. The Sampakaruma chiefdom incorporated both Shangwe and Tonga people, while Nyamhunga was a predominantly Korekore chiefdom. These Shona speakers were latecomers to the Zambezi Valley (Saidi and Matanzima 2021), with many of them, no doubt, coming originally as refugees from the Ndebele invasion in the 19th century, though more recent immigrants continued to add to their numbers. Above the Kariba gorge, these Shona immigrants were absorbed into Tonga populations. They thus spoke the *CiTonga* language and did not form separate villages or communities vis-à-vis local Tonga populations (Colson 1960).

Those Tonga who lived along the Zambezi River practised riverine cultivation, and they depended upon the river for its fertilising floods. The river landscape was shaped by the seasonality of rainfall in the Upper Zambezi catchment, such that annual floods brought floodwaters to the mid-Zambezi in the dry season thereby allowing for a second crop harvest (McGregor 2009). They also practised hunting and fishing, with fish forming part of their "everyday diet" (Scudder 1962). Their livelihood activities, mainly fishing and riverbed farming, were entangled in their "riverine" identity. They were often referred to as "riverbed farmers" or "the fishermen of the Zambezi" (Scudder 1960). However, the entangled identities were later disrupted by the Kariba Dam construction.

Kariba Dam and Resettlement Experiences

The construction of the Kariba Dam along the Zambezi River significantly impacted the lives and livelihoods of the Tonga who were directly and heavily reliant upon the Zambezi River landscape (Colson 1971; Cliggett 2005; Matanzima 2022a; Tischler 2014). The forced relocation meant that communities were separated, identities became reconfigured, religio-cultural activities were torn asunder and livelihoods ceased to be River-focused. Overall, Tonga people experienced significant precarity and uncertainty during the Kariba Dam construction, and in the years immediately thereafter.

Though only those residing in the immediate vicinity of the River were displaced, Tonga villagers on the plateau also experienced effects indirectly, either by becoming hosts of the displaced or by experiencing secondary displacements (Matanzima 2022c). For instance, in Nyaminyami District, the Negande chiefdom was pushed further inland to create space for the settlement of the Mola chiefdom, such that the Negande people left behind their homes and ancestral shrines. This history continues to shape relations between the two chieftaincies, with chief Negande reclaiming his former territory and ancestral lands 60 years after displacement.

Kariba dam was constructed between 1955 and 1959 at a gorge on the Zambezi River where it flows between Zimbabwe and Zambia. The dam extends over a length of about 300 kilometres and covers a surface area of 5,500 square kilometres at full supply level. The water storage volume of the Kariba reservoir translates into a mass of 180 billion metric tons (Reynolds 2019). The flooding of Kariba dam necessitated the displacement of the Tonga river-people residing along the Zambezi River. Before the construction of the dam, it was estimated that 29,000 Tonga people would have to be resettled once the land was flooded, but in fact 57,000 lost their homes and fields and were forced to move (Reynolds 2019; Scudder 1962).

The governments of Northern and Southern Rhodesia, then vassal states of the United Kingdom, assumed responsibility for the resettlement of people in their own domains. Approximately 34,000 were resettled from the Northern Rhodesian side of the River, and 23,000 from the Southern Rhodesia riverbank. In effect, some 66% and 74%, respectively, of the Valley Tonga lost their land (Reynolds 2019). The proportion resettled was large because much of the Tonga population was concentrated along the Zambezi River, clustering around the rich soils deposited in the flood plain and in the deltas of the Zambezi's tributaries (Colson 1960).

On the south bank, the resettled Tonga were affected more detrimentally by the move than those on the north bank. On the north bank, baseline studies for the move were conducted by Elizabeth Colson and Thayer Scudder, but these were considered an unnecessary expense on the south bank (Tischler 2013). Colson and Scudder were commissioned by the then Director of the Rhodes-Livingstone Institute (RLI), Henry Fosbrooke, to document the lives and livelihoods of the Tonga before they were displaced by Kariba (Colson 1971). McGregor (2009) reports that the move on the south bank was very hasty and under extreme compulsion, so that people were never given adequate time to prepare for the move. In quoting a World Commission on Dams Kariba case study report, Reynolds (2019: 6) highlights that: "It was reported that the people to be resettled were treated like animals or things rounded up and packed in lorries to be moved to the barren hills away from the water".

The immediate post-resettlement conditions of the displaced Tonga in Southern Rhodesia (later Rhodesia) were particularly pitiful. Most of the resettlement land was of poor quality and susceptible to erosion, and the amount of land available was too small for adequate distribution to the number of people dislocated (Reynolds 2019). The area was in agricultural region V and thus received little rainfall throughout the year. As a result, hunger, famine and poverty became the order of the day in the 1960s among the resettled Tonga. Additionally, the networks of kinship and friendship across the river that had existed before the flooding of the land were foreclosed. It became very difficult for the Tonga to visit and see relations across the River due to the presence of the Dam which they could not travel across using their traditional dugout canoes. With the building of the dam, the colonial border was further solidified, and most Tonga lacked (and still lack in many instances) the resources required to acquire formal travel documents. Furthermore, intangible losses were experienced because of the resettlement, including Tonga people's cultural identity (which had been inextricably connected to the Zambezi), as well as a focused sense of self and belonging. The move altered Tonga identity (i.e. being Tonga) beyond recognition, and for an extended period, to such an extent that reviving their identity in the post-resettlement dispensation required an almost total reconfiguration.

During Zimbabwe's Liberation War

The precariousness of the Tonga people subsequent to Kariba Dam displacement was worsened by Zimbabwe's liberation war which emerged in the late 1960s and intensified dramatically by the late 1970s. During the war, the Tonga lived in fear and their livelihood strategies such as farming were severely disrupted. The role and significance of the territorial border during the war also brought the marginal rural areas inhabited by the Tonga under the scrutiny and surveillance of the Rhodesian state and its security and intelligence apparatus (McGregor 2009).

The operations of both the guerrilla army (ZIPRA) and Rhodesian forces in the region destabilised Tonga lives. ZIPRA guerrillas moved through north-western Zimbabwe on route to and from Zambian bases, across the Zambezi River and Lake Kariba. They sought different forms of assistance from local Tonga people. Tonga villagers showed guerrillas the way to and from the Lake and helped them cross the Zambezi (McGregor 2009); as well, they provided them with food. Some young Tonga men, especially from Binga, were even trained and incorporated into the ZIPRA forces. To garner support from the Tonga, the guerrillas promised them that – after independence – their immense socio-economic problems (including those arising from Kariba Dam displacement) would be addressed (though this was never done). At times, during the war, some Tonga were labelled as "sell-outs" and those identified as sell-outs were harassed by guerrillas. In fact, stories about harassment and intimidation are part of the memories of the war in Tonga villages today. In Musampakaruma (in Nyaminyami District), for example, the first author was informed by elders of men who "disappeared" during the war because they were suspected of "sell-outs" (Matanzima 2017; Matanzima 2020).

Simultaneously, the Tonga experienced problems from Rhodesian security. As McGregor (2009: 147) argues: "To prevent such [guerrilla] crossing [and interactions between guerrillas and the Tonga], the Rhodesian government built a new road along the river and lakeshore, positioned army camps at key points along it, patrolled regularly, used floodlights and mined the riverbank from Victoria Falls to Binga". In Mola and Musampakaruma, the Rhodesian forces moved and confined the Tonga villagers in "Keeps" (so-called protected villages) to minimise their contact with guerrillas. This had implications for their livelihoods, as people stopped farming and had to survive on food handouts. However, food handouts were inadequate, and absolute hunger became common. Though people were allowed to farm in areas surrounding the "Keeps", the land was insufficient as a basis for providing sufficient food crops.

From Independence

Though the independence era is an extended period, our narrative is relatively short because the ensuing chapters tend to focus on independent Zimbabwe, particularly events over the past few years.

By the end of the colonial era, Tonga communities were in dire straits. For example, a nationwide nutritional survey, funded by donors in 1980, highlighted exceptional levels of distress in Binga District, with half of the district's children malnourished (*The Herald*, 12 October 1980). In many cases, hunger soon reduced Tonga villagers to dependency, reliant on charitable organisations (such as Save the Children – United Kingdom) for food. As a general tendency, Tonga's impoverishment and marginalisation caused by colonial government neglect, forced resettlement and war continued into the post-colonial era starting in 1980. The post-colonial government, just like its colonial predecessor, has largely ignored the plight of the Tonga (Mashingaidze 2013; Matanzima 2021; McGregor 2009).

The ZANU-PF post-colonial government, amounting it seems to a Shona ethnocracy (Ndlovu-Gatsheni 2012), has tended to exclude and dominate a range of ethnicities in relation to economic development and political inclusion. The fate of Ndebele people (particularly in Matabeleland) from the early 1980s is now well known and is most dramatically and ruthlessly visible with reference to the *Gukurahundi*. Tonga people have also suffered in a multiplicity of ways. After Dam construction, and until 1980, the colonial state never gave Tonga villagers adequate and necessary social, cultural and economic access to the Lake. In a similar way, since 1980, Shona, Ndebele and whites have controlled to varying degrees the fishing, tourism and wildlife industries surrounding the Lake, and Tonga villagers accessed menial work only because of a lack of suitable qualifications.

Some Tonga communities were incorporated into the Communal Areas Management Programme for Indigenous Resources (CAMPFIRE) programme initiated by the Zimbabwean government in the late 1980s. This natural management system was meant to benefit villagers by ensuring that they acquire financial and infrastructural benefits though income generated by safari hunting and tourism on their lands. Through specific CAMPFIRE projects in rural Zimbabwe, villagers used to obtain revenues for spurring local development like the construction of boreholes and roads. These benefits were provided because, in terms of CAMPFIRE, villagers were expected to be involved in the management and preservation of wildlife (Sibanda 2004; Dzingirai 2003; Murphree 1995). As Murphree (1995: 48–49) writes: "In keeping with community-based management practices, the programme proposed the passing of management benefits – in particular, game meat, wildlife-generated revenue and protection from animal crop raids – to the "producer community", i.e. those people who lived alongside wildlife". However, the benefits accruing to Tonga villagers were not meaningful over the long term in relation to local livelihood enhancement. Proceeds from CAMPFIRE are believed to have been embezzled at times by corrupt leaders of the Rural District Councils, with CAMPFIRE now existing on billboard displays but not in actual practice (Matanzima and Marowa 2022).

In the case of the fast-track land reform programme starting in 2000, Tonga villagers did not gain access to redistributed land (Marowa 2010). To worsen matters, many Tonga households were disadvantaged through fast track because of loss of employment, as they had one or several members working on white farms near the towns of Karoi and Kwekwe prior to the white farmer evictions (Matanzima 2022a). In June 2000, in the context of their long-term poverty and marginalisation, the Tonga in Binga District and elsewhere expressed their deep dissatisfaction with the ruling party by voting for the new opposition, the Movement for Democratic Change (MDC), in the national parliamentary elections. In fact, Binga District delivered the highest opposition vote for the MDC of any rural constituency in the country. As Helliker et al. (2021: 189) note:

> In this context, ZANU-PF tried to use former ZIPRA guerrillas as proxies against the MDC in this area, including by way of occupations. However, ZANU-PF's discourse on land (and race) did not fully resonate with the memories of local Tonga people, as those in Binga did not lose land to white farmers but to state conservation bodies. Hence, "they did not want to be resettled on former commercial farms but wanted access to state resources and reparations for unsettled grievances relating to the [Kariba] dam and displacement" (McGregor 2009:170) dating back many decades.

Tonga villagers' oppositional stance has been ongoing since then. For instance, the first author found that at, one time in 2017, Binga District (with more than 20 wards) had only one ZANU-PF ward councillor (Informal discussions with Tonga politicians, 2017).

Overall, demand for regime change among the Tonga "grew dramatically as the state failed to deliver on promises of material transformation and as anger deepened over politicians prepared to enrich themselves through the poverty of others" (McGregor 2009: 154). Poverty amongst the Tonga continues to be widespread (Mashingaidze 2013, 2020). In a piece titled "*Letting Them Starve*", Dhodho (2022) discusses the experiences of the Tonga during the post-2000 food crises and how their support for the opposition has translated into ruling party withdrawal of food aid. In response to hunger, some Tonga in Binga capitalise on their proximity to the border to cross it illegally into Zambia in desperate searches for food and to carry out illegal activities, such as smuggling, for survival purposes (McGregor 2008).

Social differentiation within Tonga communities does exist though. A limited number of Tonga people (both living in and out of the Zambezi Valley) now have improved lives due to migration and the attainment of education, with migrants, the educated and local politicians using their exposure, access and connections to the outside world to enhance their livelihoods. Some presently own cattle and goats; others run local stores and grinding mills; and some are involved in the fisheries industry (not simply as low-level gillnetters, but as *kapenta* rig owners).

However, these are the exception. As well, as indicated earlier, spatial differentiation is present in part because of the legacy of colonially constructed chieftainships. In Nyaminyami District, Chiefs Mola and Musampakaruma are pursuing a politics of the waterscape in which they question the government's granting to Chief Nyamhunga the right to engage in spiritual appeasement in Lake Kariba, and as they are left out of this arrangement despite being, from their perspective, the "rightful" owners of the Lake (Matanzima 2018; Matanzima 2022a; Tombindo 2016). At the same time, Tonga traditional leaders (and politicians) are also lobbying the state and local Lake Kariba authorities to give Tonga people collectively "adequate" access to Lake Kariba for cultural and livelihood purposes.

Identifying Knowledge Gaps in Tonga Lives

In surveying the literature on the Tonga historically, there are a number of important, path-breaking fieldwork-based studies by Thayer Scudder and Elizabeth Colson about the Tonga people of Zambia exclusively, concentrating on both their pre- and post-resettlement situation (Colson 1960, 1971, 1997; Colson and Scudder 1988; Scudder 1960, 1962, 2009). As anthropologists, Scudder and Colson founded the Gwembe Tonga Research Project (GTRP) in the 1950s, which has been tracing the longitudinal impacts of the Kariba Dam construction among those Tonga displaced on the north bank (Zambia) for over 60 years (Scudder and Colson 2002; Cliggett 2002). From the research of the GTRP, the many negative socio-economic consequences for the Tonga of the involuntary displacement have been thoroughly shown. These include the breakdown of kinship ties that once extended beyond the river and women's pronounced loss of land tenure (Colson 1971; Cliggett 2003, 2005; Scudder 2005).

The GTRP was later joined by other scholars including Lisa Cliggett, Alison Harnish, Sam Clark and Joshua Matanzima (one of the editors of this volume). Matanzima has only carried out archival research in Zambia, though he has carried out extended ethnographic research among the Tonga people of north-western Zimbabwe. As a general tendency, and with the exception of Matanzima, these scholars have published widely on the Tonga in Zambia and not Zimbabwe (see Cliggett 2002, 2003; Clark et al. 1995; Harnish et al. 2019). For instance, Cliggett (2003) examines Tonga people's migration from their original post-Kariba Dam resettlement areas into other parts of Zambia, showing the drivers for migration as well as the importance of migrants in terms of contributing to local economies. Meanwhile, Clark et al. (1995) underscore the nexus of demography and resettlement in the Tonga case, focusing on morbidity and mortality. There are many reports that, after forced resettlement, there was increased morbidity and mortality among the displaced due to psychological, socio-cultural and physiological stresses (Scudder 2005).

Unfortunately, there is no equivalence of such a detailed longitudinal archive for the Tonga people of Zimbabwe. Indeed, many scholars who have studied the history of the Tonga in Zimbabwe have partly depended on the GTRP archive, given that life for the Tonga on either side of the Zambezi was for the most part similar historically, as discussed later. Major themes identified and developed by scholars focusing on the Zambian Tonga (such as morbidity, migration and beer brewing) simply have not been studied for the Tonga on the Zimbabwe side. Currently, there are two edited volumes that focus on the Tonga in both Zimbabwe and Zambia. However, these volumes have very few contributions about the Tonga of Zimbabwe. The edited volume entitled, *The Tonga-Speaking Peoples of Zambia and Zimbabwe*, has 16 chapters and only 3 focus on the Tonga of Zimbabwe (Lancaster and Vickery 2007). The themes covered by these three chapters are the history of settlement in the Zambezi Valley (Matthews 2007), puberty and adolescents (Reynolds 2007) and marginalisation (Langely 2007). The other edited volume is by Cliggett and Bond (2013) and is entitled, *Tonga Timeline*, and it has 12 chapters, of which only two focus on Zimbabwe. The themes in these two chapters are ethnic identity, agency and development (Manyena 2013) and cultural artefacts and scared practitioners (Mukova and Chikovore 2013). These two edited volumes in large part reflect the relative lack of literature on the Tonga in Zimbabwe, compared to the Tonga in Zambia. From the 1950s to the 1990s, little research was published regarding the Tonga people of Zimbabwe (see, for example, Jarosz 1992; Weinrich 1977).

It was only in the 21st century that local scholars became interested in documenting the lived experiences of the Tonga people in the pre- and post-displacement eras. For example, Ncube (2004) traces the history of the Tonga people of Zimbabwe throughout time, from the pre-colonial to post-colonial periods. Ncube's work is a general social, economic and political history which, however, overlooks important lines of differentiation amongst the Tonga, including in terms of chieftaincies. A burgeoning literature now unearths and analyses the social, economic and political effects of the Kariba Dam construction and ensuing relocation on the Tonga people on the south side of the Zambezi (Mashingaidze 2013, 2020; Matanzima 2022a; Matanzima and Saidi 2020; Saidi and Matanzima 2021), including in relation to livelihoods. Central to the effects have been processes undercutting Tonga livelihoods, notably the overall dwindling of access to well-established riverine livelihoods (such as fishing, hunting and flood-fed agriculture) due to the flooding of the Kariba Lake and the forced resettlement.

Reporting in the 2000s, Langely (2007: 263) wrote that "although the resettlement of the Tonga occurred more than forty years ago, policies associated with the Kariba Dam project still impact the daily lives of those living in the region today". In this regard, the existing literature demonstrates a number of key points about the post-resettlement lives of the displaced Tonga. Firstly, from the time they were first settled in their new emplacements, the Tonga had limited access to the fisheries and water resources of the Lake. They depended upon gillnet fishing in the few fishing camps reserved for them. Secondly, they were not able to hunt wild animals, unlike their earlier conditions of existence in the Zambezi Valley. When the Dam was constructed, the surrounding areas endowed with wildlife became the state's protected areas. Tonga communities in these areas had virtually survived on hunting at times (Jeke 2014; Matanzima and Marowa 2022). Due to the growing conservationist interests along the Lake's littoral, though, no hunting by the Tonga was permitted (Hughes 2010; Matanzima 2022a). Thirdly, the resettlement areas had poor agricultural potential (Langely 2007; Mashingaidze 2020). For instance, Tombindo (2018) reports the extreme vulnerability of Tonga riverbed farmers in Negande Chiefdom of Nyaminyami District. Fourthly, the area was marginalised from the urban centres in Zimbabwe, and it lacked basic infrastructural services like clinics and schools. Schools and clinics were only introduced in the 1980s in most of the Tonga communities (Matanzima 2022a). Even today and indeed throughout the post-colonial era, "many villages do not have electricity or irrigation, and the fisheries industry has not adequately benefitted the local people" (Reynolds 2019: 6).

Thematically, with reference to livelihoods, recent studies highlight key issues pertaining to Tonga livelihoods. One issue is the significance of climate change in the Zambezi Valley region of north-western Zimbabwe (Ndhlovu et al. 2017). However, this literature does not strictly speaking examine the intricacies of climate conditions in relation to Tonga livelihoods. For example, while climate change has been considered by scholars working in the fishing communities in the immediate vicinity of Kariba town (Muringai et al. 2019; Ndhlovu et al. 2017), the majority of fishers there are not Tonga.

A second crucial theme is that of growing human-wildlife conflicts in the Zambezi Valley (Dzingirai 1996; Jeke 2014; Mhlanga 2001; Langely 2007; Matanzima and Marowa 2022; McGregor 2005). Studies of this conflict report the negative livelihood impacts of wild animal's attacks on humans (including injuries and loss of life) and the destruction of property and crops amongst the resettled Tonga. In local Tonga villages, humans and livestock fall prey to lion, leopard and hyena predation. In the fishing camps where some people live, stories of people attacked by crocodiles and hippos are very common (Marowa et al. 2021; Muringai et al. 2020).

A third area of study is cross-border movement (McGregor 2003, 2008; Chipere-Ngazimbi 2020). The dam displacement also displaced social capital as Tonga villagers on the south bank became far removed from relatives resettled away from the Zambezi on the north bank. Social support systems and barter trade that existed before the dam construction no longer existed, and Tonga people in Zimbabwe over an extended period have struggled to maintain social connections with their Zambian counterparts (Cliggett 2005). Often without travel documents, many resort to border jumping along the Lake when visiting their northern kin. While the Tonga in Binga have been given border passes to visit their relatives in Zambia, that is not the case in Nyaminyami District where the Lake is much wider.

Related to this is a fourth prominent theme in the literature: the post-2000 crisis in Zimbabwe. Lake Kariba and the Zambezi border achieved a new prominence as the Zimbabwean economy declined and then plummeted after 2000, with many Tonga people turning to cross-border trading to offset the effects of the crisis. The burgeoning irregular activities on and across the Lake soon became normalised to the point of being considered "illegal yet licit": These practices were "justified in terms of the economics survival and invocation of Tonga traditions of crossing the river and entitlement to the Lake as river people who had borne the costs of its creation" (McGregor 2009: 176). This theme thus considers the lives and livelihoods of Tonga people in the context of the multi-layered social, economic and political crisis bedevilling Zimbabwe and Zimbabweans over an extended period. Matanzima and Saidi (2022) for instance examine the impact of the cash crisis on the religious practices of the Tonga people of Sinakatenge in Binga District.

Finally, questions around Tonga language, identity and belonging are increasingly central to the Zimbabwean literature on the Tonga, with important literature now existing on the socio-cultural lives of the Tonga people (Manyena 2013; Matanzima 2018; Matanzima and Saidi 2020, 2022; Mumpande and Barnes 2020; Nyota 2015). Both failures and successes in the revival of Tonga cultural practices have been indicated in the literature, including the recognition and introduction of the *CiTonga* language in local primary and secondary schools in 2011 (Manyena 2013; Mumpande and Barnes 2020). Other scholars have mainly focused on Tonga identity by showing the strategies utilised by the Tonga to reclaim their diminishing identity in post-colonial Zimbabwe (Manyena 2013). These strategies include the formation of civil society organisations like Basilwizi Trust and Tonga Language and Cultural Association (TOLACO) which have been advocating for the recognition of Tonga language and culture within broader processes of socio-economic development. This demonstrates the possible linkages between projects of identity-belonging and livelihood projects (Helliker et al. 2022). There have been calls by Tonga people for increased access to resources in the Zambezi Valley so that they can overcome their impoverished lives (McGregor 2008, 2009). Indeed, the politics of landscape and livelihoods intensified in the 1990s and 2000s among the Tonga, who continue to claim entitlement to the Zambezi River as well as Lake Kariba (as they bore the cost of its creation) (Hughes 2006).

All of the studies cited are of great significance in enhancing our understanding of Tonga livelihoods in Zimbabwe. At times, though, they tend to be quite sweeping in their claims about Tonga lives. In other words, these studies might obscure specificity as well as the variegated lives and livelihoods amongst the Tonga, which this volume seeks to bring to the fore. In this regard, it is important to reiterate that not all Tonga people were compelled to move to resettlement areas because of the Kariba Dam's construction in colonial Zimbabwe, though they might have accommodated some of those displaced. In addition, amongst those displaced, their post-resettlement lives have followed particular livelihood trajectories, involving differentiated access to livelihood resources and diverse livelihood outcomes. This volume demonstrates this by drawing upon original fieldwork for all the chapters. Combined, the chapters incorporate a unique range of research sites for purposes of providing nuanced and in-depth accounts of Tonga livelihoods. This includes nine chapters focusing on Binga District and one chapter each on the districts of Gokwe and Nyaminyami, and, for Binga itself, the chapters cover different wards and chiefdoms. As well, importantly, a significant number of the chapters offer a gender analysis or at least centre on the particular livelihood activities and challenges of Tonga women.

This is all pursued thematically by presenting the chapters under three sections: Part I (*Climate Change, Resource Access and Livelihoods*); Part II (*Health, Hunger and Livelihoods*); and Part III (*Water, Borders and Livelihoods*).

Volume Outline

Part I on *Climate Change, Resources Access and Livelihoods* has five chapters. In Chapter 2, Quegas Mutale and Taruvinga Muzingili examine the effects of present-day climate change on marginalised Tonga crop farming communities in Binga District. In Binga, Tonga villagers have been farming on flood plains (called *bbonzye*) along the Zambezi valley and its tributaries since antiquity. Based on fieldwork amongst Tonga farmers in Luunga ward in Binga, this chapter explores the contribution of the *bbonzye* system of farming to the reduction of vulnerability to climate change. Results indicate that the various practices and methods of the *bbonzye* system of agriculture not only underpin the livelihoods of these marginal Tonga farmers but also limit their vulnerability to climate change. Compared to the rainy season, *bbonzye* as a form of winter-farming gives the Luunga farmers relatively high crop yields, which enables food security at household level and facilitates the accumulation of household and productive assets. *Bbonzye* farming is relevant in the face of climate change as it is practised in the context of agro-biodiversity conservation, water resource management, soil health maintenance, thereby facilitating a level of climate change mitigation and adaptation. Nevertheless, the study reveals several challenges related to *bbonzye*, which include animal-human conflicts, shortage of land, lack of agricultural, technical and extension services and perpetual conflicts with law enforcement agents.

In Chapter 3, Pottar Muzamba highlights that the effects of climate change are far-reaching and do not affect all categories of people in the same way. Women are vulnerable in a disproportionate way to the vagaries of climate change and variability because of their intimate relationship with, and dependence upon, natural resources. This chapter analyses the gendered character of climate change with reference to the Tonga people in Binga District in Zimbabwe, by focusing in particular on the basket-weaving of Tonga women in Ward 7. This entails interrogating basketry as a source of livelihoods for women in the face of climate change, including any mitigation, coping and adaptation strategies adopted by women in trying to undercut the negative effects of climate change on basket-making. Of particular significance is the implication of climate change for the local availability of the *ilala* plant and reeds used for basket-production, with declining precipitation and rising temperatures in Binga making the growing of *ilala* plants near impossible, thereby causing their increasing scarcity.

Chapter 4 by Shumirai Nyota focuses on the lives and livelihoods of the Tonga of Mkoka (in Gokwe South) in the context of their displacement because of the Kariba dam's construction and their subsequent contact and interaction with Shona settlers. The Tonga of Mkoka have lived in extreme poverty from the time of displacement from their original home, namely, the Zambezi Valley, and they have been subjected to cultural marginalisation. Prior to the forced resettlement of Shona in the Tonga's area of displacement (Mkoka), the latter were able to pursue reasonably meaningful livelihoods. However, the arrival of the Shona soon undercut these livelihoods, as Shona villagers encroached upon and made use of Tonga land and the diverse range of natural assets in the area. In addition, while the Tonga were moved to Mkoka without any belongings, the Shona were able to bring moveable assets to Mkoka and subsequently received government agricultural support. Over time, this unevenness in resettlement practices led to the Tonga together with their children undertaking menial jobs for the Shona in return for food, as a poverty cycle set in amongst the Tonga. Post 1980, the Zimbabwean government has not reversed the decades-long marginalisation of the Tonga in Gokwe South, as the chapter demonstrates.

Christopher Mweembe, in Chapter 5, considers the changing livelihoods of the Tonga people in the Sikalenge ward in Binga District over the period circa 1950–2022. It looks at, firstly, the Tonga's livelihoods prior to their forced resettlement from the Zambezi River, and then, respectively, the period from post-displacement in Binga to independence in 1980 and the independence period until now. Similarities and differences across the various periods are evident, reflecting the dynamic character of Tonga livelihoods temporally. The study used focus group discussions, key informant interviews and observations to gather data from the Tonga villagers and key stakeholders. The study reveals that, prior to the forced resettlement, the Tonga's primary livelihoods entailed riverine, alluvial and upland farming, livestock rearing, hunting, fishing and manufacturing. However, due to the relocation under colonialism and, later, the character of the post-colonial Zimbabwean political economy, long-established livelihoods were disrupted because of new contexts of vulnerability marked by systemic (structural, legal and policy) disadvantages which served to marginalise the Tonga people of Sikalenge ward. Today, their livelihoods focus mainly on fishing, subsistence farming, arts and crafts and livestock production, with significant community development programmes and projects initiated by and implemented by development agents. Overall, the Tonga of Sikalenge continue to live extremely precarious lives.

The last (sixth) chapter in Part I by Felix Tombindo and Simbarashe Gukurume focuses on Nyaminyami District. They highlight that, on the Zimbabwean side of the lake, colonialists divided the littoral into several protected areas, including a recreational park, safari areas and a national park. A relatively smaller part of the littoral was set aside to allow the displaced people access to the lake mainly for gill-net fishing. The host population (predominantly Tonga people) was then subjected to several alienating natural resource and lake management laws. The restrictive colonial regulations have largely continued in the post-colonial era, putting the livelihoods of Zambezi Valley communities at risk. This chapter discusses the struggle for natural resource access, livelihoods and belonging in Mola, Nyaminyami district. Through micro-ethnography, we analyse a case study of resistance against natural resource enclosure practices by a local rural council and a safari operator – Bulembi Safaris. The chapter argues that Mola, like other Zambezi Valley communities in

Zimbabwe, typifies a "marginal frontier", in which the state and powerful conservation and tourist interests frequently displace and restrict local people's rights of access to the lake, leading to increased livelihood vulnerability and precarity.

In Part II, with three chapters, the focus turns to *Health, Hunger and Livelihoods*. In Chapter 7, Jennifer Muderedzi brings to the fore that women in Binga District have less access than men to productive resources and opportunities, with the gender gap amongst the Tonga of Binga existing in relation to many assets, inputs and services, including land, livestock, labour, education, extension and financial services and technology. The particular characteristics of Binga District, particularly its size, remoteness, lack of resources, history, culture and politics have a unique influence on gender roles and relations that create and perpetuate these gender inequalities. Among the Tonga, patriarchy is a significant factor in defining power relations between genders. In this context, and based on extensive and extended fieldwork amongst the Tonga of Binga, this chapter examines the specific day-to-day challenges faced by Tonga women in constructing household-based livelihoods, with a particular focus on food insecurity. These challenges include HIV and AIDS, local politics and domestic labour. In seeking to overcome these challenges and enhance their food security, Tonga women engage in a fluctuating livelihood portfolio involving livelihood-diversification, with some livelihood activities (such as sex work) characterised by serious risks.

Codelia Govha Dhodho in Chapter 8 notes that, upon the attainment of independence of Zimbabwe in 1980, Binga was one of the poorest districts of the country suffering from perennial hunger. Existing studies attribute the livelihood challenges of the Tonga of Binga to neglect by the colonial government following involuntary displacement from the banks of the Zambezi River and resettlement onto barren land on the plateau in 1958. This study discusses the impact of displacement and marginalisation on crop production amongst the Tonga after displacement. The focus in particular is on how and why women in Sikalenge and Binga chiefdoms failed to establish viable livelihoods which could support their families and communities during times of shocks, as the Tonga are a matrilineal society. This entails understanding the overall failure by women to access key assets to rebuild livelihood in farming and fishing. The study establishes that marginalisation after involuntary displacement impoverished the Tonga overall, but that women found ways of coping and adapting to livelihood challenges without external support, drawing upon their indigenous knowledge systems in the process.

In Chapter 9, Lizzy Zinyemba offers an intriguing analysis of the role of traditional and spiritual birth attendants in maternal health care amongst Tonga women in Binga District, with a specific emphasis on the motivations of these different types of birth attendants in providing their maternal health services. The research for this study entailed a qualitative research design in order to identify and understand local perspectives and practices around maternal health care. It is clear that the birth attendants perform a diverse array of roles, including in both the prenatal and postnatal phases, including at times direct involvement in the delivery of babies. In the past, birth attendants typically provided their maternal health services free of charge. However, today, it is quite clear that forms of gratuities are expected by the attendants and indeed offered by women and their families. In this sense, being a birth attendant has become a livelihood strategy for many Tonga women in Binga. Tonga women continue to be appreciative of both traditional and spiritual birth attendants, but there is a possibility that pregnant women at times may be subject to exploitative practices by birth attendants, and hence some sort of monitoring of their work is required.

In Part III, the volume ends with three chapters on *Water, Borders and Livelihoods*. In Chapter 10, Ivan Marowa and Joshua Matanzima examine the ways in which the Tonga have had ongoing constrained and restricted access to the waterscape because of Kariba Dam construction. Much of the waterscape and its littoral have been reserved for conservancies, national parks, tourism and recreational activities. The waterscape is governed by the Zimbabwean state through the Department of National Parks and Wildlife Management (DNPWM). However, in response to this alienation of their historical resource, the Tonga people have developed multiple forms of agency in dealing with the Zimbabwean government in seeking to access Lake Kariba and the Zambezi River. This agency, involving fishing and hunting, raises significant questions around landscape and contestations over the construction and use of landscapes. The study for this chapter is grounded in fieldwork conducted in the chiefdoms of Sinakatenge and Siamupa in Binga district.

Vimbainashe Garaiza, in Chapter 11, first notes how small-scale fishing communities worldwide are confronted with serious problems throughout the stages of the fishing cycle, from fish catching and processing to distribution and marketing. The chapter then focuses on the small-scale fishing activities of Tonga women at Mujele fishing camp, Siabuwa, Binga District and the many challenges they face in pursuing their lives and livelihoods as fishers. These challenges include poor market access, lack of capital, dwindling fishing stocks and the absence of proper equipment and storage facilities. Their fishing activities at Mujele camp are administrated by the Parks and Wildlife Management Authority and they also have to contend with the Authority's regulations and practices, which at times undermine their fishing prospects. In the context of these various challenges, the Tonga fishers (including female fishers) are involved in a range of coping mechanisms, which at times entail acting beyond the reach of the Authority. These mechanisms include fishing at night, accepting EcoCash rather than hard cash in their fishing transactions, and enacting alternative livelihood activities.

Last but not least, in Chapter 12, Teverayi Muguti analyses the interplay between border (in)security and economic development for the Tonga people in Binga District, since the year 2000. The district is a border area along the Zimbabwean-Zambian border. Challenges exist around border (in)security in the Binga district, and these are partly explained by the absence of a completely functional formal border in the district, as juxtaposed to the already functioning border post at Nemafulo on the Zambian side of the borderline. Smuggling, poaching, cattle rustling and border-related disputes regarding Lake Kariba and the lack of safe modes of transport for crossing the border are among the problems that act counterproductively in pursuing and attaining effective economic development for the district. Using interviews, ethnography and government records as sources, this chapter shows that effective border security is vital for enhanced economic development in Binga and Zimbabwe at large, therefore enriching the understanding of border experiences and practices in Africa.

References

Chipere-Ngazimbi, M. (2020). Invisible-visible borders between Zambia and Zimbabwe along the Zambezi Valley: Tonga fishermen, cross-border livelihoods and monetary practices. In C. Nshimbi and I. Moyo (eds), *Borders, mobility, regional integration and development*. New York: Springer, pp 101–111.

Clark, S., Colson E., Lee, J., and Scudder, T. (1995). Ten thousand Tonga: a longitudinal anthropological study from southern Zambia, 1956–1991. *Population Studies: A Journal of Demography*, Vol. 49: 91–109.

Cliggett, L. (2002). Multigenerations and multidiscipline inheriting fifty years of Gwembe Tonga research. In R.V. Kemper and A. P. Royce (eds), *Chronicling cultures: longterm field research in Anthropology*. Lanham: Altamira Press, pp 239–251.

Cliggett, L. (2003). Gift remitting and alliance building in Zambian modernity: old answers to modern problems. *American Anthropologist*, Vol. 105(3): 1–10.

Cliggett, L. (2005). *Grains from grass: aging, gender and famine in rural Africa*. Cornell: Cornell University Press.

Cliggett, L. and Bond, V. (eds) (2013). *Tonga timeline: appraising sixty years of multidisciplinary research in Zambia and Zimbabwe*. Lusaka: Lembani Trust.

Colson, E. (1950). A note on Tonga and Ndebele. *NADA*, Vol. 2: 35–41.

Colson, E. (1960). *The social organisation of the Gwembe Tonga*. Manchester: Manchester University Press.

Colson, E. (1971). *The social consequences of resettlement*. Manchester: Manchester University Press.

Colson, E. (1997). Places of power and shrines of the land. *Paideuma*, Vol. 43: 47–57.

Colson, E. and Scudder, T. (1988). *For prayer and profit: the ritual, economic, and social importance of beer in Gwembe district, Zambia, 1950–1982*. Stanford: Stanford University Press.

Dhodho, C. G. (2022). Letting them starve: the 2008 food crisis and marginalisation of the Tonga of Binga in Zimbabwe. In: K. Helliker, P. Chadambuka and J. Matanzima (eds), *Livelihoods of ethnic minorities in rural Zimbabwe*. Cham: Springer, pp 157–172.

Dzingirai, V. (1996). Every man must resettle where he wants: the politics of settlement in the context of community wildlife management programme in Binga, Zimbabwe. *Zambezia*, Vol. 13(1): 19–30.

Dzingirai, V. (2003). "CAMPFIRE is not for Ndebele migrants": the impact of excluding outsiders from CAMPFFIRE in the Zambezi Valley, Zimbabwe. *Journal of Southern African Studies*, Vol. 29(2): 445–459.

Harnish, A., Cliggett, L. and Scudder, T. (2019). Rivers and roads: a political ecology of displacement, development, and chronic liminality in Zambia's Gwembe Valley. *Economic Anthropology*, Vol. 6(2): 250–263.

Helliker, K., Bhatasara, S. and Chiweshe, M. K. (2021). *Fast track land occupations in Zimbabwe: in the context of the Zvimurenga*. Cham: Springer.

Helliker, K., Chadambuka, P. and Matanzima, J. (eds) (2022). *Livelihoods of ethnic minorities in rural Zimbabwe*. Cham: Springer.

Hughes, D. M. (2006). Whites and water: how Euro-Africans made nature at Kariba Dam. *Journal of Southern African Studies*, Vol. 32(4): 823–838.

Hughes, D. M. (2010). *Whiteness in Zimbabwe: race, landscape, and the problem of belonging.* Palgrave: Macmillan.

Jarosz, L. (1992). Constructing the dark continent: metaphor as geographic representation in Africa. *Geografiska Annaler. Series B, Human Geography* Vol. 74(2): 105–115.

Jeke, L. (2014). Human-wildlife coexistence in Omay communal land, Nyaminyami rural district council in Zimbabwe. *Mediterranean Journal of Social Science,* Vol. 5(20): 809–818.

Lancaster, C. and Vickery, K. P. (eds) (2007). *The Tonga speaking peoples of Zambia and Zimbabwe.* Lanham: University Press of America.

Langely, S. (2007). Marginalization and response: lingering effects of the Kariba Dam project in Zimbabwe. In C. Lancaster and K. P. Vickery (eds), *The Tonga speaking peoples of Zambia and Zimbabwe: essays in honour of Elizabeth Colson.* Lanham: University Press of America, pp 263–285.

Manyena, S. B. (2013). Ethnic identity, agency and development: the case of the Zimbabwean Tonga. In L. Cliggett and V. Bond (eds), *Tonga timeline: appraising sixty years of multidisciplinary research in Zambia and Zimbabwe.* Lusaka: Lembani Trust, pp 25–66.

Marowa, I. (2010). The Tonga people of Zimbabwe: historical memories and contemporary challenges of a minority society. In M. U. Umbansao and C. J. Korich (eds), *Minorities and the State in Africa.* Armhest: Cambria Press, pp 171–191.

Marowa, I., Matanzima, J. and Nhiwatiwa, T. (2021). Interactions between humans, crocodiles, and hippos at Lake Kariba, Zimbabwe. *Human–Wildlife Interactions,* Vol. 15(1): 212–227. https://doi.org/10.26077/765a-76f4

Mashingaidze, T. M. (2013). Beyond the Kariba Dam induced displacements: the Zimbabwean Tonga's struggles for restitution, 1990s–2000s. *International Journal on Minority and Group Rights,* Vol. 20(1): 381–404. https://doi.org/10.1163/15718115-02003003

Mashingaidze, T. M. (2020). The Kariba Dam: discursive displacements and the politics of appropriating a waterscape in Zimbabwe, 1950s–2017. *LIMINA: A Journal of Historical and Cultural Studies,* Vol. 25(1): 1–15.

Matanzima, J. (2017). Fieldwork Report for Mola Chiefdom. Unpublished.

Matanzima, J. (2018). Changing and continuities in the cultural significance of the Nyaminyami water spirit among the Tonga people of northwestern Zimbabwe. MA Thesis, Rhodes University.

Matanzima, J. (2020). Fieldwork Report for Sinakatenge Chiefdom. Unpublished.

Matanzima, J. (2021). Lived experiences of cross-border traders: the case of Kariba. In: K. Helliker, S. Bhatasara and M. K. Chiweshe (eds), *Everyday crisis-living in contemporary Zimbabwe.* London: Routledge, pp 143–154.

Matanzima J. (2022a). Thayer Scudder's four stage framework, water resources dispossession and appropriation: the Kariba case. *International Journal of Water Resources Development,* Vol. 38(2): 322–345. doi: 10.1080/07900627.2020.1866505

Matanzima J. (2022b). Stereotyping, exploitation, and appropriation of African traditional religious beliefs: the case of Nyaminyami, water spirit, among the Tonga people of Northwestern Zimbabwe, 1860s–1960s. *Journal of Africana Religions,* Vol. 10(1): 72–99. https://doi.org/10.5325/jafrireli.10.1.0072

Matanzima, J. (2022c). "We were displaced several times since 1956": Tonga-Goba involuntary resettlement experiences at the Kariba Dam. *Water International* https://doi.org/10.1080/02508060.2022.2085851

Matanzima, J. and Marowa, I. (2022). Human-Wildlife conflicts and precarious livelihoods of the Tonga speaking people of north-western Zimbabwe. In K. Helliker, P. Chadambuka and J. Matanzima (eds), *Livelihoods of ethnic minorities in rural Zimbabwe.* Cham: Springer, pp. 107–122.

Matanzima, J. and Saidi, U. (2020). Landscape, belonging and identity in northwest Zimbabwe: a semiotic analysis. *African Identities*, Vol. 18(1–2): 233–251. https://doi.org/10.1080/14725843.2020.1777839

Matanzima, J. and Saidi, U. (2022). Religious rituals and socio-economic change: the impact of the Zimbabwe "cash crisis" on the Tonga *Masabe* (alien spirits) ceremony. *African Identities*, Vol. 20(1): 57–72, doi: 10.1080/14725843.2020.1811637

Matthews, T. (2007). Notes on the precolonial history of the Tonga, with emphasis on the Upper River Gwembe and Victoria Falls Areas. In C. Lancaster and K. P. Vickery (eds), *The Tonga speaking peoples of Zambia and Zimbabwe: essays in honour of Elizabeth Colson.* Lanham: University Press of America, pp. 13–33.

McGregor, J. (2003). Living with the river: landscape and memory in the Zambezi Valley Northwest Zimbabwe. In W. Beinart and J. McGregor (eds), *Social history and African environments*. Oxford: James Currey, pp 87–105.

McGregor, J. (2005). Crocodile crimes: people versus wildlife and the politics of postcolonial conservation on Lake Kariba, Zimbabwe. *Geoforum*, Vol. 36: 353–369.

McGregor, J. (2008). Patrolling Kariba's waters: state authority, fishing and the border economy. *Journal of Southern African Studies*, Vol. 34(4): 861–879. https://doi.org/10.1080/03057070802456797

McGregor, J. (2009). *Crossing the Zambezi: the politics of landscape on a Central African frontier.* Harare: Weaver Press.

Mhlanga, L. (2001). Conflicts between wildlife and people in Kariba town, Zimbabwe. *Zambezi*, Vol. xxviii(i): 39–51.

Mukova, M. and Chikovore, J. (2013). Art and the sacred practitioner among the Zimbabwe Tonga: An analysis of the symbolic interaction. In L. Cliggett and V. Bond (eds), *Tonga timeline: appraising sixty years of multidisciplinary research in Zambia and Zimbabwe.* Lusaka: Lembani Trust, pp 67–80.

Mumpande, I. and Barnes, L. (2020). The revitalisation of the Tonga language in Zimbabwe: the strategies. *Language Matters*, Vol. 51(3): 43–65.

Muringai, R., Naidoo, D. and Mafongoya, P. (2020). The challenges experienced by small-scale fishing communities of Lake Kariba, Zimbabwe. *The Journal for Transdisciplinary Research in Southern Africa*, Vol. 16(1): 1–6.

Muringai, R., Naidoo, D., Mafongoya, P. and Sibanda, M. (2019). Small-scale fishers' perceptions of climate change and its consequences on fisheries: the case of Sanyathi fishing basin, Lake Kariba, Zimbabwe. *Transactions of the Royal Society of South Africa*, Vol. 74(3): 248–257. doi: 10.1080/0035919X.2019.1639564

Murphree, M. W. (1995). Optimal principles and pragmatic strategies. Creating an enabling politicolegal environment for community based natural resource management. In: E. Rihoy (ed), *The commons without the tragedy: strategies for community based natural resources management in Southern Africa.* Lilongwe: SADC Wildlife Technical Coordination Unit, pp 47–52.

Ncube, G. T. (1986). Study of the Tonga people of Sebungwe District (Binga District) under British South Africa Company (1896–1923) and their response to colonization. Honours thesis. University of Zimbabwe.

Ncube, G. T. (2004). *A History of Northwestern Zimbabwe, 1850–1960.* Gweru: Mambo Press.

Ndhlovu, N., Saito, O., Djalante, R. and Yagi, N. (2017). Assessing the sensitivity of small-scale fishery groups to climate change in Lake Kariba, Zimbabwe. *Sustainability*, Vol. 9: 2209. doi: 10.3390/su9122209

Ndlovu-Gatsheni, S. J. (2012). The death of the Subject with a capital 'S' and the perils of belonging: a study of the construction of ethnocracy in Zimbabwe. *Critical Arts*, Vol. 26(4): 525–546. doi: 10.1080/02560046.2012.723844

Nyota S. (2015). Language shift among the Tonga of Mkoka? Assessing ethnolinguistic vitality in Gokwe South. *South African Journal of African Languages*, Vol. 35(2): 215–224. doi: 10.1080/02572117.2015.1113010

Reynolds, P. (2007). Adolescents and individuality in a Zimbabwean Tonga community. In C. Lancaster and K. P. Vickery (eds), *The Tonga speaking peoples of Zambia and Zimbabwe: essays in honour of Elizabeth Colson*. Lanham: University Press of America, pp 171–202.

Reynolds, P. (2019). *The uncaring intricate world: a field diary, Zambezi valley, 1984–1985*. Durham: Duke University Press.

Saidi, U. and Matanzima, J. (2021). Negotiating territoriality in North-Western Zimbabwe: locating the multiple-identities of Tonga, Shangwe, and Karanga in history. *African Journal of Inter/Multidisciplinary Studies*, Vol. 3(1): 61–74. doi: 10.51415/ajims.v3i1.864

Scudder, T. (1960). The fishermen of the Zambezi. *Northern Rhodesian Journal*, Vol. 27: 41–49.

Scudder, T. (1962). *The ecology of the Gwembe Tonga*. Manchester: Manchester University Press.

Scudder, T. (2005). The Kariba case study (Social Science Working Paper 1227). California Institute of Technology.

Scudder, T. (2009). Resettlement theory and the Kariba Case: an anthropology of resettlement. In A. Oliver-Smith (ed), *Development and dispossession: the crisis of forced displacement and resettlement*. Santa Fe: School for Advanced Research Press, pp 25–48.

Scudder, T. and Colson, E. (2002). Long-term research in Gwembe Valley, Zambia. In R. V. Kemper and A. P. Royce (eds), *Chronicling cultures: Longterm field research in anthropology*. Lanham: Altamira Press, pp 197–238.

Sibanda, B. (2004). Community wildlife management in Zimbabwe: the case of CAMPFIRE in the Zambezi Valley. In C. Fabricius, E. Koch, H. Magome and S. Turner (eds), *Rights, resources and rural development: community-based natural resource management in Southern Africa*. London: Earthscan, pp 248–431.

Tischler, J. (2013). *Light and power for a multiracial nation*. New York: Palgrave Macmillan.

Tischler, J. (2014). Cementing uneven development: the central African federation and the Kariba Dam Scheme. *Journal of Southern African Studies*, Vol. 40(5): 1047–1064.

Tombindo, F. (2016). Critical analysis of landscape and belonging in Mola. Master Thesis. Rhodes University.

Tombindo, F. (2018). Livelihoods vulnerability among riverbed farmers in Negande, Nyaminyami District. In K. Helliker, M. K. Chiweshe and S. Bhatasara (eds), *The political economy of livelihoods in contemporary Zimbabwe*. London: Routledge, pp 154–169.

Weinrich, A. K. H. (1977). *The Tonga people on the Southern Shore of Lake*. Kariba: Mambo Press.

PART I

Climate Change, Resource Access and Livelihoods

2

ADDRESSING VULNERABILITY OF CROP FARMERS TO CLIMATE CHANGE THROUGH FLOOD PLAIN CULTIVATION (*BBONZYE*) IN LUUNGA, BINGA

Quegas Mutale and Taruvinga Muzingili

Introduction

The world is in a state of imminent danger as the bio-space continues to suffer due to the deleterious effects of climate change. This has significant crisis-consequences for humans, such as poverty, death, diseases, inequalities, famine, land contamination, pollution and other related challenges. Perhaps predictably, an environmental paradigm is central to the policies and politics of sustainable development as encapsulated in the Millennium Development Goals (MDGs) as presented at the United Nations (UN) General Assembly in 2015 (United Nations 2015). For instance, Sustainable Development Goal (SDG) 13 highlights the need to "take urgent action to combat climate change and its impacts" and Goal 15 speaks about the necessity to "protect, restore and promote sustainable use of terrestrial ecosystems, sustainably manage forests, combat desertification, and halt and reverse land degradation and halt biodiversity loss".

Anthropogenic activities, including agricultural activities, have contributed to global warming and to climate change more broadly (Muzingili 2017), while climate change in turn undercuts the viability of crop agriculture, as evident throughout sub-Saharan Africa. Presently, modern scientific knowledge is being applied to manage the impacts of climate change on agriculture, but communities have been also applying their own indigenous knowledge systems as coping and adaptation mechanisms. Of course, Zimbabwe is no exception to the challenges of climate change and agricultural decline. This is seen for example in the case of the tropical cyclone Dineo which hit Tsholotsho District in Zimbabwe in February 2017 and caused flooding and destruction for many local villages. Likewise, cyclone Idai in March 2019 pummelled Zimbabwe's Chimanimani District and proximity areas, and heavy flooding in Binga District in February 2020 left a trail of agricultural and infrastructural damage.

DOI: 10.4324/9781003278580-3

In this context, this study examines the lives of Tonga farmers in Binga District in the northwestern part of Zimbabwe. In particular, it focuses on the possible contribution of flood plain cultivation (called *bbonzye*) in reducing the vulnerability of Tonga crop farmers to the effects of climate change in Binga. The major themes covered include local perspectives of crop farmers about *bbonzye* in relation to climate change, and the contribution of *bbonzye* in reducing the vulnerability of crop farmers to climate change. The study findings reveal that food plain cultivation has been crucial in reducing the vulnerability of Tonga farmers to climate change in Binga.

Context

Climate change refers to any change in climate over time (including variability in climate), whether due to natural variability or human activity (UNFCC 2011). Climate change and variability relate to both temperature and rainfall patterns and already have had substantial impacts globally on ecological systems and the small-scale crop farmers which depend on them for their lives and livelihoods (Thornton et al. 2014). This adds to their level of vulnerability, with climate change vulnerability being a function of exposure, sensitivity and adaptive capacity (Warner et al. 2017). Overall, vulnerability speaks to the degree to which a system is susceptible to, or unable to cope with, the adverse effects of climate change, including climate variability and extremes (Dumenu and Obeng 2016). It is thus understood as the potential for small-scale farmers to experience harm or loss from some event, condition or process, and this potential is related to the many factors that affect the likelihood of the event, condition or process occurring and the ability to cope with (or adjust to) the ensuring effects (McLeman and Smit 2006).

While exposure and sensitivity to a climate threat are crucial to identifying and understanding vulnerability, so is the resilience or adaptive capacity of a system (such as a local agricultural system) vis-à-vis the threat (Smit and Wandel 2006). Generally, subsistence farmers are vulnerable to the effects of climate change, as noted in Kenya where decreases in rainfall contributed to hunger (Thorlakson and Neufeldt 2012). Similarly, cocoa farmers in West Africa (Cameroon, Côte d'Ivoire, Togo and Nigeria) are affected by increases in temperature leading to the reduction in their cocoa production. The vulnerability of agriculture to climate change has led to food insecurity in different settings around the world (Mase et al. 2017). Some of the strategies that farmers practise in response to climate change involve conservation practices, off-farm jobs to stabilise household income and diversifying the type of crop production. In some settings, flood plain cultivation has been pursued by crop farmers to cope with the negative effects brought about by climate change.

Flood plain cultivation is practised in Africa and elsewhere (Entwistle et al. 2019). Different local terms are used in speaking about flood plain cultivation, such as *molapo* in Botswana where farmers practise flood plain cultivation along the Okavango Delta, despite the inundation of flood plains (Shinn 2016). Though flood plains are prone to flood hazards and associated risks, farmers across the world continue to make use of them to boost (or forestall drops in) agricultural production in the face of climate change. At the same time, flood plain agriculture has been practised extensively in some areas in the past, prior to climate change concerns. The practice of flood plain cultivation is most common in places where crop farmers rely on rain-fed agriculture. In Bangladesh, farmers cultivate in the Padma flood plains (Rahman et al. 2012). In Bangladesh, agroforestry activities conducted by farmers along the flood plains contributed to a reduction in vulnerability of farmers to climate change by enhancing economic security, household resilience and livelihood opportunities of rural households. With reference to Nigeria, flood plains have fertile soils with increased water-holding capacity compared to upland areas, which have attracted farmers to the plains (Ogbodo 2011). In this light, it becomes important to investigate the contribution of flood plain cultivation to a reduction in the vulnerability of crop farmers to climate change, as this study does in relation to Tonga people in Binga in Zimbabwe, and specifically Luunga ward.

Climate change in Binga has led to shifts in agricultural seasons, low crop productivity, pest infestations, perennial droughts and increased human-wildlife conflicts. In response to problems faced by Tonga crop farmers, the government of Zimbabwe and Non-Governmental Organisations (NGOs) sought unsuccessfully to introduce conservation agriculture measures in Binga, while also providing emergency food aid on occasion. Tonga farmers in Luunga in fact have long been practising flood plain cultivation along the Sengwa and Kasambabezi Rivers, and they continue to do in the face now of climate change. Indeed, with the rising intensity of climate change, the crop farmers in Luunga in large part abandoned dryland crop farming to concentrate more exclusively on flood plain cultivation. The impact of flood plain cultivation in relation to reducing climate change vulnerability amongst crop farmers in Luunga ward remains unknown, though anecdotal evidence suggests significant problems.

Study Site and Methods

The study was conducted in Luunga ward of Binga District. The area is located almost 150 kilometres from Binga centre, the administrative town for the district. In Luunga ward, crop farmers rely on rain-fed agriculture. Due to population growth in the ward, scarcity of land for crop farming exists. As well, the fertility of the soil is on the decline and overall land degradation has led to reduced crop productivity. In the face of climate change, Tonga farmers in Luunga are increasingly reliant on flood plain cultivation. Luunga ward belongs to the Gwayi catchment area. Tyunga River is a tributary of Sengwa River which makes its way onto the Zambezi River, and the ward is located on the mouth of Sengwa River. There is a flood plain there which is utilised by crop farmers for cultivating mainly maize. The area is usually affected by bouts of drought, and it also experiences flooding in frequencies of five-to-ten-year cycles.

The study used qualitative and quantitative data collection methods, with fieldwork conducted in June 2021: in-depth interviews and a survey questionnaire, respectively. From a qualitative perspective, the focus was on evidence about the experiences of Tonga farmers practising flood plain agriculture. Since farming involves degrees of production, the study employed quantitative analysis as well to facilitate the quantification of certain patterns around production patterns and levels. Research participants were first selected through simple random sampling to participate in the survey, and the sample incorporated 105 crop farmers in Luunga. For qualitative data collection, availability sampling was used to select 15 participants (crop farmers) for the in-depth interviews. From an ethical perspective, the participants consented voluntarily to their involvement in the study, and their confidentiality and anonymity have been ensured. Permission to conduct the study was sought and received from the District Development Coordinator's Office, and the letter of permission from the office was presented to the Luunga ward's local leadership (ward councillor, chiefs and village heads) prior to undertaking the research.

Bbonzye as a Climate Change Response Strategy

The realities of climate change in the ward, including reduced incidences of rainfall, have limited crop production and yields. The Tonga people in Luunga ward cultivate along the flood plains of Sengwa River, a tributary to the Zambezi River. Farming is seasonal, though at times it happens throughout the year. Practising *bbonzye* has minimised the crop farmers' vulnerability to climate and weather patterns. One farmer aired that:

> The *bbonzye* have assisted us a lot. If you observe what happens in Tyunga and Sizemba and other areas, crops are wilting permanently because of lack of rains, but ... [because of] *bbonzye* the crops are ever green.

However, the study findings reveal that the Tonga living along the Zambezi basin have shifted their agricultural activities from summer to winter seasons. Usually, rains are expected during the summer season but, due to poor soils and the existence of some excessive flooding during this time, engaging in agriculture post the rainy season (i.e. in winter) is now the best option. Rain-fed agriculture still took place; however, the main attention was on the winter season because of better harvests. One of the study participants thus brought to the fore:

> I do both summer and winter ploughing but I prefer winter more because it gives us better harvests [*butebuzi*]. During the rainy seasons we focus on small grains but soils are poor and the harvests are low .... Crops do well in floods plains since soils are fertile.

In concurrence, another Tonga farmer noted that:

> Unlike in traditional times, where rain patterns were normal, these days it's either there are not enough rains or there is too much, [both of which] ...

affect agriculture. Our soils in the higher lands are poor and even small grains sometimes fail to grow. As a coping mechanism, we now resort to *bbonzye* because it provides us better harvests and it's done several times per year.

A further response made similar points:

> Instead of relying on the normal rainy season, people utilise the winter and riverbank cropping to sustain themselves. It is imperative to note that while the [agricultural] season has changed, our people remain along the banks of the rivers cropping until November and mostly even throughout the year.

In this way, the study provided evidence on how *bbonzye* contributed to the reduction in vulnerability of Tonga crop farmers, given climate change's impacts such as short and unreliable seasons, especially for rain-fed agriculture. As a well-established form of agriculture amongst the Tonga, existing long before climate change, flood plain cultivation remains embedded in the repertoire of livelihood strategies available to the Tonga of Luunga and is enacted when necessary and where possible. The *bbonzye* system acted as a complementary livelihood activity to fishing in the Luunga community. Its significance comes across clearly in the following words of one informant:

> At some point, people managed even to sell their harvests and bought housewares like building materials and some have built infrastructure such as tuck-shops out of flood plain cultivation.

Crop farmers in the study area have managed to purchase livestock and household commodities through the proceeds from *bbonzye*, thereby forming part of a livelihood diversification strategy. The Tonga saw flood plain cultivation as a way to not only improve their livelihoods but reduce their vulnerability to climate change as well.

The Tonga people use a variety of indigenous knowledge in the implementation of flood plain agriculture. For instance, instead of using common shallow seed pits, they resort to deep ones, because the latter maintained moisture and crops could survive from germination to harvest with little or no irrigation. One of the farmers indicated that:

> We use deep pits and we got this knowledge from our elders. Since winter seasons have no rains in Zimbabwe, shallow pits are not suitable for crop survival. Therefore, we resort to deep pits to ensure that crops have moisture throughout the farming period.

In an interesting twist on the importance of deep pits, another farmer noted:

> We use deep pits for pest control. So often crops from deep pits are not affected by termites and other crops. During germination periods, deep pits are safe from birds like *bakwale* and *nkanga* [guinea fowl] which eat planted seeds.

In this respect, indigenous knowledge as applied to *bbonzye* is quite central to the Tonga's attempts to cope with climate change. Other related observations were that when crops were at the knee-height stage, farmers would fill the pit and crops would be covered with soil up ground level, a practice similar to modern-day conservation agriculture.

Bbonzye agriculture is not a once-off farming process as it is pursued throughout the year, which enhances food security. Crops are planted in March and harvest is expected in June. After this, another batch of crops are planted and harvested around September and October. One study participant indicated:

> We farm in *bbonzye* throughout the year as long as there is enough moisture to sustain the crops. This gives us enough food to the extent that summer agriculture [November to February] may not be necessary. With *bbonzye*, you are guaranteed two or three harvest points per year depending on the land or moisture availability.

One farmer elaborated on this:

> Flood plains especially along Sengwa River guarantee moisture throughout the year. If you observe, the situation is like this: during the rainy reason, land is flooded and in March floods will be gone and we start our agriculture. Another advantage is that from April to June, the water level in Kariba Dam will be rising and flooding certain tributaries and this water level drops in July onwards, creating another tract of land for farming.

In addition, for some Tonga households, the higher lands which were used for crops in the past now remain unused during the rainy season to boost grazing lands for livestock. Clearly, then, *bbonzye* boosts agricultural harvests for the Tonga, despite climate-related challenges of low and erratic rainfall. Without access to irrigated crop farming, Tonga crop farmers understand changing temperature and rainfall patterns and, as a result, increasingly recognise the necessity of flood plain farming.

Besides maize, the farmers also planted other crops in their food plain fields, such as beans, cucumbers, watermelon and okra. Other crops were included to ensure food availability even before maize harvests, as different crops matured over different time-periods. One of the farmers practising *bbonzye* stated:

> I use other crops to ensure that there is a high opportunity for food availability before the main harvest. Crops like cucumbers and watermelon can be eaten within the space of two months. So, we are assured of food availability [at all times].

Another farmer reflected upon this as well:

> I learnt from my elders that including different crops is the cornerstone of Tonga farming. It's part of [our] adaptation to drought. Other crops have a short-life span and this [diversity] give our families food.

Some of the vegetable crops were also used to substitute for meat and fish in meals. The array of different crops through *bbonzye* ensured at least two meals a day, thereby enhancing food security in the context of climate change. Flood plain cultivation reduced the vulnerability of crop farmers to drought and, even without food aid and assistance, the Luunga community survived well in terms of access to food during dry years.

One key point coming out of the study is the attempt by the Tonga to ensure that everyone could partake in *bbonzye*. The extent of flood plain lands is limited compared to the higher elevation lands, and all families are provided with at least a small piece of land. One of the farmers noted that:

> Flood plain land is limited compared to our usual farms. As a result, we ensure that no one controls everything [all the land] but give every family a small piece of land. This is done to ensure that every family has access to food.

In this way, the *bbonzye* system is embedded in kinship and other social ties (i.e. social capital) and, in turn, it strengthens these ties. Additionally, households in possession of food obtained through *bbonzye* share this with especially relatives from other villages or communities.

This practice is related to what is called *kusunza* locally, by which families without food are allowed to visit those with excess food and receive it for free or a small payment. This could be reciprocated in the future, when those without food might have good harvests later. A Tonga proverb brings this to the fore, namely, "*nzala nkalonga ilakunguluka*". This means that starvation in a particular village is not permanent and, as a result, this village will have better harvests in future. To show the importance of such communal values, one farmer indicated:

> We don't just share land but also food. [There is] no way one can have a good harvest and not think of others. Apart from relatives from distant villages, even those within our villages, we help them.

Bbonzye therefore helped the Tonga to cement their communal values and relationships in the midst of livelihood complications induced by climate change, including reducing their vulnerability to food shortages.

Despite the importance of *bbonzye* to Tonga crop farmers, the Zimbabwean government – notably through the Environmental Management Agency (EMA) – demonstrated opposition to this farming practice; in fact, the practice is illegal, as flood plains are considered wetlands and are protected areas. This is because of the damage that *bbonzye* poses to both land and aquatic life. For instance, some farmers applied inorganic fertilisers, while others used pesticides to control pests. Such practices have long-term effects on the environment and can even accelerate the rate of climate change. Regardless of this, *bbonzye* remained at the heart of Tonga crop farmers' livelihoods as it reduced their vulnerability to climate change.

Bbonzye and Livelihood Effects

This chapter examines the effects of flood plain agriculture on the livelihoods of Tonga farmers in Luunga, focusing on patterns and trends with regard to crop and livestock production, agricultural marketing, food security and social capital.

Agricultural Production and Marketing

The mean crop production (maize) for the rainy and post-rainy (*bbonzye*) seasons were compared as measured in terms of kilogrammes harvested, and this was found to be statistically significant at the 95% confidence interval. The average harvest for the rainy season was 162 kilogrammes and, for the post-rainy season, it was nearly double at 307 kilogrammes. To confirm the findings, one of the farmers indicated:

> The impact of bbonzye cannot be compared with normal rainy season farming. We use fertile lands [with *bbonzye*] and also use different stages of farming like twice per year which gives us better harvests. … We also have different crops which improve harvests.

This significant level production under *bbonzye* exists even though the Tonga farmers are using small plots of land for cropping.

Amongst the Tonga of Luunga, crops are grown both for subsistence and marketing purposes, therefore giving crop production a commercial element. A significant minority of households (37%) noted that they market their crop products "often", and another 27% indicated "very often". Additionally, 17% "sometimes" marketed their products and only 19% were "not at all" involved in this. The commercial transactions might entail cash sales or barter trading. One Tonga farmer stated:

> I always sell my maize locally. I start selling cobs before the final harvest. It is either for cash or I exchange maize for goods like fish which I use for relish.

In contrast to this, other farmers simply did not produce enough for commercial sales, as indicated in the following quotation:

> Sometimes I produce enough but I fear to sell because I do not know what the future holds. As a result, I stock my food. In some seasons, rains might not come and flood plains might not support our winter ploughing.

Insofar as sales did take place, these were done locally, with those in the local community or in nearby communities. These crop sales at times became the basis for asset accumulation, including livestock.

In this light, the average number of livestock (cattle, goats and chickens) before and after intensifying *bbonzye* activities for the Tonga under study increased significantly for each of the livestock types, especially cattle. Tested at the 95% confidence interval (.05), the findings reveal that the difference between levels of livestock before and after *bbonzye* is statistically significant. The marketing of agricultural crop products via flood plain cultivation performed an important role in increasing the numbers of livestock. To support the statistical findings, one of the farmers noted that:

> Through barter trade I managed to acquire six goats which multiplied. Now I bought 2 cows. This farming helped me a lot in acquiring livestock.

Another Tonga farmer brought to the fore:

> In a good harvest, we produce enough food for families and the remaining crops I sell to get money for domestic uses. I can also purchase livestock from households which do not have enough food.

Food Security

Food security at household level is crucial for rural Tonga households. Of significance in this respect is food availability throughout the year, and a food-secure home should have ongoing access to food throughout the year. The study findings show that 75% of those households which practise *bbonzye* are marked by regular food availability (i.e. food every day), while 25% are not. One Tonga farmer said:

> I don't deny the existence of severe droughts in these communities but I can tell you that *bbonzye* is a game changer. People plant different crops and this gives them food security. It's not about maize alone but other types of food as well.

On probing some of the farmers, it became clear that some households simply did not have food throughout the year, largely due to the small pieces of land in their possession. Further, some small crops were destroyed by animals. As a farmer put it:

> I don't own land and my piece of land is extremely small to have enough food throughout the year. In some cases, animals such as elephants and hippopotamus destroy crops. This results in huge losses and ultimately some food challenges.

Thus, land shortages and animals continue to affect Tonga harvests, with food-deficient households relying upon NGOs at times.

Critical to food security is also the availability of in particular nutritious food. Overall, 70% of households indicated access to nutritious food and 30% spoke in the negative about this. The majority of households benefit from a diverse variety of crops planted in the flood plains. One farmer explained:

> From knowledge I have on nutrition, I can tell you that *bbonzye* has helped us to have different types of plants. Apart from indigenous education, NGOs have taught us on various nutrients which are important. So we have incorporated those guidelines even in our farms.

Another participant noted that:

> I enjoy eating different types of food. It is not about sadza [*nsima*] [the staple mealie-meal food] only but also vegetables are available and these are also recommended by health practitioners.

The nutritional food consumed was important in preventing malnutrition and stunted growth among Tonga children.

Finally, regarding household food security, the number of meals consumed per day is relevant. In this regard, the average number of meals in a normal rainy season was 2.11, and it was 3.18 during the winter season *(bbonzye)*. This means that *bbonzye*, on average, enabled Tonga households to have at least three meals per day. Most households did not have to wait for a particular harvest-time to be food secure, as multiple harvested crops with different growing-periods and life-spans were typically available on an ongoing basis.

Challenges in Practising *Bbonzye*

Like all agricultural practices, whether with reference to climate change or not, the pursuit of flood plain cultivation by the Tonga faces major challenges. The range of challenges appears in Table 2.1.

As depicted in the table, the study findings reveal that animal-human conflict is the greatest challenge and it is experienced by all Tonga farmers. This relates in particular to the damage caused to crops by different animals. One of the farmers lamented:

> Elephants and hippos are a menace in these areas. As you can see, we try to protect farms with fencing using logs but elephants destroy these. More so, we even have cases of people killed by animals in trying to protect their crops. This is a traditional challenge and there is a little help from government to end this problem. These animals move freely and they are not in a national park.

Another major challenge is that of conflicts with environmental legislation which is supposed to be implemented by the local council and the state's EMA: nearly all

TABLE 2.1 Challenges associated with *Bbonzye*

Challenge	*Yes*	*No*
Animal-human conflicts	100%	0%
Conflicts with legislation (Council and Environmental Management Agency)	95%	5%
Poor infrastructure such as roads to market agricultural produce	91%	9%
Shortage of land (limited access to flood plain land including communal land conflicts)	85%	15%
Crops prone to flooding (rising water levels from Kariba Dam and rains during rainy seasons)	67%	33%
Crops damage due to pests and other plan diseases	57%	43%
Lack of modern scientific knowledge on farming (including poor timing of farming)	50%	50%
Limited access to AGRITEX services	42%	58%

farmers (95%) confronted this problem. As noted earlier, flood plains are classified as wetlands in Zimbabwe and these lands are protected through legislation. More so, the district council encourages people to not use water-zone farming to ensure that dams are not silted due to flood plain agriculture. One of the farmers confirmed that:

> We always get warnings from council and from Environmental Management Agency about farming in flood plains. Some people end up not taking part in agriculture [because of this]. However, we have nothing else to do because we can die with hunger.

Conflicts with legislation and the administering bodies was one of the reasons why farmers using *bbonzye* did not receive the services of AGRITEX (the central state's agricultural extension department). This issue limited access to AGRITEX services to only 42%, and these services related to agricultural activities which were not associated with flood plain cultivation. Research participants also noted that AGRITEX officers worked with other legislative bodies to discourage flood plain agriculture. The limited involvement of AGRITEX likely explains why half of the farmers cited lack of modern scientific knowledge about farming as an agricultural challenge, as AGRITEX tends to promote so-called scientific farming. While AGRITEX's refusal to engage with *bbonzye* is understandable, this possibly affects – negatively – how farmers use flood plains while conserving the environment at the same time.

Shortage of land was cited as a major factor by the farmers (85%). Land for flood plain cultivation is very limited, which resulted in farmers using very small pieces of land. One farmer thus highlighted:

> There is not enough land for everyone to farm. As you can see, most land available is small. As much as we try to share it, sometimes people fail to access any or sufficient land. This also affects the harvest levels.

Another participant added that:

> For the past two years, I only got access to [flood plain] land once as competition is high and sometimes it results in communal land ownership conflicts. This is a serious challenge but it's difficult to manage it.

Another key challenge was poor infrastructure such as roads to market agricultural produce (91%). Lack of proper roads was a major challenge for people to market their product and access agricultural support services. One of the study participants noted that:

> There are no roads here to go and sell our produce in other wards. Roads are bad and we rarely get transport this side. As you are aware, it's now 10 years with no bus coming into these areas. This also affects our fish marketing too.

Farmers were not spared other problems as well, such as flooding and crop damage due to pests and plant diseases, with the relative absence of AGRITEX affecting detrimentally the capacity of Tonga farmers to control pests which attacked their *bbonzye* crops.

Bbonzye and the Lives of the Tonga

With the calamitous impact of climate change on local livelihoods, Tonga people resorted to flood plain agriculture which typically takes place in the winter months. This form of agriculture (*bbonzye*) is characterised by the application of various farming knowledge and practices, including the use of a variety crops in a single field, deep-seed basins and multi-stage farming phases, with farmers sensitive to factors such as moisture and soil type in this regard. The adoption of flood plain cultivation, and its increasing relevance in the face of climate change and variability, is not unique to the Tonga or to Zimbabwe. In the case of Botswana, Singh et al. (2021) found out that, along the Ganga River, farmers use the moisture-laden and nutrient-rich soils of the flood plains for growing crops after water levels recede, and then harvest them before flooding of the river. Turning to flood plain cultivation is part of the broader repertoire of adjustments and adaptive strategies crafted by small-scale farmers in dealing with fluctuations in rainfalls and increasing high temperatures associated with climate change in the Okavango Delta (Kolawole and Kashe 2019). Because of the myriad of issues brought about by climate change, the *bbonzye* system, which has been widely practised across Africa, Europe and the Americas, remains as a crucial and common livelihood practice that reduces the vulnerability of crop farmers to climate change impacts.

Flood plain agriculture has been adopted as an immediate livelihood strategy in response to varying climatic conditions in diverse cases, and this often entails the usage of local indigenous knowledge passed on across multiple generations. Certainly, the drawing upon indigenous knowledge pertaining to *bbonzye* farming is not peculiar to Tonga people alone. For instance, Motsumi et al. (2012) for Botswana, Coomes et al. (2016) for Peru, Chimweta et al. (2018) for Zimbabwe, Balana et al. (2019) for Ghana and Peraza-Villarreal et al. (2019) in the case of Mexico are all examples of studies covering different aspects of flood plain agriculture. In these studies, different aspects and developments of flood plain agriculture have been uncovered, such as the role of indigenous knowledge in this form of agriculture (Motsumi et al. 2012), the effect of flood-stage reversals on crop production (Coomes et al. 2016), the fertility status of flood recession fields (Chimweta et al. 2018), assessment of food security using optimisation modelling (Balana et al. 2019) and estimation of potential area under flood plain agriculture (Peraza-Villarreal et al. 2019). These and other studies highlight that the contribution of the *bbonzye* system to reducing the vulnerability of crop farmers to climate change cannot be underrated.

Supported by both qualitative and quantitative insights, the findings of this particular study demonstrate the importance of flood plain agriculture for Tonga people along the Zambezi valley. Of key significance is the increased productivity of *bbonzye* which, in turn, led to increased food security, asset accumulation and strengthening of social capital. The increased productivity hence brought about many benefits for the marginalised Zambezi valley communities, which helped them to weather the shocks of climate change. Despite differences in ecological locations with other African communities, the practice of bbonzye is productive in diverse areas, as confirmed by other studies across the world. Numerous African communities use this practice to increase food production and thereby enhance food security and livelihoods (Motsumi et al. 2012; Balana et al. 2019). Flood plain agriculture is enormously productive when the output is compared with the initial input costs (Nederveen 2012). It gives high returns compared to the low input of energy and natural resources, and potentially also paves the way for improving environmental sustainability (Nederveen 2012; Sidibe et al. 2016). However, observations show that it is also environmentally unfriendly if eco-friendly farming methods are not used.

Despite the benefits of *bbonzye* farming, this climate change adaption strategy is characterised by a host of problems which range from nature to legislative frameworks. These include human-animal conflicts, shortage of land, conflicts with state bodies enacting environmental legislation and limited access to agricultural technical and extension services. These issues, notably wild animal-human conflicts, are reoccurring amongst people living along the Zambezi River (New Zimbabwe 2019). The Tonga communities of Luunga are discouraged by law enforcement agents, even though it is known that intercropping (which is often undertaken by Tonga farmers) increases biodiversity, improves soil quality, insures against crop failure, enhances crop resilience and, consequently, promotes sustainability of food production, livelihoods and environmental health (Alcon et al. 2020). The discouragement of people engaging in *bbonzye* emanates from the desire on the part of the Zimbabwean state to protect wetlands and ultimately the ecosystem, as also appears in other countries in the region, like Botswana (Vanderpost 2009).

Conclusion

Developing the capacity to adapt to climate change, and to build resilient livelihoods in the process, is critical in the years ahead. Among the Tonga along the Zambezi valley, flood plain agriculture (*bbonzye*) has been crucial historically when it comes to riverine livelihoods and it is now of great significance for local villagers in the face of the adverse implications of climate change in the area. Indeed, winter flood plain farming backed by indigenous Tonga knowledge has been used to cope with the challenges of perennial droughts in the Zambezi valley. Despite its relevance for addressing and possibly overcoming the precarity of Tonga livelihoods in the harsh environment of Binga, *bbonzye* is mired in controversy. These controversies relate in part to the importance of preserving the wetlands of Zimbabwe and the government's associated attempt to inhibit and limit the practice of flood plain cultivation, such that agricultural extension services (including pest controls) are not provided for the Tonga in Luunga. Other problems also exist, including human-animal conflicts and land shortages. Undoubtedly, the Tonga of Luunga will continue to engage in flood plain agriculture unless meaningful alternative livelihoods arise in the near future.

References

Alcon, F., Marín-Miñano, C., Zabala, J. A., De Miguel, M. D., & Martínez-Paz, J. M. (2020). Valuing diversification benefits through intercropping in Mediterranean agroecosystems: a choice experiment approach. *Ecological Economic*, Vol. 171: 106593.

Balana, B. B., Sanfo, S., Barbier, B., Williams, T., & Kolavalli, S. (2019). Assessment of flood recession agriculture for food security in northern Ghana: an optimization modelling approach. *Agricultural System*, Vol. 173: 536–543.

Chimweta, M., Nyakudya, I. W., &. Jimu, L. (2018). Fertility status of cultivated floodplain soils in the Zambezi Valley, northern Zimbabwe Phys. *Physics and Chemistry of the Earth*, Vol. 105: 147–153.

Coomes, O. T., Lapointe, M., Templeton, M., & List, G. (2016). Amazon River flow regime and flood recessional agriculture: flood stage reversals and risk of annual crop loss. *Journal of Hydrology*, Vol. 539: 214–222.

Dumenu, W. K. & Obeng, E. A. (2016). Climate change and rural communities in Ghana: social vulnerability, impacts, adaptations and policy implications. *Environmental Science and Policy*, Vol. 55(1): 208–2017.

Entwistle, N. S., Heritage, G. L., Schofield, L. A., & Williamson, R. J. (2019). Recent changes to floodplain character and functionality in England. *Catena*, Vol. 174: 490–498.

Kolawole, O. D. & Kashe, K. (2019). Food security and flood recession farming in the Okavango Delta, Botswana: policies and practices. In, *Smallholder farmers and farming practices: Challenges and prospects*. New York: Nova Science Publishers, pp 139–150.

Mase, A. S., Gramig, B. M. & Prokopy, L. S. (2017). Climate change beliefs, risk perceptions, and adaptation behavior among Midwestern U.S. crop farmers. *Climate Risk Management*, Vol. 15: 8–17.

McLeman, R. & Smit, B. (2006). Vulnerability to climate change hazards and risks: crop and flood insurance. *The Canadian Geographer*, Vol. 50(2): 217–226.

Motsumi, S., Magole, L., & Kgathi, D. (2012). Indigenous knowledge and land use policy: implications for livelihoods of flood recession farming communities in the Okavango. *Physics and Chemistry of the Earth*, Vol. 50(52): 185–195.

Muzingili, T. (2017). Moving together in environmental discourse: call for social work intervention towards environmental justice in Africa. *International Journal of Politics and Good Governance*, Vol. 13(4): 1–16.

Nederveen, S. (2012). *Flood recession farming: an overview and case study from the upper awash catchment, Ethiopia*. Available at: www.semanticscholar.org/paper/Flood-Recession-Farming%3A-An-Overview-and-Case-Study-Nederveen/03eba87943e16228e75336c9829155ed7bbcc07b

New Zimbabwe (2019). Zimparks petitioned over human-wildlife conflict. Available at: www.newzimbabwe.com/zimparks-petitioned-over-human-wildlife-conflict/

Ogbodo, E. N. (2011). Assessment of some soil fertility characteristics of abakaliki urban flood plains of South-East Nigeria, for sustainable crop production. *World Journal of Agricultural Sciences*, Vol. 7(4): 489–495.

Peraza-Villarreal, H., Casas, A., Lindig-Cisneros, R. & Orozco-Segovia, A. (2019). The marceño agroecosystem: traditional maize production and wetland management in Tabasco, Mexico. *Sustainability*, Vol. 11(7): 1978.

Rahman, S. A., Imam, M. H., Snelder, D. J., & Sunderland, T. (2012). Agroforestry for livelihood security in Agrarian landscapes of the Padma floodplain in Bangladesh. *Small-Scale Forestry*, 10 pages. doi 10.1007/s11842-012-9198-y

Shinn, J. E. (2016). Adaptive environmental governance of changing social-ecological systems: empirical insights from the Okavango Delta, Botswana, *Global Environmental Change*, Vol. 40: 50–59.

Sidibe, Y., Williams, T. O., & Kolavalli, S. (2016). Flood recession agriculture for food security in northern Ghana: literature review on extent, challenges, and opportunities. GSSP Working Paper 42, IFPRI: Washington, D.C.

Singh, R., Patel, S. K., Tiwari, A. K., & Singh, G. S. (2021). *Assessment of flood recession farming for livelihood provision, food security and environmental sustainability in the Ganga River Basin*. Available at: www.sciencedirect.com/science/article/pii/S2666049021000141

Smit, B. & Wandel, J. (2006) Adaptation, adaptive capacity and vulnerability. *Global Environmental Change*, Vol. 16: 282–292.

Thorlakson, T. & Neufeldt, H. (2012). Reducing subsistence farmers' vulnerability to climate change: evaluating the potential contributions of agroforestry in Western Kenya. *Agriculture & Food Security 2012*, Vol. 1: 15, www.agricultureandfoodsecurity.com/content/1/1/15

Thornton, P. K., Ericksen, P. J., Herrero, M. & Challinor, A. J. (2014). *Global Change Biology*, 20(11): 3313–3328. doi: 10.1111/gcb.12581

UNFCC (2011). Fact sheet: Climate change science – the status of climate change science today. Accessed at https://unfccc.int/files/press/backgrounders/application/pdf/press_factsh_science.pdf

United Nations (2015). Transforming our world: The 2030 agenda for Sustainable development. Available at: https://sustainabledevelopment.un.org/content/documents/21252030%20Agenda%20for%20Sustainable%20Development%20web.pdf

Vanderpost, C. (2009). *Molapo farming in the Okavango Delta*. Gaborone: University of Botswana: Harry Oppenheimer Okavango Research Centre.

Warner, B. P., Schattman, R. E. & Hatch, C. E., 2017. Farming the floodplain: ecological and agricultural tradeoffs and opportunities in river and stream Governance in New England's changing climate. *Case Studies in the Environment*, Vol. 1(1): 1–18.

3

CLIMATE CHANGE AND LIVELIHOODS OF TONGA WOMEN IN WARD 7, BINGA DISTRICT

Pottar Muzamba

Introduction

The effects of climate change are far-reaching and do not affect all categories of people in the same way. Women are vulnerable in a disproportionate way to the vagaries of climate change and variability because of their intimate relationship with, and dependence upon, natural resources. This chapter examines the gendered character of climate change with reference to the Tonga people in Binga District in Zimbabwe by focusing in particular on the basket-weaving of Tonga women in Ward 7. This entails interrogating basketry as a source of livelihoods for women in the face of climate change, including any mitigation, coping and adaptation strategies adopted by women in trying to undercut the negative effects of climate change on basket-making. Of particular significance is the implication of climate change for the local availability of the ilala plant and reeds used for basket-production, with declining precipitation and rising temperatures in Binga making the growing of ilala plants near impossible, thereby causing their increasing scarcity.

Context

Binga District in Matabeleland North Province is the home of many Tonga people, who are known as one of Zimbabwe's finest basket-weaving communities. The Tonga, together with Korekore people, were forcibly relocated from the banks of the Zambezi River in the late 1950s to pave way for the construction of the hydroelectricity generating Kariba Dam. While the Kariba Dam brought about national-strategic economic benefits for the country, those removed suffered the social, political, religious and economic costs of resettlement (Matanzima 2021). Indeed, dispossession and appropriation via the Kariba Dam resulted in the overall impoverishment of the Tonga. In this context, Tonga women coped with, and

DOI: 10.4324/9781003278580-4

adapted to, dam-induced poverty through the commodification and commercialisation of baskets.

In the pre-colonial past of Africa broadly, baskets were embedded in the lifestyle of the hunter-gatherers, pastoralists and fishing and agricultural communities which made them. Including amongst the Tonga, baskets were used in virtually every part of the food production cycle and for other purposes – in planting and harvesting, seed-sowing, winnowing, transporting, storage, sleeping mats, sandals, wine straining, food processing and serving food. Basket-making represented a fine blend of environment, culture and technology amongst pre-colonial African communities. Well into the colonial period, and specifically during the 1970s, there arose a dramatic increase in international appreciation of African basketry as a form of art, leading to the export of African baskets to collectors, interior designers and museums in the United States and Europe (Cunningham and Milton 1987). This culminated in a considerable expansion of basketry production by private entrepreneurs to meet the demands of the commercial market, including baskets for use as wall decorations and souvenirs. All natural and harvested materials for baskets – such as wild grasses, small vines, reeds, papyrus, rushes and palm leaves dyed with tree bark ilala palm – are sourced from local ecosystems (World Bank 2010).

Concurrently, climate change is having massive effects on the presence and distribution of plant species across the globe (Parmesan and Yohe 2003), with all sorts of serious consequences for the future of biodiversity (Pachauri et al. 2014; Ngingi 2016; Dube et al. 2017). Prolonged and frequent droughts, floods, heat waves, changes in seasons and precipitation patterns and water stress are some of the key dimensions of climate change which also have direct and indirect effects on rural livelihoods (Mubaya et al. 2012; Shaw et al. 2011; UNDP 2007; Stern 2007). This is deepening the livelihood risks of rural populations which are already experiencing severe conditions of vulnerability, especially those involved in ecosystem-dependent livelihoods in developing countries (Davies et al. 2013). This is certainly the case for Tonga women in Binga, as the ilala palm and reeds (as raw materials for basketry production) are gradually getting depleted, rendering the plants to be classified under the category of endangered plant species. Critical to mitigating the vagaries of climate change for Tonga women is the possibility of devising local coping and adaptation approaches and strategies.

A livelihoods perspective highlights the structural context of vulnerabilities within which rural households regularly exist, and how they make use of available assets (including natural, human, financial, physical and social assets) in constructing livelihoods (Dube et al. 2021; Kollmair and Juli 2002). Livelihood activities might include agricultural activities, petty trading and formal and casual employment. Households at times are subjected to various livelihood risks, both long-term trends (such as climate change) and short-term shocks (such as the death of a household member), which affect negatively household-livelihood capacities (Ellis and Allison 2004; Serrat 2008). Various institutions and processes, including the presence and performance of state entities and non-governmental organisations (NGOs) as well as societal norms and formal regulations, either enable or disable these capacities.

In the end, households seek livelihood outcomes which entail enhanced household resilience incorporating ongoing food security, an increased asset base and physical and emotional well-being for household members. Ideally, this would be accomplished without degrading the local ecological system (land, water and so forth).

As the rural livelihoods literature demonstrates, climate change is a major challenge for rural households and addressing this challenge at local levels entails coping, adaptation and resilience measures (Cline 2007; Lamichhane 2010). For some time now, Africa has been experiencing increased water stress, decreased yields from rain-fed agriculture, increased food insecurity, growing expanses of arid and semi-arid land and depletion of ecological systems, in part as a result of climate change (IPCC 2014). Changes in rainfall and temperature patterns, as well as extreme weather events, are increasing crop failures, leading to pest and disease outbreaks, and heightening the degradation of land, forestry, fisheries and water resources in sub-Saharan Africa (Seneviratne et al. 2012). These climatic changes are undermining rural livelihoods, especially amongst those households dependent upon rain-fed agriculture in the region, as the vitality of natural assets is central to household-livelihood sustainability in rural spaces. This impact is often more pronounced for rural women, as they typically have fewer options – compared to men – for pursuing alternative livelihoods as part of a process of diversification.

Research Site and Methods

The research for this chapter adopted a case study research design in order to understand the relationship between climate change and basketry. As indicated by Creswell (1994), case studies do not allow for statistical generalisation but, importantly, they are generalisable to theoretical propositions. There was no attempt therefore to identify and establish statistically formulated causal relationships. But the evidence is generalisable to theory in the sense that investigating the case study is facilitated and illuminated by a theoretical framing; additionally, the case study findings may be used in refining prevailing theory about the particular social phenomenon under investigation (such as climate change and basketry production). In this study, the theoretical framework, as briefly outlined, is the livelihoods perspective.

The case study approach entails studying social phenomena through the understanding and analysis of an individual case, which forms part of a broader class of cases of that particular social phenomenon. The unit of study (or case) then becomes the subject of in-depth examination and investigation. On this basis, it is quite likely that this case study and its findings resonate with the livelihoods of rural women residing elsewhere in Zimbabwe who, like the Tonga women, are experiencing livelihood challenges in the face of climate change. The research methodology underpinning this study entailed a purely qualitative approach consistent with interpretive sociology, including key informant interviews, semi-structured interviews, focus group discussions and primary documentation. The adoption and use of various research methods facilitated the triangulation of empirical evidence and, in the process, enhanced the study's reliability and validity.

The fieldwork was conducted from December 2021 to January 2022 in Manjolo Ward (Ward 7) in Binga District, in Matabeleland North Province, with a population of 5,158 (2,298 males and 2,860 females) and 1,231 households (ZimStat 2012). This ward lies in Agro-Ecological Regions IV and V in Zimbabwe which have historically received the least amount of rainfall nationally. Coupled with declining precipitation as a result of climate change, the effects of climate change have been particularly severe in these regions. For this study, three villages were selected, that is, Bulawayo Kraal, Siangwemu and Dumbwe comprising 528 households and a total population of 2,210 (985 males and 1,225 females) (ZimStat 2012). These villages incorporate many women engaged in basketry production. A total of 176 households consisted of the sample from the three villages. Every third household was sampled using a systematic random sampling technique. A total of 352 interviewees (that is, two people per household) participated in the study: 300 were women mainly involved in basketry, while 52 were men. This sampling approach captured a population that was representative of the villages.

For the key informants, the study adopted purposive sampling. The main aim of purposive sampling in qualitative research is to select a small number of important people or unique cases to study, which then produces a wealth of detailed information and an in-depth understanding of people, programmes, cases or situations studied (Yilmaz 2013). Purposive sampling was used to select key informants at district level (local heads of state institutions) and village level (traditional leaders, notably village heads). These informants were people in positions of authority and they had specialised knowledge or long-term experience about local conditions in Ward 7, including with reference to climate change and basketry livelihoods – thereby providing particularly deep and insightful narratives about the focus of this study, albeit based on their own interpretation of developments. The key informants include the Natural Resources Manager, Binga Rural District Council Manager for Binga Craft Centre, District Officer for Forestry Commission, Executive Director of Zubo Trust, District head for the Ministry of Women Affairs, Community, Small and Medium Enterprises Development, head of Binga Rural District Council-CAMPFIRE, and Department and District Environmental Officer for the Environmental Management Agency (EMA).

Climate Change and Basketry

Before their relocation in 1957, the Tonga people subsisted on riverine- and fishing-based livelihoods. The dam-induced displacement moved them from their age-old riparian settlements to arid places (even prior to major forms of climate change) where meaningful crop farming was unviable. Their dispossession from the river and lake created innumerable problems for the Tonga, including food insecurity, human-wildlife conflict and diseases. In Tonga society, because of culturally rooted patriarchal tendencies, women have tended to be confined to the private sphere, while men dominated the public sphere. In their new arid environment, Tonga women in Binga District started to venture into basketry on a commercialised basis.

Basketry is the art and craft of making interwoven objects (usually containers) from flexible vegetables and associated objects, such as twigs, grasses, osiers, bamboo, reeds and rushes or from plastic or other synthetic materials. In Binga, women utilised their traditional weaving and coiling techniques to create a diverse range of intricately patterned items – mats, purses, bags, pots, basket containers, lamp shades, flower pots, chairs, hats, bangles, stools and cups. In doing so, they harvested natural materials such as reeds, ilala, sisal, bamboo, wild grasses, small vines and palm leaves dyed with tree bark. Historically, the shapes, styles and functions of weaved baskets and other items were determined by the established lifestyles of local communities. Over time in post-relocation Binga, though, the objects found a growing international market in art and design which began to bring in significant levels of revenue for the Tonga women.

Learned during processes of family apprenticeship, the basket-weaving techniques have enabled many Tonga women to meet household needs which they would not otherwise be able to do, including sending their children to school. Marvis Mwembe, a female from Dumbwe village, said that:

> Basketry has taken the place of our husbands [as an income source] since it is now our main source of income to buy other commodities, domestic animals and send our children to school. The craft is done all year round and is not physically demanding as one can make the baskets while seated and leisurely. I sell baskets on a monthly basis and, by so doing, have constant flow of income.
>
> *Interview, 28 December 2021*

This and other testimonies are a clear indication that women are being economically empowered in a small way, as basket-making has granted them a degree of economic autonomy or independence from their husbands. They now have the capacity to educate their children and buy household assets. A level of economic empowerment amongst women was confirmed by a male village head (Sijoke), who also spoke about its relationship to reducing gender-based violence:

> I have seen a reduced number of cases of gender based violence (GBV) and increased peace in my village due to the economic emancipation of women. Most of the GBV cases I have presided over in my village court were as a result of economic issues at home.
>
> *Interview, 28 December 2021*

Most GBV locally is a result of poverty and lack of access to resources to sustain households. Hence, besides being simply a source of livelihoods, the basketry business has been instrumental in the maintenance of peace and social cohesion in Manjolo Ward communities.

Basketry production by Tonga women expanded considerably to meet the demands of the commercial market. Basket-making became a virtual cottage industry due to the combination of low-capital input, locally available resources and traditional skills. Along with increased production, there have been significant changes in styles and designs of baskets and in the raw materials used for the production of baskets and other items.

The basketry industry in Ward 7 in Binga District depends heavily on natural capital, such ilala, reeds, sticks for rings, barks for colouring the ilala, clean water and timber and fuel wood. However, whatever natural capital exists in Binga District has come under pressure because of severe overexploitation and poor resource-management over a number of years, and it is now subject to further depletion through climate change. Interviewees thus spoke about visible changes in the local ecological system and attributed this to climate change. They claimed that, particularly since the year 2000, average temperatures have increased and average rainfall decreased. In this light, they referred to the failed growth of the ilala palm as well as the scarcity of reeds along Lake Kariba due to the drastic reduction in the water level – leaving the area without water for the growth of reeds. Maria Munkuli from Siangwemu village said:

> The sleep mats made from reeds are no longer a common product due to scarcity of reeds along the rivers. Producers attempt to produce some using the ilala palm, but these are not strong and durable. River reeds used to produce very strong mats.
>
> *Interview, 3 January 2022*

Another participant lamented as follows:

> Yes, I have noticed climate change; there are less rains now and high temperatures. The last three years have been miserable; we didn't receive any rains and as a result our dams, wetlands, rivers and streams, whose banks are appropriate sites for reed germination, are empty. The wetland, rivers and streams are silted and now completely dry. In the past these … never used to dry up. We would get to the next season with lots of water.
>
> *Siangwemu Village Focus Group Discussion, 3 January 2022*

The fieldwork evidence shows that communities from Siangwemu, Dumbwe and Bulawayo Kraal travel on average 20 kilometres to the ilala palm fields, and communities from other wards (such as Ward 12) travel 50 kilometres to palm-field sites. Before the conundrum of climate change, palm fields were 200 metres away from homesteads in Dumbwe and Bulawayo Kraal and 7 kilometres for Siangwemu. Also, Kamata village, the custodian of ilala sites, is now charging people from other villages USD1 per day for harvesting the palm. In order for a woman to have adequate palm, she needs five days of harvesting and this costs a total of USD5. These challenges have reduced basketry output by Tonga women and the ensuing income accrued. Local Tonga women are deeply worried about the worsening situation and, if no urgent action is taken to curb the disappearance of ilala palm and reeds, they fear that they will slide back into a deep poverty trap. Minor Muleya from Dumbwe village submitted that:

> Drying up of the water bodies has affected the growing of the much needed … reeds. The non-availability of reeds has led to the disappearance of sleeping mats. Women are now focusing on baskets and they do not fetch enough money as compared to mats.
>
> *28 December 2021*

The basketry industry in Manjolo Ward is dominated by women, while men are involved in the carving industry. Because of the patriarchal structuring of local households, women are responsible for unpaid domestic care duties. A normal day for Tonga women, particularly at the height of the agricultural season, starts at 5 am and ends at 9 pm and it is jam-packed with activities. The women of Manjolo also revealed that the seasons are no longer the same. Further, in terms of physical capital, the Tonga women lack basic infrastructure in undertaking their basketry. Basket-weaving is done under trees or in a "*Nganzi*" (a Tonga traditional upstairs house), and possibly at times of heat waves and extremely cold temperatures, which can disrupt the work flow. By the end of the day, the women might be exhausted, particularly under conditions of intense heat. As such, the pace of basket production is affected detrimentally, as is the delivery of baskets for sale. Mayobo Mumpande from Dumbwe village said that:

> We do not have proper shelter. The intensity of the heat caused by heat waves makes it practically impossible to go under these modes of shelter.
>
> *28 December 2021*

Susan Muleya from Bulawayo Kraal village added:

> The other challenge is that we are overburdened with unpaid care work. We wish the unpaid care work could be distributed between the family members. Currently, all is being shouldered by women and this has affected other productive activities.
>
> *30 December 2021*

Lack of basic infrastructure for the basketry operations has exposed women to harsh weather conditions, thereby impeding the basketry production process. Also, the unpaid care work inhibits women in applying maximum effort in basketry production to meet the demands of the market.

The lack of financial capital is a major setback for the Manjolo basketry producers because of low incomes, limited cash flows and insignificant savings, thereby inhibiting them from pursuing alternative livelihoods in the absence of basketry.

This is related as well to their rural remoteness, leading to erratic access to markets for their basket products. The Tonga women bewailed the lack of firm linkages to sound and established markets with high uptakes of basketry products, including the far distances to urban centres like Victoria Falls, Bulawayo and Harare. Further, weak market linkages deprived them of the opportunity to sell their produce at competitive prices.

The Tonga women identified two market-systems whereby they sell their products, namely, freelancer buyers and fixed places such as Binga Craft Centre. Freelancers visit the producer community in Ward 7 at their production sites. The female producers bemoaned the negotiated selling prices because of compromises made on their part and, sometimes, their wares are exchanged or bartered for commodities whose prices are not congruent with the price of a basket. For example, a 20-litre empty bucket with a lid costing USD2 will be exchanged for a basket that costs USD2 to make, and a 90-litre plastic container priced at USD5 would be traded for two baskets. In the case of Binga Craft Centre, the women's products are collected and sold by the centre on behalf of producers, with the latter paid at a later stage. Through this system, the producers complained about the lack of transparency and accountability on the part of the centre as the payments are always delayed and sometimes these are remitted in part-payments. As one woman from Bulawayo Kraal village claimed:

> We don't access international markets for our products. The current marketing system is robbing us in day light. We sell our products very cheaply and payments for the products are not fully remitted.
>
> *30 December 2021*

With the outbreak of Covid-19, resulting in lockdowns and closure of borders, the basketry markets (both local and international) have shrunk. Without stable and reliable markets, the realisation of sustainable livelihoods by the Tonga women is compromised.

Because of this, young women from Manjolo are migrating to town in search of employment as maids and other menial work, as agriculture and basketry are longer dependable sources of livelihoods. This has relegated the function of basketry production to middle-aged women (40–45 years) and older women (50–60 years). This is leading to the failure to transfer basketry skills to the younger generation. It also results in older women doing more and more of the household-based domestic chores.

Climate Change Mitigation and Adaptation

Mitigation involves minimising the potential risks and effects of climate change in the future by seeking to reduce the anthropogenic causes of climate (Brazier 2015), while adaptation encompasses the enhancement of the coping and absorptive capacities of households and communities by making them more resilient to the risks of climate change (Wisner et al. 2003), Ideally, basketry producers should adopt both mitigation and adaptation measures, thereby lessening their own contribution to climate change and heightening their capacity to handle the climate change effects taking place. This entails minimising the vulnerability of communities, including people and the ecological mechanisms they rely upon, and strengthening adaptation and resilience in order to inhibit the risks arising from climate change.

In this context, in trying to mitigate and adapt to the anthropogenic effects of climate change, a wide range of strategies exist amongst the Tonga people in Ward 7. These include tree growing, preservation of forests, protection of wetlands, prevention of veld fires and practising conservation farming.

Tree Growing and Protecting Forests

Every first Saturday of December, Zimbabwe commemorates national tree planting day and engages in a reforestation project for schools and other institutions. This day is set aside to motivate the nation to plant and conserve trees, enlighten the nation on the importance of forests and woodland resources and enhance biodiversity and household food security, thereby mitigating the impacts of climate change (Mapira 2017). According to the Forestry Officer:

> We provide seedlings for tree species for communities to plant on the tree planting day. However, communities often do not go far enough regarding the maintenance of the trees. We have been working with Community Based Organisation (CBOs) such as Binga Craft Centre and the defunct Binga Trees to raise awareness on the importance of planting trees, through the use of messages such as "do not grow old, grow trees". We have assisted communities with seeds to establish ilala plots. Ironically, the tree planting never goes beyond the planting. Trees need to be looked after by being watered and protected from fire, livestock and wild animals, especially during the first two years of their life. Simply planting trees is highly unlikely to guarantee that they survive to maturity, ... Communities need to grow trees rather than just plant trees.
>
> *7 January 2022*

In Ward 7, 82% of the sampled villagers in fact professed ignorance of the National Tree Planting Day. Another 10% have heard about the day but have no information on what happens on that particular day, and 8% were fully aware of the day but never participated in the process. In the case of planting trees as part of a national programme, one basket producer Makwe Munenge of Bulawayo Kraal village thus said:

> We are not consulted or involved in decision making processes regarding location of the plots [where trees are planted]. These plots are situated far away from our homestead and pose challenges to safeguard and maintain them.
>
> *30 December 2021*

Marvis Munsaka, a female basket producer in Dumbwe village, added:

> National Tree Planting Day is a noble programme and a panacea to mitigate the depletion of the endangered fauna and flora. However, as villagers, we do not have much information about the day. We are not involved in the planning of such events thereby leading to its unpopularity.
>
> *28 December 2021*

As an alternative to this national planting programme, one villager suggested:

> The most practical situation is to give seedlings to people with vested interests in planting, so they can go and plant in their homestead. By so doing, the maintenance of the plant will be enhanced.
>
> *Sophia Mwinde of Siangwemu village, 3 January, 2022*

Overall, then, the local communities in Ward 7 are not actively involved in planting trees, let alone growing them. It does not appear that this event is being properly advertised by the EMA and Forestry Commission through the Tonga villagers' traditional leadership, in order to raise awareness of the need to enhance biodiversity through growing and preserving trees and the environment more broadly.

Tonga villagers do speak about the importance of local forests, but they tend to emphasise the protection of what already exists. Thus, in Ward 7, only 25% of the respondents prefer reforestation (planting trees) as a mitigation strategy, while the rest (75%) mainly focus on forestry preservation by avoiding veld fires. There is a general consensus within the community to protect the local forests from veld fires and hence to save the natural resources contained within the forests, mitigating climate change in the process. Maphios Munenge (male) of Siangwemu hence declared:

> We have huge tracks of forest areas. What is important in this era of climate change is to preserve and protect these forests from veld fires and deforestation.
>
> *3 January 2022*

Musaanje Munkuli of Dumbwe village added that:

> Our traditional leaders should ensure that they do not allocate land to new settlers in these forest areas and we should make a deliberate effort to maintain some fire guards around our forests.
>
> *28 December 2021*

Protection of Wetlands and Rivers

Protection of wetlands, streams and rivers enhances climate change mitigation, as these water bodies trap carbon, thereby reducing greenhouse gases. In rural areas, they play a pivotal role in enhancing household resilience to climate change and they can be vital sites for planting endangered plant species (such as ilala palm and reeds) as well as a source of water for supporting trees. Plants along the banks of wetlands, rivers and streams also minimise and control land degradation by preventing soil erosion.

However, it is worrying to observe how human activities are causing significant alterations to the function, integrity and quality of wetlands, rivers and streams in Zimbabwe. In the country, more than 50% of the wetlands, rivers and streams were lost between 1980 and 2020 and this is negatively affecting the balance of ecosystems (ZELA 2021). Wetlands have dried up due to interference with the overall ecosystem, and rivers and streams have been silted due to river bank cultivation. The EMA officer explained that:

> Water bodies play an important role in environmental, economic, and social services and they need to be preserved and protected at all cost. We are collaborating with local partners such as Basilwizi Trust, to sensitise communities to avert disrupting the rivers, streams and wetlands ecosystems; however, communities have been very stiff-necked. They argue that rainfall in Binga district is very low, since it falls in ecological region V. Hence, [they argue], we are dependent on these water bodies for livelihoods.
>
> *7 January 2022*

The last part of the quotation implies that local Tonga people rely so significantly on the very limited water bodies existing in Binga that seeking to protect them over the long term may undermine their short-term livelihoods. At the same time, though, 98% of the interviewees expressed a willingness to preserve wetlands, streams and rivers because they recognised that endangered plant species require preserving. This is because they remembered how reeds and ilala palm grew and flourished close to water streams in times past, yet these water streams have dried up. Sofia Munkuli from Siangwemu village, for example, referred to this, highlighting that Manjolo Primary School's nearby springs, streams and wetlands once provided water throughout the year.

Conservation Farming

Conservation farming is an integral part of agro-ecological approaches which seek to conserve and improve soil fertility and water moisture content. It involves using the surface cover (mulch) to maintain soil fertility and minimise rainfall run-off and, in turn, this improves the conditions for crop growth. It also incorporates the digging of plant basins, minimal or zero tillage of the land and crop rotation. The Zimbabwean government has sought to encourage Tonga villagers to adopt this "modern" conservation farming system. According to the Department of Agricultural, Technical and Extension Services (AGRITEX) officer:

> The department of AGRITEX has been educating communities to adopt agro-ecological approaches in their farming activities to avert shifting from

> one field to the other and prevent unnecessary deforestation. However, communities are resistant to change as they continue with their old system of cultivation. They cite that modern conservation agriculture (*Gatshompo/fumvudza*) was time- consuming and demanding in terms of labour-intensity.
> *7 January 2022*

Hence, in Manjolo, 95% of the sampled villagers were still implementing some version of their "traditional" agricultural methods, including the long-established method of shifting cultivation. During land clearance and preparation, they would burn grass and crop stocks, thereby minimising soil regeneration, with the soil suffering loss of fertility over time. They would then abandon the field and clear a new piece of land for planting crops, causing deforestation in the process.

The villagers spoke themselves about failing to adopt "modern" conservation farming, in the following ways. During a focus group discussion, Moonga Mudenda (male) of Siangwemu village for instance said:

> The introduced modern conservation farming methods are difficult to adopt due to lack of corresponding technologies to till big sizes of fields/farms and this is not going well with us. In this era of climate change, you are required to manually dig holes in intense heat and this is affecting our health.

Another villager added that:

> We wish the government could introduce a technology for cultivation to minimise labour intensity. This will influence people to migrate from shifting cultivation to conservation farming, thereby leading to conservation of forests.
> *6 January 2022*

The Manjolo community were very comfortable with their conventional farming methods. However, the villagers strongly recognise that shifting cultivation should be stopped and they now thoughtfully consider the importance of using cow and goat dung for manure while also not burning the grass, leaves and crop stocks during the land preparation process.

Conclusion

This chapter has examined the impact of climate change on basketry as a source of livelihood for marginalised women in Ward 7 in Binga District, Zimbabwe. The study established that the impact of climate change on the basketry livelihood activity is unequivocal and that basketry producers are increasingly aware of the unfolding detrimental events surrounding local ecological changes. The Ward 7 villagers show great concern about prolonged and frequent droughts, floods, heat waves, changes in seasons and precipitation patterns, water stress and ecosystem changes, especially the depletion of the flora, as all these undercut the basketry work of women. Despite recognising that climate change does exist and is a key contemporary challenge for local livelihoods, the Tonga villagers simultaneously continue to express bitterness over the loss of the riverine livelihoods because of the Kariba Dam construction decades ago. Today, communities from Siangwemu, Dumbwe and Bulawayo Kraal travel long distances to access ilala palm fields, reducing their level of production and income. If no urgent action is taken to curb the disappearance of ilala palm, the local Tonga women fear that they will soon slide back into the poverty and depravation. This is because their households do not have access to alternative forms of capital, such as human, physical and financial capital, which could sustain them in the face of long-term losses to their natural capital base. Further, living and remaining at the margins of state power, the Tonga in Ward 7 are not receiving significant support and assistance from the Zimbabwean government to cushion this blow to their livelihoods.

References

Brazier, A. (2015). *Climate change in Zimbabwe: facts for planners and decision makers*. Harare: Konrad-Adenauer-Stiftung.

Cline, W. R. (2007). *Global warming and agriculture: impact estimates by Country*. Washington, DC: Centre for Global Development, Peterson Institute for International Economics.

Creswell, J. W. (1994). *Research design: qualitative and quantitative approaches*. Thousand Oaks, CA: Sage.

Cunningham, A. B. and Milton, S. J. (1987). Effects of basket-weaving industry on mokola palm and dye plants in northwestern Botswana. *Economic Botany*, Vol. 41(3): 386–402. Springer. www.jstor.org/stable/4254989

Davies, M., Béné, C., Arnall, A., Tanner, T., Newsham, A., and Coirolo, C. (2013). Promoting resilient livelihoods through adaptive social protection: lessons from 124 programmes in South Asia. *Development Policy Review*, Vol. 31: 27–58.

Dube, T., Intauno, S., Moyo, P., and Phiri, K. (2017). The gender differentiated impacts of climate change on rural livelihoods labour requirements in Southern Zimbabwe. *Journal of Human Ecology*, Vol. 58(1–2): 48–56.

Dube, T, Ncube, C, Moyo, P, Phiri, K., and Moyo, N. (2021). Marginal communities and livelihoods: san communities' failed transition to a modern economy in Tsholotsho, Zimbabwe. *Development Southern Africa*. https://doi.org/10.1080/0376835X.2021.1955660

Ellis, F. and Allison, E. (2004). Livelihood diversification and natural resource access. Access to Natural Resources Sub-Programme Livelihoods Diversification and Enterprise Development Sub-programme Overseas Development Group, LSP Working Paper 9, University of East Anglia UK.

IPCC. (2014). Summary for policymakers. In: *Climate change 2014: impacts, adaptation and vulnerability. Part A: global and sectoral aspect. contribution of working group II to the fifth assessment report of the intergovernmental panel on climate change*. Cambridge, United Kingdom and New York, NY: Cambridge University Press, pp 1–32.

Kollmair, M. and Juli, G. (2002). *The sustainable livelihoods approach: input paper for the integrated training course of NCCR North-South Aeschiried*, Zurich: University of Zurich, Switzerland.

Lamichhane, K. (2010). *Sustainable livelihood approach in assessment of vulnerability to the impacts of climate change: a study of Chhekampar Vdc, Gorkha district of Nepal*. Kathmandu: Kathmandu University Centre for Development Studies National College, Baluwatar.

Mapira, J. (2017). Zimbabwe's forestry commission and the quest for sustainable development. *Journal of Social Science Research*, Vol. 11(2): 2415–2423. https://Doi.Org/10.24297/Jssr.V11i2.6305

Matanzima, J. (2021). Thayer Scudder's four stage framework, water resources dispossession and appropriation: the Kariba case. *International Journal of Water Resources Development*. doi: 10.1080/07900627.2020.186650

Mubaya, C. P., Njuki, J., Mutsvangwa, E. P., Mugabe, F. T., and Nanja, D. (2012). Climate variability and change or multiple stressors? Farmer perceptions regarding threats to livelihoods in Zimbabwe and Zambia. *Journal of Environmental Management*, Vol. 102: 9–12.

Ngingi, S. N. (2016). *Climate change adaptation strategies: water resources management options for smallholder farming systems in sub-saharan Africa*. New York, NY: The Earth Institute at Columbia University.

Pachauri, R. K., Allen, M. R., Barros, V. R., Broome, J., Cramer, W., Christ, R., and Dasgupta, P. (2014). Climate Change 2014: Synthesis Report. Contribution of Working Groups I, II and III to the Fifth Assessment Report of the Intergovernmental Panel on Climate Change. Cambridge University Press, Cambridge, UK.

Parmesan, C. and Yohe, G. (2003). A globally coherent fingerprint of climate change impacts across natural systems. *Nature*, Vol. 421: 37–42. http://dx.doi.org/10.1038/nature01286

Seneviratne, S. I., Nicholls, N., Easterling, D., Goodess, C. M., Kanae, S., Kossin, J., Luo, Y., Marengo, J., McInnes, K., Rahimi, M., Reichstein, M., Sorteberg, A., Vera, C., and Zhang, X. (2012). Changes in climate extremes and their impacts on the natural physical environment. In: *Managing the risks of extreme events and disasters to advance climate change adaptation. A special report of working groups I and II of the Intergovernmental Panel on Climate Change (IPCC)*. Cambridge, UK and New York, NY: Cambridge University Press, pp 109–230.

Serrat, O. (2008). *The sustainable livelihoods approach*. knowledge@adb.org www.adb.org/knowledge solution

Shaw, M. R., Pendleton, L., Cameron, D. R., Morris, B., Bachelet D. et al. (2011). The impact of climate change on California's ecosystem services. *Climatic Change*, Vol. 109: 465–484.

Stern, N. (2007). *The economics of climate change*. Cambridge, UK: Cambridge University Press.

UNDP. (2007). *Human development report: fighting climate change. Human solidarity in a divided World*. London: Palgrave Macmillan.

Wisner, B., Blaikie, P., Cannon, T.Y. and Davis, J. (2003). *At Risk: natural Hazards, peoples' vulnerability and disasters*. 2nd ed. Wiltshire: Cromwell Press.

World Bank. (2010). The Zambezi river basin a multi-sector investment opportunities analysis. Volume 3 state of the Basin. *The international bank for reconstruction and development, the World Bank*. Washington, DC: The World Bank.

Yilmaz, K. (2013). Comparison of quantitative and qualitative research traditions: epistemological, theoretical, and methodological differences. *European Journal of Education*, Vol. 48(2). New York: John Wiley & Sons Ltd, pp 311–325.

Zimbabwe Environmental Lawyers Association (ZELA). (2021). *ZELA press statement: let us restore our wetlands*. www.zela.org/zela-press-statement-let-us-restore-our-wetlands.

ZimStat. (2012). Zimbabwe National Census Report. Causeway, Harare.

4

TONGA LIVELIHOODS IN MKOKA, GOKWE SOUTH, IN THE CONTEXT OF CONTACT WITH SHONA SETTLERS

Shumirai Nyota

Introduction

This chapter examines the livelihood activities of the Tonga people of Mkoka in Gokwe South in the context of their displacement from the Zambezi Valley as well as contact and interaction with Shona people. Prior to living in the Mkoka area, this group of Tonga (like all other Tonga found in Zimbabwe today) lived along the Zambezi Valley where, particularly before the rise of colonialism, they pursued productive lives and livelihoods Accounts by many scholars describe the Tonga's time in the Zambezi Valley as the "golden age" of their history and identity (Tremmel 1994; Gambahaya and Muhwati 2010; Sibanda 2015). In relation to the link between Tonga identity and the natural environment, the Zambezi River and the river valley call to mind abundant game, crops and fish, and social belonging, unity and sovereignty (Reynolds and Cousins 1989). The golden age also evokes anecdotes of the many fruits the Tonga used to eat, their ability to predict and adjust to the weather of the valley, and their vibrant political institutions. The Tonga's relative prosperity and good health in the golden age are indirectly reflected in their vast knowledge of varieties of fish and wild plants (some of which were used as edible vegetables), alongside an intimate knowledge of many plants and trees which served as grain substitutes (Gambahaya and Muhwati 2010). Further, through indigenous "knowledge and technology" (Chiwome 2000: vi), they developed local technologies to process vegetables and fruits that would not normally be fit for human consumption and drew upon over 100 plants with healing properties.

At that time in the valley, the Tonga lived in harmony with nature and with minimum impact on the ecosystem, and the Zambezi River was central to this. They relied on the river, its valley and the surrounding forests for food and general sustenance. The large pools of the Zambezi River provided substantial fish while the nearby forests ensured access to game meat, poles for building shelters

DOI: 10.4324/9781003278580-5

and firewood, among other things. There was interdependence between themselves and the surrounding flora and fauna nurtured by the river. The Zambezi Valley was indeed their lifeline and they looked after it – hence their name, BaTonga that originates from the term "BaLonga" which means "people of the Great River" (Tremmel 1994: 14). However, after the emergence of colonialism and, in particular, subsequent to their displacement from the Zambezi River in the 1950s and resettlement because of the construction of Kariba dam and lake (Calamita et al. 2019), the Tonga had to painfully learn and unlearn many knowledges and practices in order to survive under new circumstances.

Livelihoods in the Context of Displacement

This study locates livelihoods in the context of displacement, an idea that was originally developed after the Second World War to refer exclusively to the displacement of refugees. However, this restricted definition was soon seen as excluding other forms of displacement, such as forced resettlements under government policies or due to projects of private corporations, as well as because of natural disasters. Overall, displacement entails "enforced changes in interweaving spatial, social and symbolic conditions and relations" (Cottyn 2018: 9). In both colonial and post-colonial Zimbabwe, there have been significant and diverse forms of state-induced displacement. Hammar (2008) cites several scholars who record such displacements since independence in 1980. These include: the violent eviction of migrant Shona and Ndebele small-scale farmers from Vumba in northwest Gokwe in the late 1990s; large-scale evictions from commercial farms from 2000 onwards as a result of the state's fast track land reform programme; and the military-style campaign of mass urban demolitions and evictions named Operation *Murambatsvina* carried out in 2005 and 2006.

Displacement is paradoxical in that there are not only experiences of destruction, dislocation and confinement, but also possible livelihood opportunities and moments of creativity (Cottyn 2018). However, these effects of displacement take place unevenly across particular displacements and are experienced by "displacees" in variegated ways. Disruptions and shocks to livelihood activities because of displacement are common (Tawng 2020), and the likelihood of particular post-displacement livelihood activities and strategies are conditioned in part by policies and institutions governing the contexts of the displaced (Potts 2008; Jaysawal and Saha 2018). The absence of resettlement and livelihood planning aid and assistance usually leads to an overall decline in living conditions and well-being of those displaced (Cottyn 2018). In fact, post-displacement lives are typically marked by vulnerability and precariousness, and displacees need to cope with displacement-induced stress (Arnall et al. 2013) while also seeking to build new livelihoods and livelihood resilience, as many studies have shown (Hong et al. 2009; Tischler 2014; Mashingaidze 2013). The Kariba dam is a prime example of development-induced displacement, and one in which post-displacement support was not forthcoming for the Tonga of Mkoka, leading to excessive poverty and exposure to exploitation by Shona villagers.

The construction of the Kariba dam and lake was a massive project that is well documented and it was meant to benefit both Northern and Southern Rhodesia, present-day Zambia and Zimbabwe, respectively, including in relation to energy generation (Noyoo 2007). As "river people", the Tonga lost their unfettered access to the river because of displacement. They lost their homes, grazing land, woodlots, ancestral graves and burial grounds and overall livelihoods generation due to the forced evictions. The Kariba project resulted in the Tonga of the Zambezi valley being displaced to Binga, Kariba rural, Omay and Nyaminyami, Hwange, Gokwe North and Chirundu (Hachipola 1998; Makoni et al. 2008; Manyene 2013; Ndlovu 2009).

In terms of research undertaken about the post-displacement Tonga, the Tonga of Mkoka in Gokwe South have not received sufficient scholarly attention. This chapter thus focuses on the Tonga that trekked to Gokwe South under their paramount chief, Mkoka, who still presides over them to this day. The Tonga of Gokwe South were soon joined by other groups, notably Shona who occupied the land to the north of the Kana River and the Ndebele who moved onto land south of the Kana. These arrivals became Mkoka residents after being displaced from different areas in (then Southern) Rhodesia due to the implementation of the Land Apportionment Act (LAA) of 1931 and the 1950/1951 Native Land Husbandry Act (NLHA) (Hanyani-Mlambo et al. 2000). In this context, the chapter examines the livelihoods of the Tonga of Mkoka in the context of their evictions from the Zambezi Valley and their subsequent contact with Shona people who also settled in the same area.

Methodology

The study uses a qualitative research methodology as it focuses on the perspectives, experiences and practices of the Tonga. The fieldwork took place from August 2021 to February 2022 and involved informal face-to-face interviews as well as *WhatsApp* audio and text messages. Face-to-face interviews were carried out with three participants purposively selected as they were rich repositories of both the Mkoka Tonga and Shona histories. The three were an elderly Tonga person, an elderly Shona woman and an elderly retired Shona teacher. These elderly interviewees were all present in Mkoka at the time of the initial contact between the Tonga and Shona, with these two groupings interacting in the Mkoka area for the first time in the late 1950s following their respective displacements. The two groups were well established elsewhere before displacement, that is, the Zambezi Valley in the case of the Tonga, and Rhodesdale in the case of the Shona. The three interviewees provided very useful recollections of events which took place over half a century.

As well, *WhatsApp* audio and texts messages were exchanged with four participants: a Tonga teacher and a Shona teacher both teaching in schools in the area, a young Tonga man working at the local Grain Marketing Board depot, and a young Tonga man in the local police force. *WhatsApp* audios and texts were chosen because they are cheaper than voice calls, and they allow for lengthy discussions or conversations. The advantages of these texts and audios is also that they can be recorded even when the recipient is offline and will be delivered when they come online. This was very helpful because network connectivity is erratic in Mkoka. In this regard, the researcher assisted the interviewees with data bundles. These youthful professionals were also purposefully selected because they were in a strong position to offer pertinent information about the livelihood strategies of the Tonga in the context of contact with the Shona settlers.

The interviews with the Tonga and Shona elders were undertaken in the Shona language because the Tonga elder (like the other Tonga in the area) is fluent in Shona. Interviews with the professionals were done mainly in English. I also draw upon my own observations and experiences as a Shona person who grew up in the area under study (indeed, the elderly Tonga resides in a Tonga village next to my home village).

Livelihoods of the Tonga on Arrival in Mkoka from the late 1950s

Most Tonga of Mkoka are settled along the Kana River since the time they arrived in the late 1950s to date. The river is the main landmark that delineates the boundary between Gokwe South, which is mainly Shona speaking, and Nkayi and Lupane, which are both Ndebele speaking areas. Though these areas are known as Shona and Ndebele speaking, respectively, it was the Tonga who settled in both places first. Some Tonga people also settled along smaller rivers on the Gokwe side in the Shona speaking area. It is likely that the Tonga named these rivers on arrival in the area since the rivers bear Tonga names, such as Lufuse, Lutope, Dongalonga, Manzialisalala, Lukugwe and Ndandulo. The Shona arrived in the area after the Tonga and this affected the latter's livelihood strategies. I focus on the Shona-Tonga interactions but draw parallels with Ndebele-Tonga relations where relevant.

My elderly Tonga participant pointed out that, when the Tonga first settled in Mkoka area, they continued with their cultural practices and livelihood activities as existed in their former home, the Zambezi valley. This included socialising their children in the Tonga cultural ways of life. For example, boys spent evenings with male adults and elderly men of their extended family around a fire, during which time the boys were taught such skills as fishing, hunting and preparing animal skins (used as cloth to cover their lower back and front parts). The boys were also taught carpentry skills to make: walking and hunting sticks; stools for use in the home by both men and women; a mortar and pestle for preparing mealie meal from the small grains they grew in the valleys; and utensils such as wooden dishes and plates. Further, they learnt how to make mats and baskets from reeds that grew in the rivers. Girls associated with adult and elderly women who taught them the following skills: cooking Tonga dishes; cleaning and mending floors with cow dung; and making pottery plates, cooking pots, water pots and beer pots. They were instructed as well about making traditional smoking water pipes with which the Tonga smoked a mixture of water and tobacco known as *ndombonda*. The water pipe, it seems, was mainly smoked for pleasure (Interview with the elderly Tonga participant held on 12/08/21).

In terms of livelihoods, the Tonga in the Mkoka area tried to live their lives as they did in the Zambezi valley, despite the fact that the natural conditions in Mkoka did not match those they experienced in the valley. To begin with, the rivers in Mkoka (including Kana) were very small compared to the mighty Zambezi River, such that these rivers could not match what the Zambezi offered them (for instance, in terms of fish for consumption). The same applied to the local woodlots, as they were not as expansive as those along the Zambezi. They, thus, grudgingly settled in their new post-displacement environment, trying to construct familiar livelihood practices. One informant (a Shona teacher) said the following about the way the Tonga of Mkoka felt about their new home:

> Settling in Gokwe, … after being forced out of their rich hunting and fishing grounds in the Zambezi Valley was not easy for the Tonga and this, coupled with the bitterness of leaving their ancestral lands, was a bitter pill to swallow. They had to contend with the knowledge that their lives would never be the same again. The rivers in Gokwe were small as compared to the mighty Zambezi river which had more and bigger fish.
>
> *WhatsApp call with a Shona teacher, on 26/09/21*

Indeed, weather conditions in Mkoka were different from what the Tonga experienced in the Zambezi valley, where there was high levels of rainfall. As Ncube (2017) indicates, the Mkoka area is tsetse infested with poor rainfall patterns. Gokwe is in agro-ecological regions III and IV marked by "low and erratic rainfall patterns" and only "suitable for drought resistant crops such as cotton".[1] Other major constraints in Mkoka included:

> Unfavourable geo-physical conditions, an inadequate resource base, restricted access to inputs, labour bottlenecks, pests and diseases, inappropriate post-harvest technology, poor animal nutrition, poor animal health delivery systems, …, insufficient infrastructure for disposal of marketable produce, and lack of institutional support.
>
> *Hanyani-Mlambo et al. 2000: 3*

Though this assessment relates to more contemporary times (compared to the late 1950s and 1960s), it does speak to the challenges of constructing livelihoods in the Mkoka area at the time the Tonga arrived in the area.

Despite the shortcomings of their new home, the Tonga tried as much as possible to live in harmony with nature. The minor rivers in Mkoka provided small fish, and the Tonga only fished quantities enough for daily consumption. They grew small grains, namely, sorghum and millet, using the *chitemene* method, an agricultural method involving shifting cultivation (Sibanda 2015). They practiced this from the time of their displacement in Mkoka but the possibility of continuing with this became problematic after the arrival of Shona people. This farming system entailed crop rotation, and it allowed the Tonga to remove a piece of land from the crop rotation cycle to allow that land to lie fallow during one or two agricultural seasons, so that it becomes productive again after resting and regeneration. As well, the woodlots provided wild animals for food, with the Tonga hunting kudus and small animals such as hares, which were then used for relish. Reeds in the rivers were cut for mat-making and constructing baskets for use in their homes. As with their livelihoods prior to displacement, they tried not to disrupt the local ecosystem for purposes of sustainability.

Arrival and Presence of the Shona

The Tonga were the first to settle in Gokwe South before the arrival of Shona and Ndebele people soon afterwards. The Ndebele people who settled in certain parts of Gokwe South were pushed from areas around Gwanda, Fort Rixon and Filabusi by the colonial government, while Shona people were forcedly removed by white settlers from the area named Rhodesdale (a name that earned these Shona the nickname, *MaRhozidheyi*, literally meaning "those from Rhodesdale") which is an area between the Gweru and Zibagwe rivers. The first amongst the Shona victims of Rhodesdale were 1,100 families under headmen Muyambi and Selima who were dumped in the area between the Lutope and Kana rivers in Mkoka (Ncube 2017). My Shona elderly woman interviewee spoke about how the Shona ended up in Mkoka to live with the Tonga:

> Though we were young I remember we were loaded into lorries with our property like furniture, grain, goats, chickens. Those who resisted had their legs and hands tied up and thrown into lorries. Men drove cattle for days on end from *Rhozidheyi* to Mkoka. We were displaced together with teachers, nurses, pastors, [and] agricultural officers, such that schools, clinics, [and] churches (Catholic, Methodist, Salvation Army and other churches) were opened up on arrival. … [T]he agricultural officers had beautiful houses built for them at Land Development Offices (LDO). These officers taught agriculture while their wives taught home economics.
>
> *Interview with a Shona elderly woman participant on 20/08/21*

Though the Tonga were the first indigenous people in the area, the Shona and Ndebele settlers soon after arrival began to dominate and ill-treat the Tonga people. At first, there appeared to be some possibility of inter-ethnic cooperation. Hence, on their initial relations with the Tonga, the retired Shona teacher had this to say:

> On arrival for the first time, we feared the Tonga, who did not wear clothes but animal skins. They moved around in groups with weapons like spears. But they were helpful people. Whenever they saw a Shona walking alone, they would walk behind you until you were in a safe place. We ended up realising

> that they did this to protect the newcomer from marauding animals like hyenas. They ended up helping us in our gardens and fields.
>
> *Interview with the former Shona teacher on 15/12/21*

Cultural Marginalisation of Tonga

Generally, though, from the time they originally arrived, the Shona did not treat the Tonga with dignity. For example, they addressed the Tonga by the derogatory term *MaZambezi* ("those of the Zambezi"), a term meant to constantly remind the Tonga of where they came from (and belong) and how they ended up in Kana. Ill treatment of the Tonga is also confirmed by Ncube (2017: 23) who discovered from her interview with a Tonga headman that some Shona migrants forcibly displaced indigenous Tonga people who they found in the Muyambi area to more arid areas like Lukukwe, Mwambani and beyond. This was corroborated by another Tonga interviewee of Ncube (2017) whose parents settled at Muyambi but, according to her mother, were then chased away by "*vabvakure*" (immigrants). My Tonga policeman interviewee additionally spoke about cultural marginalisation by Shona-speakers vis-à-vis Tonga people:

> Life was relatively better for some of the Tonga before the arrival of the so called *maRhozideyi* people who came with their arrogant and bullish personalities to dominate the otherwise docile Tonga people. The first thing these Shona people did was to belittle Tonga culture, language and religion. The Shonas also made Tonga children their herdsmen while they sent their own children to school resulting in Tongas being left behind in terms of development. The other thing that irked the Tonga people was that the Shonas and Ndebeles came with their own chiefs, village heads and headmen who imposed themselves on the Tonga.
>
> *WhatsApp audio message from a Tonga policeman interviewee on 22/11/21*

The Tonga in retaliation referred to the Shona as *MaRhozidhey* in reference to the displacement they suffered at the hands of the white settlers. However, this term of address did not tarnish the Shona to the extent that *MaZambezi* did to the Tonga.

As Manika (2014: 11) points out, the collapse of the Tonga social, cultural and economic fabric could also be attributed to colonial and post-colonial policies and practices. For instance, during registration of birth and national identification certificates, state officials forced the Tonga to change their names to Shona ones; those who converted to Christianity were given new Shona and bible names; and those who went to school were compelled to change their names to Shona and to learn Shona. Despite such actions, the Tonga tried by all means to hold on to their culture.

The Shona also corrupted the spelling and pronunciation of the names of the rivers found in the area (i.e. the names given by the Tonga) to be read and pronounced as follows:

Tonga Name of River	Name Corrupted/Rephonologised by the Shona
Lufuse	Rufuse
Lutope	Rutope
Dongalonga	Dhongaronga
Manzialisalala	Mandisarara
Lukugwe	Rukugwe
Ndandulo	Ndanduro

The Tonga meanings for the named rivers are lost in the rephonologised spellings, and the river names now reflect Shona phonology and semantics. Any visitor to the area would be forgiven to believe that these rivers were named originally by the Shona.

As confirmed by the Shona and Tonga professionals interviewed, a number of other issues negatively affected Tonga culture after the arrival of the Shona. The Shona propagated many myths about Tonga culture, customs and religion. Generally, the Shona believed that the Tonga would kill one of their own at religious ceremonies such as *mubuyiso*, a ceremony to appease a dead relative. The Shona claimed that a man would be struck to death with either a spear or an axe so that another *mubuyiso* would be held the following year. Such myths presented Tonga villagers as murderers and backward morally from the perspective of Shona people. Shona youngsters apparently feared to be in the vicinity of the Tonga because of these myths. These stories about the Tonga reiterate the observations made by Manyene (2013: 26) regarding the labels placed on the Tonga, with negative descriptions such as "marginalised, poor, isolated, backward, minority, primitive, dangerous and degraded". In this context, some Tonga people in Mkoka sought to assimilate themselves into aspects of Shona culture, such that assimilation was not based entirely on compulsion. As one informant (a Tonga teacher) put it:

> The Tonga people had to try to adopt some aspects of Shona culture and language in order to be acceptable. Today it is not surprising to find Tonga people with Shona names or to find people at a Tonga home speaking in Shona; that's how far things have gone in the subjugation of the Tonga people by Shonas and Ndebeles.
>
> *WhatsApp audio interviewee with a Tonga teacher 19/11/21*

Overall, compared to the Shona, the Tonga have always seemed voiceless by virtue of their lowly position in society, as if the Shona now treat the Tonga in the same manner the colonialists treated blacks in the past (including the Shona). One of my young Tonga professional informants had this to say about the relations which developed over time between the Tonga and their Shona (and Ndebele) neighbours:

> These Shona and Ndebele people were totally different from them [the Tonga] and relations were never good. The Ndebeles and Shonas were a

> dominant people who, in spite of the fact that they were newcomers, tried successfully to dominate the Tongas. The Tonga people were forced to adopt Shona/Ndebele ways of life to the detriment of theirs. Meanwhile, the Tonga tried to make sure that it was very difficult for their children to learn the Shona language, culture and customs all the time, and this has helped them to maintain a Tonga identity up to this day despite the onslaught on their culture by the Shona.
>
> *WhatsApp audio interviewee with a Tonga professional, 21/11/21*

The Tonga are very proud of their language and customs and, in terms of their identity, they have sought, if only in part successfully, to remain Tonga.

Marginalisation of Tonga Livelihoods

The displacement of the Shona decades ago to Mkoka was a planned and forced one undertaken by the Rhodesian state. Those who "cooperated" with the agencies of displacement were accorded the opportunity of bringing at least some of their assets with them to Mkoka, thus possibly enabling the building of livelihoods along the lines pursued at Rhodesdale. The assets they brought with them meant that they could reconstruct a built environment that was in some way similar to *Rhozidheyi*, their place of origin. Compared to the manner in which the Tonga were displaced, the Shona were at a distinct advantage in terms of managing their displacement and reconstructing livelihoods, as there was a level of post-displacement state planning in the case of the latter. As Cottyn (2018: 4) argues more generally: "[H]ouseholds with better access to capital have been found to be more resilient while those constrained in accessing resources are vulnerable".

Initially, the Tonga were able to pursue reasonably viable livelihoods in Mkoka despite the dramatic disruption arising from displacement, but this changed significantly with the arrival of the Shona. This is corroborated by the elderly Tonga interviewee's recollections:

> Our elders moved from place to place looking for good areas. This is why you see us living along valleys. When we first arrived, these rivers had fish, the woodlots had animals, we hunted for relish. We grew sorghum in the valleys for food, beer brewing and for *ndombonda*. Things have changed such that we do not get what we used to get; we are in poverty.
>
> *Interviewee with the elderly Tonga interviewee on 12/08/21*

My informants spoke about the negative effects of the Tonga people's contact with Shona speakers with regard to the former's food security in Mkoka. The Shona had initially been settled further inland than the Tonga, with the Tonga people residing along river valleys. However, the Shona soon began to encroach into the river valleys. It is claimed that the Shona aggressively pursued and practiced an intensive crop-cultivation economy about which the Tonga were not familiar or experienced. The Shona started market gardening by developing vegetable gardens along the river valleys occupied by the Tonga. They grew vegetables for own consumption and sold any surpluses to those further inland, where water to irrigate vegetables was not easy to come by. As more and more Shona villagers realised the importance of the vegetable-growing ventures, the more land they took away from the Tonga for their gardens. This reduced substantially the land available to the Tonga for growing their small grains.

My informants also reported that the encroachment and activities of the Shona made it impossible for the Tonga to continue with the *chitemene* (i.e. shifting cultivation). The Tonga in Mkoka no longer had the luxury of letting pieces of land lie fallow and uncultivated because, in absolute terms, they now had very little land available for growing their grains. Moreover, the Shona did not practice any form of soil conservation, thus leading to siltation of the local rivers. Some of the small rivers have since disappeared due to siltation while those that remain are fast filling up with sand. This, in turn, undercut the fishing-based livelihoods of the Tonga. In addition, the number and sizes of the gardens developed by the Shona required the cutting down of many trees in the woodlands in order to make poles for constructing wooden security fences around their gardens for protection against wild animals and livestock. Over time, as their children grew up, they also needed houses and gardens of their own, so the Shona continued cutting down trees to use as construction materials (as well as for firewood). This entailed direct competition with the Tonga, as the Tonga needed wood for energy and poles as well, and for brewing beer (*vukande*) on a regular basis as per their cultural requirements.

The general result was pressure on the local natural habitat, leading to land degradation and deforestation. Deforestation meant that the woodlands along river valleys were now depleted of the wild animals that had once provided the Tonga with food. Moreover, some of the Shona are said to have hunted using nets that enabled them to catch many animals at a time, thus depleting the woodlots of wild animals at a rapid rate. This "over-kill" disturbed the ecosystem and impacted detrimentally on the Tonga who had always hunted just enough for immediate consumption (as relish).

As well, the Shona drove their cattle to the rivers for drinking water and grazing in the valleys because, further inland, they did not have readily available water for livestock. They made use of drilled boreholes that often ran empty of water especially in the dry season. Some Tongas also kept a limited number of cattle. Combined, this put significant strain on available grazing land and left all the cattle prone to diseases due to lack of enough nutritious food. To make matters worse, there were not sufficient cattle dipping facilities in the area to protect the cattle from diseases, leading to loss of cattle for both the Tonga and the Shona.

The early activities of the Shona in areas designated for the Tonga pushed the Tonga into dire poverty. Meanwhile, the Shona continued with market gardening and growing subsistence crops. When cotton was introduced into the area in the late 1970s, the Shona embraced this commercial crop and enjoyed income from cotton growing up to the late 1990s. The Shona used some of the earnings from commercial cotton farming to send their children to school, even up to university in some cases. The Tonga, whose livelihoods had been eroded by the Shona, could not do the same for their children. They could not afford food, let alone generate surplus crops to sell in order to raise school fees for their children.

Instead, the Tonga and their children often ended up being forced to look for menial work from the Shona in exchange for food. When asked what the Shona gave to the Tonga for working in their gardens and fields, one interviewee said that they gave them sadza and some grains which would last just a few days (Interview with the elderly Shona woman, 20/08/21). The Shona did not perceive that they were exploiting the Tonga, or that there was anything wrong morally in making the Tonga work for food, with the Tonga labour helping the Shona settlers to produce enough crops for food and resale. Some elderly Tonga worked in the fields owned by the Shona while their sons and daughters were employed by the Shona as herdsmen and domestic servants, respectively. Thus, there is evidence suggesting that a vicious poverty circle emerged among the Tonga, while the Shona prospered (relatively speaking) on the backs of the Tonga, both the young and the old. Some Tonga, who were skilled in mat and basket making or carpentry, sold their wares "for peanuts" to the Shona who, in turn, sold these wares to lucrative markets in towns such as Bulawayo.

As a general tendency, including in the post-1980 period, the Tonga in Mkoka have been left out of developmental programmes that were availed to the area by local development officers. This is despite the fact that there were efforts made by government and Non-Governmental Organisations to protect if not improve the livelihoods of Zimbabweans (including those of residents of Mkoka) from the 2000s, the period known for Zimbabwe's devastating economic collapse which did not spare even the Shona of Mkoka. The Basic Education Assistance Module (better known by its acronym BEAM) was one such initiative, coordinated by the Department of Social Services. The BEAM was established in 2001 by the government of Zimbabwe as part of the Enhanced Social Protection Programme (ESPP), which was meant to provide basic education (at primary and secondary school level) to everyone in the country including students who could not afford the school fees (such as orphans and other vulnerable children). This was part of the overall policy of the government as well as pertaining to global agreements to which the Zimbabwean government is a signatory (Smith et al. 2012). My informants, both Shona and Tonga professionals, report that very few Tonga children have had fees paid through BEAM. The Tonga children had to compete with those from among the Shona and the Ndebele for chances with BEAM, and they did so largely unsuccessfully. Some of the few Tonga youths who participated in government strategies like BEAM, mostly Tonga male youths, joined the civil service such as the police, army and teaching after receiving their BEAM-funded education. Very few female Tonga children received the same educational opportunities.

Schemes by state agencies like the Agricultural Research and Extension Services (AREX) and companies such as Cotton Company of Zimbabwe (COTTCO) have sought to improve the agricultural livelihoods of residents of Mkoka, but these have benefited primarily the Shona. Most Tonga could not join the agricultural schemes supported by these external institutions because they did not have access to land to enable them to participate. The Tonga are deeply dissatisfied with this, as they feel that they have been side-lined in favour of Shona and Ndebele people. One informant thus lamented:

> Tongas as a people are still very bitter about the way they were treated by all concerned i.e. colonialists, Shonas and Ndebeles. They feel they were marginalised throughout by being made to feel inferior by all the above groups. They also feel they did not benefit much from education strategies such as BEAM, [as] since up to now only a few Tonga people are educated. AREX officers did not help much as they were in most cases Shona. Hence, [they] were only interested in empowering their fellow Shona communities, leading to marginalisation of the Tonga communities.
>
> *WhatsApp audio with a Tonga employee of the Grain Marketing Board on 05/02/22*

The current evidence shows that the Tonga live in poverty, in part because they lack access to natural capital (notably, land, the river valleys and woodlots). Though these were in abundance during the few years they lived on their own in the immediate post-displacement period, the arrival of the Shona changed this situation drastically. For example, an interviewee (in Ncube 2017: 23) narrates how the Shona displaced and restricted the Tonga along very narrow river valleys which the Shona continued to deplete of assets. In this respect, many studies on rural displacement highlight the importance of assets (notably natural capital) to combat the negative effects of displacement on livelihoods (Jaysawal and Saha 2018; Speranza et al. 2014). The case of the Tonga in Mkoka illustrates this. The Tonga of Mkoka are exposed to ongoing precariousness because their resilience and adaptive capacity are very low considering that they do not have a ready pool of assets and resources to mobilise for livelihood purposes.

Conclusion

The story of the Tonga of Mkoka, as discussed in this chapter, has been one of suffering double domination, first as a result of their displacement and now oppression by the Shona (both under colonialism and then in post-colonialism). Their story fits well in the overall story of the Tonga of Zimbabwe. From the time they were displaced by the colonialists, their lives have never been the same up to today. Dam construction did not consider the consequences for the Tonga, leading to long periods of neglect. This neglect arose, because after making way for the construction of Kariba Dam, they were moved into areas where they soon were forgotten about. For decades, they have remained victims of development (Chiwome and Mguni 2003). Lessing (1992) thus describes how the great dam, which deprived the Tonga of their homes, has not benefited them. The lake does not irrigate the land along its long shoreline; instead, Kariba is a vast lake which is a lifeline for people other than those it displaced. Similarly, Kayawe (2013) describes the plight of the Tonga who had no access to electricity generated by the dam whose construction resulted in their displacement. The description by Tremmel (1994: 10) of the displaced Tonga in general is thus apt, as it refers to "realities such as excessive drinking, unemployment, ... poor health, ..., poor self-image, ..., illiteracy, ...". All these observations are true for the Tonga of Mkoka more specifically.

Note

1 http://fnc.org.zw/wp-content/uploads/2021/04/Gokwe-District-Zimbabwe_FNS-Response-Strategy-in-the-Context-of-COVID-19.pdf (accessed 21/02/22).

References

Arnall, A., Thomas, D. S., Twyman, C., and Liverman, D. (2013). Flooding, resettlement, and change in livelihoods: evidence from rural mozambique. *Disasters*, Vol. 2013(37): 468–488.

Calamita, E., Schmid, M., Kunz, M., Ndebele-Murisa, M. R, Magadza, C. H. D., Nyambe, I., and Wehrli, B. (2019). Sixty years since the creation of Lake Kariba: thermal and oxygen dynamics in the riverine and lacustrine sub-basins. *PLOS ONE*. https://doi.org/10.1371/journal.pone.0224679 (Accessed 10/11/21).

Chiwome, E. (2000). *A social history of the Shona Novel*. Gweru: Mambo Press.

Chiwome, E., and Mguni, Z. (2003). *The discourse on Zimbabwean women in the war of liberation and the land reform programme: myth and reality*. University of Zimbabwe. www.gwsafrica.org/knowledge/zifikele (Accessed 16/01/22).

Cottyn, I. (2018). Livelihood trajectories in a context of repeated displacement: empirical evidence from Rwanda. *Sustainability*, Vol. 10: 3521.

Gambahaya, Z., and Muhwati, I. (2010). Tonga orature as historical record: an Afrocentric exegesis of the dialectics between African human factor agency and the European enslavement of place. *Journal of Black Studies*, Vol. 41(2): 320–337.

Hachipola, S. (1998). *A survey of the minority languages of Zimbabwe*. Harare: University of Zimbabwe Publications.

Hammar, A. (2008). In the name of sovereignty: displacement and state making in post-independence Zimbabwe. *Journal of Contemporary African Studies*, Vol. 26(4): 417–434.

Hanyani-Mlambo, B. T., Sibanda, S., and Rukuni, M. (2000). Farming systems in Zimbabwe's smallholder agricultural sector: the case of Gokwe South District. AEE Working Paper no. 2/2000. UZ, Mt. Pleasant, Harare: DAEE.

Hong, P.Y. P., Singh, S., and Ramic, J. (2009). Development-induced impoverishment among involuntarily displaced populations. *Journal of Comparative Social Welfare*, Vol. 25: 221–238.

Jaysawal, N., and Saha, S. (2018). Impact of displacement on livelihood: A case study of Odisha. *Community Development Journal*, Vol. 53: 136–154.

Kayawe, B. (2013). *Electricity for all but those the Kariba Dam displaced*. www.ipsnews.net/2013/03/electricity-for-all-but-those-the-kariba-dam-displaced/ (Accessed on 22/05/22).

Lessing, D. (1992). *African laughter: four visits to Zimbabwe*. New York: Harper Collins Publishers.

Makoni, S., Makoni, B., and Nyika, N. (2008). Language planning from below: the case of Tonga in Zimbabwe. *Current Issues in Language Planning*, Vol. 9: 413–439.

Manika, T. (2014). A History of the Tonga People's Relocations from Binga to Settlement in Kana Valley. Dissertation submitted in partial fulfilment of the requirements for the BA Honours Degree in History and International Studies Midlands State University.

Manyene, S. B. (2013). Ethnicity, identity, agency and development: the case of the Zimbabwe Tonga. In L. Cliggett and V. Bond (eds), *Tonga timeline. Appraising sixty years of multidisciplinary research in Zambia and Zimbabwe*. United States: Lembeni Trust, 2(10): 25–65.

Mashingaidze, T. (2013). Beyond the Kariba Dam induced displacements: the Zimbabwean Tonga's struggles for restitution, 1990s–2000s. *International Journal on Minority and Group Rights*, Vol. 20: 381–404.

Ncube, A. (2017). *Cultural dynamism as a solution to the ethnic conflict: the case of Gokwe South District 1950–2017*. Gweru: B. A. project Midlands State University.

Ndlovu, F. (2009). *The politics of language and nation building in Zimbabwe*. Bern: Peter Lang, AG, International Academic Publishers.

Noyoo, N. (2007). Indigenous Knowledge Systems and Sustainable Development: Relevance for Africa. Tribes and Tribals, Special Volume No. 1: 167–172.

Potts, D. (2008). Displacement and livelihoods: The longer term impacts of Operation Murambatsvina. In M. Vambe (ed), *The Hidden Dimensions of Operation Murambatsvina in Zimbabwe*. Pretoria: Weaver Press:, pp 53–64.

Reynolds, P., and Cousins, C. C. F. (1989). *Lwaano Lwanyika: Tonga book of the earth*. Harare: C. C. Cousins and SCF (UK), pp 250.

Sibanda, N. (2015). An analysis of the significance of myths and proverbs as African philosophies of peace and justice: a case of the Ndebele, Shona and Tonga tribes from Zimbabwe and the Igbo from Nigeria. *IOSR Journal of Humanities and Social Science (IOSR-JHSS)*, Vol. 20(4): 01–06. Ver. V.

Smith, H., Chiroro, P., and Musker, P. (2012). Zimbabwe: Evaluation of the Basic Education Assistance Module Programme, UNICEF, Published: 2012, Accessed: 01 Oct 2021.

Speranza, C. I., Wiesmann, U., and Rist, S. (2014). An indicator framework for assessing livelihood resilience in the context of social–ecological dynamics. *Global Environmental Change*, Vol. 28: 109–119.

Tawng, L. H. (2020). Exploring the Livelihoods of Internally Displaced Persons in Kachin State Myanmar. A thesis submitted to Victoria University of Wellington in partial fulfilment of the requirements for the degree of Master of Development Studies School of Geography, Environment, and Earth Sciences, Victoria University of Wellington.

Tischler, J. (2014). Cementing uneven development: the Central African Federation and the Kariba Dam scheme. *Journal of Southern African Studies*, Vol. 40(5): 1047–1064.

Tremmel, M. (1994). *The people of the great river: the Tonga hoped the water would follow them*. Gweru: Mambo Press.

5

"NEITHER ELEPHANT NOR MOSQUITO"

Livelihoods of Tonga People in Sikalenge Ward, Binga, circa. 1950–2022

Christopher Mweembe

Introduction

Binga District is located in the Zambezi Valley, in the northwestern part of Zimbabwe. The Tonga ethnic group dominates the population of the district, with only approximately 3% comprising Shona and Ndebele speakers. The district has a population of around 138,074 people, with 63,512 males and 74,562 females (ZimStat 2012). More than 80% of the population lives below the poverty datum line (ZimStat 2017), with food insecurity threatening the everyday lives of thousands of vulnerable Tonga households. Absolute poverty is the leading cause of people's vulnerability to food insecurity in Binga, and it is the defining feature of the people once proudly known as "people of the great river". In fact, Binga falls within an agro-ecological regions III, IV and V, and in the main it is characterised by semi-arid and tropical dry savannah climatic conditions resulting in deficiencies in soil, high temperatures, low and erratic rainfall and low crop yields. These conditions have led to prolonged chronic disasters (such as droughts), with most of the population requiring humanitarian aid dating back for decades now (Tremmel 1994). Despite being richly endowed with natural resources, Binga District ranks last on the development index among all rural districts in Zimbabwe (UNDP 2010; ZIMVAC 2012). The very presence of Tonga people in Binga arose over half a century ago. The World Bank-funded Kariba Dam project in the 1950s forced the mass displacement of more than 23,000 people on the Southern Rhodesian side and 34,000 on the Northern Rhodesian territory from the fertile soils along the Zambezi River banks (Colson 1971). The forced displacement of the Tonga people disrupted livelihoods as entitlements to riverine cultivation; fishing and hunting activities were lost.

In this context, this chapter examines the changing livelihoods of the Tonga people of Binga District over the period circa 1950– 2022. It considers, firstly, Tonga livelihoods prior to the forced resettlement, and then, respectively, the period

DOI: 10.4324/9781003278580-6

from post-displacement in Binga to independence in 1980 and the independence period until now. Similarities and differences across the periods will become evident, reflecting the dynamic character of Tonga livelihoods temporally.

Research Methods

Binga district has 24 wards, each with its particular climatic conditions and belonging to different agro-ecological regions. This chapter focuses specifically on Sikalenge Ward in agro-region V, which is an extensive farming area with less than 650 millimetres of rain per year and very high temperatures. A stratified random sampling procedure was used to select the case study ward among the 24 wards, with Sikalenge Ward chosen. The procedure was as follows: the names of wards were put in three groups of wards according to the three agro-ecological regions (III, IV and V) in the district. From each of the three groups, one ward was selected at random, and these were then put in a separate box, whereupon a single ward was then picked (i.e. Sikalenge). In Sikalenge Ward, there are eight villages, namely, Sialota, Keelemenda, Damba, Delampuli, Mangogo, Chilimbana, Siabhanga and Musenampongo. The eight villages in Sikalenge Ward have 2,713 females and 2,200 males in total (ZimStat 2012).

The fieldwork for this study was undertaken for five months from October 2021 to February 2022. In the first instance, it involved four Focus Group Discussions (FGDs) which included representatives from each of these eight villages. As depicted in Table 5.1, a total of 40 respondents participated in the FGDs, with 10 respondents per group. In terms of gender and age disaggregation, there were 5 male youth and 5 female youth (below 18 years of age), and 15 female adults and 15 male adults (18 years of age and older, with the oldest person being 65 years old). The four FGDs were each conducted over a period of 1 hour with the help of two research assistants. Although Tonga was the primary language used during the discussions, respondents could use any language in which they were comfortable expressing themselves, including English.

TABLE 5.1 Focus group discussions in Sikalenge Ward

Village	*Males*	*Females*	*Total*
1. Damba	2	2	4
2. Delampuli	3	3	6
3. Chilimbana	2	2	4
4. Keelamenda	2	2	4
5. Mangogo	3	3	6
6. Musenampogo	3	3	6
7. Siabhanga	3	3	6
8. Sialota	2	2	4
Total	**20**	**20**	**40**

Source: Author 2022.

In addition to the FGDs, there were key informant interviews with stakeholders in the Binga district. In total, 16 key informants (7 Government officials, 6 NGO personnel and 3 Chiefs), 10 males and 6 females, were interviewed. Each key informant interview took roughly 45 minutes, with the lead researcher (author) asking questions and the two research assistants taking notes. These notes were triangulated amongst the research team to ensure that all crucial information and impressions from team members were captured. The research made use of participant observation as well, whereby the researcher and research assistants participated actively in the villages' social gatherings such as funerals, sporting activities and meetings, while also observing and recording people's livelihood activities. In addition, the researcher reports from government departments and development partners operating in Binga district.

Before 1957: Pre-Colonial and Colonial Livelihoods in the Pre-Dam Context

There is scant literature on the vulnerability context of the Tonga people before they were forcibly relocated from the Zambezi Valley. This can be attributed in part to the existence of only a few scholars conducting research in the Zambezi Valley during that period. Further, well-known scholars like Colson and Scudder extensively researched the lives of the River Tonga on the Zambian side of the Zambezi, while sparse research was undertaken on the Zimbabwean side.[1] Scholars like Matanzima and Saidi (2020: 3) note this gap and bemoan the fact that, though the Tonga in Zimbabwe are a very marginalised people in the country, academic scholarship has generally neglected researching and documenting their way of life. This scholarly neglect reflects the political neglect experienced by the Tonga over an extended period, as this chapter demonstrates. Certainly, the Tonga people were neglected by both the colonial government and missionaries, and this became visibly evident in the absence of roads, schools and clinics in the Zambezi Valley.

Before the late 1950s (in then-Southern Rhodesia), the homesteads of the Tonga people were located along the Zambezi River and deltas of the tributaries from Victoria Falls to what is now Kariba dam (Manyena 2009; Mashingaidze 2020). The fieldwork revealed that, according to Sikalenge villagers, the pre-displacement lives of the Tonga were marked at times by the vulnerabilities of war, disease and drought.

In times past, the Tonga faced profound livelihood shocks due to war and raiding from neighbouring Lozi warriors (from the southern part of present-day Zambia) and Ndebele warriors (from the eastern part of present-day Zimbabwe). The oral history of the local villagers indicates that the Lozi warriors mainly took young women and men and later sold them to Arab and Portuguese traders at the time of the slave trade systems (Interview, Mr. Siabulabupati Munsaka (pseudonym), Sikalenge Ward, 3 January 2022). Meanwhile, in their raids, the Ndebele warriors took food and livestock, as well as young men and women. However, according to a headman in Sikalenge Ward, these raids ended as the Tonga warriors defeated both the Lozi and Ndebele warriors at the mountain cliff called *KuliSyadogo* (Interview, with Fulunga Muleya (pseudonym), Headmen in Sikalenge Ward, 6 January 2022). Elders in the Sikalenge Ward hold that the Lozi and Ndebele raids left the Tonga people impoverished.

The FGDs revealed that the pre-dam shocks and threats experienced by the Tonga generally also included diseases. For example, most respondents highlighted that the Zambezi Valley was severely infested by mosquitoes which caused malaria. People who were infected with malaria became ill and many died possibly because the area lacked hospitals and clinics. At the same time, though, informants indicated that the Tonga people had well-established ways of treating malaria and infected people would be healed using indigenous knowledge systems. Related to malaria, villagers also noted that the Zambezi valley region was severely infested with tsetse fly, causing sleeping sickness in humans and *trypanosomiasis* in livestock (Ndlovu 2016). Tonga people lost many of their cattle due to tsetse fly.

During the FGDs, droughts and famines became a motif as one major shock experienced often by the Tonga people before the dam displacements. The older people who witnessed the forced removals from the valley to the uplands (known as "*Lusaka*" in Tonga) argued that severe droughts characterised life in the valley on many occasions. For example, one elderly woman in her 90s even challenged the view that life was better before dam displacement in saying that:

> We experienced severe droughts, and we had no food for family consumption. Most of our parents went to *"Kumbo"* searching for menial jobs to get food. *Kumbo* is the area around the Copper Belt in present-day Zambia, as we used to know it during our olden days along the Zambezi Valley. Our parents and we used to go there for days or weeks working in people's fields to get food, or at times we used to go there with art-craft products such as baskets and mats for sale to buy food.
>
> *Interview, Mrs. Violet Mulenga (pseudonym), Sikalenge Ward, 6 January 2022*

This aptly shows that, despite the common narratives that the Tonga people were riverine dwellers, that they cultivated twice a year and that they seemed mostly food secure, in fact, such claims need to be contested because they tend to romanticise the past. There were many times that they faced severe droughts that depleted their natural and other assets (including livestock), pushing them into lives of precarity. Besides going to *"Kumbo"* as articulated above, it was also discovered that, during such periods of droughts, people survived on gathering wild fruits, hunting and fishing. For example, one informant listed examples of wild fruits used as food, including bird plum or *berchemia discolor*, known as *inji* in Tonga; snot apple called *manengo* in Tonga; tamarind known as *busika* in Tonga and many others (Interview, with Chamugolya (pseudonym), Sikalenge Ward, 14 February 2022). He also highlighted that the buffalo was the most hunted animal by the Tonga people, probably because of its tasty meat and their closeness to the Chizarira National Park established by the colonial state.

Overall, then, the Tonga people prior to the construction of the Kariba Dam and their displacement tended to pursue their livelihoods in the face of numerous vulnerabilities. This was the case even though the Zambezi Valley region was abundant in natural resources. Along with social capital, natural assets were crucial to the construction of Tonga livelihoods at the time (Mashingaidze 2020; Mago et al. 2015; Matanzima and Saidi 2020; Manyena 2009).

Broadly speaking, during the pre-dam era, the main economic activities of the Tonga comprised riverine and upland crop farming, livestock rearing, hunting, fishing and manufacturing. Riverine farming was based on recession agriculture which mainly depended on the flooding system of the Zambezi River, while upland farming was practised on poor soils using a shifting cultivation system (WCD 2000). Villagers cultivated diversified crops such as maize, bulrush millet, sorghum, sweet potatoes, groundnuts, various cucurbits, tobacco and cotton (Tremmel 1994) – with tobacco and cotton grown for commercial purposes (Manyena 2009). The Zambezi River flooded annually and fertilised the riverine gardens with deposits of alluvial soils, which enabled the Tonga to harvest twice a year.

For this Binga study, the research respondents referred to past Tonga lives being animated by abundant natural resources, allowing for hunting, fishing and gathering wild foods for consumption and nutrition. This was based on access to water from the perennial (Zambezi) river with various fish, significant nearby forested areas with numerous wild animals and fruits and other forestry products like honey. However, restrictive game laws were introduced in Southern Rhodesia from as far back as 1906 (Manyena 2013; Ndlovu 2016), leading to an increase in both game and tsetse fly. The wild animals increased because the Tonga people were now restricted from hunting and killing animals using spears, dogs and snares. This restriction harmed their diets and dietary diversity. Besides eating meat from wild animals, the Tonga respondents spoke about exchanging game meat for maize, millet and sorghum grains with neighbouring villages. The animal skins were used for making drums, clothes, blankets, royal regalia and kilts, while animal horns became wind instruments during musical and cultural performances.

In line with the historical details of Tremmel (1994), the fieldwork evidence demonstrates that fishing was one of the main economic activities in which both men and women actively participated. While men and women both participated in fishing activities, they used different methods. Women used the more straightforward method of *kuzuba baswi* using a big basket (called *mazubo* in the Tonga language) to catch fish, and they typically fished in shallow waters in groups. For their part, men had more sophisticated ways of using spears and nets to catch fish in deeper waters. The catch of fish was consumed within Tonga households, and any surplus was sold or traded for grains and other products.

The Tonga people also had robust social networks, including maintaining close relationships with kin and clansmen even in Zambia, almost on a daily basis. These interactions with their counterparts in Zambia included the performance of cultural practices such as *Ngoma butibe* (traditional music of beating drums, while singing and blowing horns), *kumpila maleende* (a traditional rain-worshipping ceremony) and *kuumpila mizimu* (a family or clan spiritual cleansing or appeasing the spirit of the dead). These social networks were maintained by walking from one village to the other along paths, and they crossed the Zambezi River with dugout canoes carved out of large trees. The beating of drums and blowing of horns provided a basis for communication over long distances, including announcing the death of an elderly person or inviting people to a community beer drink.

In terms of pre-dam livelihood conditions, as indicated, the past should not be romanticised, including the pre-colonial days. As Ndlovu (2016: 2) warns: "One should, certainly, resist the temptation to create a picture of a kind of lost paradise which emerges from the memories of elderly Tonga". At various times, life was very precarious in the Zambezi valley, including high levels of disease (such as dysentery and leprosy) and child mortality. Health care was minimal (WCD 2000) and communication and transport were virtually non-existent, making interaction with others difficult (Manyena 2009). There were no roads, only footpaths, so few vehicles could reach the valley. Travelling by footpaths was dangerous due to wild animals, and Tonga people travelled in groups whenever they had to make long journeys.

Livelihoods in the Post-Dam, Pre-Independence Context: 1958–1980

Although several shocks and threats existed before the displacement, the Kariba dam construction in 1957 has had the most severe negative impact on the lives of the affected Tonga people (Mashingaidze 2020; Matanzima 2020). With thousands of Tonga people forcibly removed, the fieldwork in Sikalenge Ward confirms that, unlike on the Zambian side where the displaced people received compensation on a *pari passu* basis (or on "a hut for a hut" basis) (Mashingaidze 2013), the Zimbabwean Tonga were not compensated. The respondents highlighted that the Southern Rhodesian government was focused on the benefits of the hydro-electric scheme to grow the white settler economy.

When the Kariba Lake was crested, it opened new opportunities for tourism, and mainly white Rhodesian settlers began to appropriate the space. As revealed in the FGDs, the creation of Lake Kariba facilitated tourism and a fisheries industry which were monopolised by white Rhodesians, and they employed Ndebele and Shona speaking people in doing so. In the process, the Tonga people were sidelined and failed to benefit from the expanding opportunities. As other Lake Kariba studies (Matanzima 2021; Hughes 2010; McGregor 2008) show, the government neglected the Tonga people after displacing them from their ancestral lands. McGregor (2008) comments that the Southern Rhodesian authorities prioritised white settlers' interests, and the landscape was appropriated for conservation and tourism, turning the new inland sea into a leisure-focused habitat for whites. Hughes (2006) makes a similar observation, claiming that conservation carried out a white cultural agenda and worked to naturalise settler's claims. Nearly all natural resources were regarded as conservancies, national parks, safari areas and forestry areas for the overwhelming benefit of the white settlers.

Instead of accessing, exploiting and utilising the newly created Lake Kariba and other natural resources centring on the river and lake, the Tonga of Sikalenge lost access to riverine livelihoods. They were in large part denied access to the water because they were dumped very far from the Lake. The Tonga people were pushed far from the shoreline to dry upland areas with poor soils for crop production. Water and fisheries conservation policies were enacted which inhibited Tonga livelihoods further. The local Tonga people were now restricted in, for instance, hunting wild animals. Scholars like Mashingaidze (2020) indicate that game wardens enforced stringent wildlife conservation systems which denied Tonga people the right to hunt wild game for subsistence purposes. Those in the FGDs noted that, soon after the relocation, the many wildlife sanctuaries, national parks and safari areas established began arresting people who hunted animals for consumption. Local people who hunted animals were regarded as poachers and faced stiff punishments to deter them and others from repeating similar offences in future. Similarly, the Forestry Management officials enforced regulations that prevented Tonga men and women from harvesting firewood, plants, herbs and wild vegetables from these protected areas.

Fishing in Lake Kariba also became a challenge for the Tonga. Indeed, the Tonga people on the Zimbabwean side had more limited access to the Lake and its resources compared to their Zambian counterparts, who had established many fishing camps and were not restricted in fishing. For the Zimbabwean Tonga, only limited fishing camps were established, and most of the shoreline was demarcated as fish breeding sites by the government where local Tonga people were not allowed to fish. The Tonga of Binga highlight that the shoreline on the Zimbabwean side was soon dominated by hotels and lodges, conservancies and state-managed National Parks. In a particularly cruel twist, they did not benefit from the hydro-electricity generated from the creation of Lake Kariba.

By the late 1960s and early 1970s, the guerrilla war in Rhodesia had affected the study site. Because (the now) Binga district was used as a corridor for the guerrillas crossing into Zambia to train and attack the white government, there were often intense and fierce clashes between the two armies (guerrilla and state army) during the war of liberation. For example, Mr. Chamugolya,[2] who served in the Rhodesian army, narrated how people's livestock were forcibly taken or killed by the guerrillas, negatively affecting people's livelihoods. He further asserted that young girls were raped by guerrillas who gave birth to fatherless children and, when they grew up, most lacked financial support to proceed with education, pushing them into deeper poverty (Interview, Mr. Chamugolya (pseudonym), 14 February 2022). The war also destroyed infrastructure such as roads, bridges, dip tanks, schools and clinics. Some schools were temporarily closed in the 1970s due to fierce fighting between the guerrillas and the Rhodesian army.

As in the pre-dam context, the period from the late 1950s to 1980 was characterised by severe droughts, floods and famines. For example, during the FGDs at Siabuzuba, a villager called Siajagi narrated that, since being forcibly relocated in 1957, there has been a clear observable trend that every ten years Binga district experiences a drought (including droughts in 1962, 1972 and 1982). It was claimed that, during droughts, villagers would resort to eating and living on wild fruits as their source of sustenance. Similarly, in 1965, some areas like Sungwale experienced flooding, which swept away people's limited assets such as crops, top soils and small livestock.

From both key informants and FGDs, it was gleaned that the Tonga people had limited assets of all kinds during this period. The forced displacement from their riverine life to the dry uplands destroyed much of the social capital (or networks) that they had enjoyed before relocation. Indeed, their sense of belonging to the river was disrupted, in part because their ancestral shrines were submerged in the vast Lake Kariba, disconnecting people from their departed ones. Social interactions with the Zambian Tonga became difficult to sustain and they no longer jointly performed traditional ceremonies like the annual Tonga cultural festival called *ilwiindi*. An elderly woman from Delampuli village bemoaned how the traditional rain-making ceremonies called *maleende* were soon neglected and how this consequently affected the rains among the Tonga people, which further impacted detrimentally the Tonga's livelihoods (Interview, Mrs. Muleya (pseudonym), 27 December 2021).[3] However, the relocated Zimbabwean Tonga did endeavour to uphold Tonga culture and traditions in their newly resettled upland areas. For example, the rain-making ceremony in fact continued to be performed by a Mr. Malila, who embodied the rain-making spirit after relocation.

Besides being denied employment, the colonial government did not invest any of the proceeds derived from the tourism and fishing industries to develop the infrastructure of the locations to which the Tonga were displaced. One of the women in the FGDs lamented the fact that, during this period, the absence of schools, roads and health facilities was clear for all to see. In the FGDs, it was highlighted that the first schools in the Binga district were established in the late 1950s after Tonga resettlement away from the Zambezi River. However, a significant challenge was that most parents were illiterate and did not know the importance of education in the making of a better life. Therefore, few children attended school and, notably, very few children completed secondary education. When questioned about this dire state of affairs, local informants mentioned that: no schools offered secondary education such that those who proceeded to secondary school went to other districts like Hwange and Gokwe; parents were far too poor to raise fees to send children to school; and there was an overall negative attitude to education amongst both parents and children. The girl child was also particularly disadvantaged as parents preferred to send boys to school ahead of girls. The absence of schooling existed despite the construction of schools from the early 1960s by missionaries attached to mainly the Catholic Church, Church of Christ and Methodist Church. Sikalenge villagers claim that, compared to elsewhere in the colony, missionaries started building schools in Binga district very late and their schools in Binga were poorly resourced and mostly provided education to only Standard three.

The early years of resettlement were particularly difficult for the Tonga people as they were just dumped in new upland areas without shelter, water and food. In the first two years of resettlement, the government provided food relief of grain, powdered milk and salt (Tremmel 1994). From the FGDs, though, it was learnt that some chiefdoms (like Sinakatenge, Sinamwenda and Sinamusanga) were able at least in part to continue the riverine life since they were settled along major tributaries of the Zambezi River. These villagers still enjoyed cultivating on floodplains and tried to harvest throughout the year as before. However, most of the chiefdoms (like Sikalenge, Sinakoma, Sianali, Saba, Siachilaba and others) were not so fortunate, and they survived on hunting and gathering of fruits to supplement subsistence agriculture (which involves mainly the cultivating of small grains like millet and sorghum). Fishing became more difficult for these communities as they were now far away from the Lake. Some chiefdoms like Simuchembu and Sinamagonde were resettled to the *lusaka* (uplands) where soils and rains are better, and they later ventured into commercial farming based on crops such as cotton and maize. Both key informants and FGDs respondents reveal that, across all the 15 relocated chiefdoms, this is the period (late 1950s–1980) when most of the migration of Tonga people to towns, mines and commercial farms of white settlers to seek employment took place. Many of these migrants reinvested their earnings in local livelihoods in Binga.

The intractability of the vulnerability context during this period is quite clear, characterised by significant trends and shocks such as the relocation of the people, the war of liberation and restrictive colonial legislation that wiped out meaningful livelihood assets and ultimately stifled people's way of life and life chances. This reduced many Tonga villagers' livelihood options, pushing them into a profound abyss of chronic poverty leading to long-term precarity. At the same time, based on the claims of fieldwork informants, the livelihood strategy of migration (of movement out of the area for purposes of formal employment) did enhance the livelihoods of many Sikalenge villagers as it gave them access to cash as a financial resource.

Livelihoods in the Post-Independent Context, 1980–2022

By independence in 1980, the Tonga in the study site had experienced major livelihood challenges and setbacks. Several further detrimental events and processes befell Binga district post-1980, including climate change and variability (Manyena et al. 2008; Manyena 2009; Tremmel 1994; Mashingaidze 2020). Perhaps the greatest negative impact of climate change has been the recurrence of severe droughts. The FGDs revealed that Binga district suffered severe droughts in 1982/1983, 1992/1993, 2007/2008, 2014/2015 and 2016/2017. All these droughts (now known to be linked to the ENSO or *El Nino* Southern Oscillation phenomenon in the southern Pacific Ocean) resulted in poor harvests and losses of livestock, leading to widespread food insecurity. Besides droughts, climate change and variability have also contributed to severe flooding in selected wards in the district. For example, Nsugwale village under Sinakoma Ward, possibly because of its topography, has been prone to flooding, leaving villagers vulnerable due to the loss of varied types of assets. The trends of droughts and flooding in the district from 1980 have pushed villagers towards a never-ending condition of precarity, including in relation to food insecurity.

Soon after independence and in the years that followed, political strife in the country became a significant shock and deeply troublesome for the villagers of Binga district. Notably, between 1983 and 1987, the Matabeleland provinces (Matabeleland North and Matabeleland South) and the Midlands province experienced the notorious *Gukurahundi* atrocities (Ngwenya 2018), involving the mass killings (genocide) of Ndebele-speaking people by the Zimbabwean state's Fifth Brigade. This period was one of Zimbabwe's darkest moments, in which an estimated 20,000 to 80,000 civilians were killed (CCJP 1992). In an interview, the Lubimbi Ward Councillor testified that, "I recall vividly one evening when the fifth brigade killed the sister to my mother. They also took our livestock – cattle, goats, and chickens – by force" (Interview, 19 November 2021). Such a practice affected people's livelihoods.

Further political strife flared up again in the year 2000 after the formation of the opposition party the Movement for Democratic Change (MDC) in 1999. Because the district was economically and politically marginalised after 1980 with reference to social development programmes implemented by the ZANU-PF government, people in Binga district, in turn, revolted against the ruling party and voted for MDC at all levels of government – presidential, parliamentary and council elections – hoping that one day the MDC would come to power and bring the dearly needed development into the district (McGregor 2008). This further widened the gulf between the ZANU-PF government and the people of Binga district, with the central government seemingly punishing the district for its heartfelt support for the MDC. During my fieldwork, one traditional chief aligned to ZANU-PF bemoaned that:

> People of Binga district do not learn. They have been voting for an opposition party that has not done anything in the district. People from other districts (Lupane, Umguza and Tsholotsho) in the province have since gone back to ZANU-PF. People in the Binga district expect the ZANU-PF government to invest in development programmes. For whom? These people are rebels. They should eat from MDC and not expect any development projects from the ZANU-PF government.
>
> *Interview, 22 October 2021*

This aptly shows that the deficient infrastructure prevailing in the district is in part deliberate, as the government actively neglects the social and economic development of the district because the majority of the people continue to vote for the MDC party. On one hand, this voting pattern clearly shows that the Tonga people in Binga district have used their political savvy to become an elephant that blocks ZANU-PF from winning both Binga North and Binga South constituencies. On the other hand, the voting pattern depicts that the Tonga people have become a mosquito that irritates the ruling ZANU-PF party by continuously voting for the opposition party. However, because of the perpetual poverty and underdevelopment, the Tonga people in Binga district are "*neither an elephant nor a mosquito*". If they were either of the above, they could have used their political assets to influence the government in developing the district for people to enjoy sustainable livelihoods.

As a major physical asset in the area, the water from Lake Kariba could be harnessed for massive irrigation development to increase crop production that would increase food security and also provide access to potable water for the Tonga people of Binga. The Zambezi River is home to various fish species, a resource that local people could exploit through gill net and *kapenta* fishing for home consumption and sales, in order to raise incomes and improve food and nutritional security. Tonga people could enhance their livelihoods by being given permission to hunt and kill wild animals for food consumption only, but these are protected within Chizarira National Park, the Chete Safari area and lands controlled by other safari operators located near Lake Kariba. The wards under agro-ecological region V (including the ward under study), most of which are adjacent to Lake Kariba, are marked by semi-arid and tropical dry savannah climatic conditions with low and erratic rainfall (Dzingirai and Madzudzo 1999). Despite the deprivations arising from this adverse ecological system, the post-independence government has not seen it fit to reverse in any meaningful way many of the colonially configured conditions hindering Tonga livelihoods, including around water supplies for agriculture, as well as fishing and hunting activities.

The expanded educational system initiated by the post-independence government and the building of many primary and secondary schools in the district from the 1980s has, however, led over time to a growing group of men and women in the district who have even completed tertiary education. Binga's human capital has improved as well through capacity development programmes led by central government departments (and development partners) for both out-of-school youth and adults in developing technical life skills. In Binga, for instance, youth have been trained in technical skills such as building, agriculture and carpentry which are meant to stimulate further livelihood activities locally. Though this has also enhanced the employability of district inhabitants on the labour market, formal employment opportunities in the district itself are exceedingly limited. Further, the structural adjustment programme implemented in the 1990s led to massive retrenchments of workers, mainly in manufacturing and mining industries and had major local effects. Thus, Kamativi tin mine, which was the only major industry employing thousands of Tonga people from Binga, was closed down. Those who lost jobs went back home to their villages and poverty deepened for the already impoverished Tonga households.

In this context, this section ends by focusing on the current livelihoods of Tonga villagers primarily in Sikalenge Ward. Fishing remains one of the key livelihood activities in Binga district, especially for Tonga communities adjacent to the lake. There are two main types of fishing. Artisanal fishing is the predominant form, which was practised even before displacement in 1957. This form of fishing consists of small-scale, low-capital and low-technology fishing practices involving gill nets, in which households engage primarily for own consumption but at times for selling purposes as well. Secondly, since independence in 1980, there has been a shift in fishing practices whereby communities have formed fishing cooperatives and adopted more technologically advanced modes of fishing. Currently, there are several *kapenta* fishing cooperatives, as well as certain individuals owning fishing rigs, that fish for commercial purposes. Although there are many fishing companies, these are predominately owned by outsiders (Ndebele or Shona), leaving local Tonga people to work as poorly remunerated labourers. Fishing licences are just too expensive for locals to afford, making them mainly bystanders to the fishing industry, surviving as subsistence fishers or labourers for others.

In most wards that fall within agro-ecological region IV and V in Binga district, farmers practice subsistence agriculture. They grow drought resistant crops such as sorghum and millet for home consumption. Besides this, they keep small livestock like goats, sheep and chickens to supplement their diets and to sell to improve household cash incomes. However, there are a few Tonga households which keep cattle usually for draught power and to generate income through sales to pay for, for example, school fees and health services. Sinamangonde Ward, with its more reliable rains and good soils, falls under agro-ecological region III. The villagers in the ward grow both food (mainly maize and sorghum) and cash crops (including cotton and tobacco). This ward is said to be the breadbasket of Binga, with farmers selling their produce to the Cotton Marketing Board and Grain Marketing Board, as well as engaging in cattle ranching. Generally, Tonga households in wards along the Zambezi valley keep small livestock, while wards further away (Sinamangonde, Lubimbi, Tinde and Chinonge Wards) focus on raising cattle.

Despite their agricultural and fishing activities, not all people in the district are food secure throughout the year. For example, during the lean months when food from their fields and livestock is scarce, food insecurity prevails. Because of this, some particularly poor households undertake casual labour such as weeding in other farmers' fields. For such households, casual labour becomes a major livelihood option during the farming season (November to February) when intensive labour is critical for working in the fields. Meanwhile, other households at times pursue small-scale mining. Binga district has no commercial mines, but several gold, diamond and coal sites are dotted across the district. There are a limited number of artisanal miners in Binga district (for instance, in Tinde and Lubimbi Wards) involved in gold panning. Although Covid-19 and the associated lockdowns have recently disrupted most small-and medium-scale enterprises, many people in all the wards are still active in petty trading. This is mainly done by women and youth, who buy clothes from Harare and Bulawayo and resell them locally. Some traders are more adventurous and purchase goods from further afield, including South Africa, Zambia and Mozambique. The crafting of cultural artefacts, by converting natural capital into financial capital, is common in many wards such as Sikalenge,

Manjolo, Saba-Luanda, Sinakoma, Chinonge and Kariangwe. These artefacts mostly comprise weaving basketry as well as manufacturing traditional tools, drums and animal artefacts. These products are sold along the road to motorists and tourists in particular. Wild foods also contribute greatly to some Tonga households' diet and income in Binga. These include fruits like *busika* and *kula*, which they sell and eat to supplement their diets. During the FGDs in Sikalenge Ward, women testified to having raised substantial levels of money from the sale of these fruits, which they use to buy basic household goods and to pay school fees for their children.

Finally, since the early 1980s, Tonga people in Binga district have mobilised themselves to improve their livelihood conditions, including by way of community-based organisations for empowering and diversifying people's livelihoods. Table 5.2 lists some of these organisations and their interventions and activities.

TABLE 5.2 Local organisations formed by Tonga people in Binga

Name of the Organisation	*Year established*	*Key interventions*
1. Fishing Cooperatives		- Livelihoods - Incomes and food security - Employment creation
2. Kulima Mbobumi Training Centre	1984	- Food security - Small holder farming - Small grains and drought resistant crops
3. Binga Craft Centre	1989	- Women empowerment - Natural resources management
4. Binga Development Association	1989	- Education and culture - Gender development - Participatory development
5. Binga Catholic Commission for Justice and Peace (CCJP)	1996	- Civic education - Social justice, governance and human rights - Livelihoods
6. Ntengwe for Community Development	1996	- HIV/AIDS - Orphans - Livelihoods
7. Basilwizi Trust	2002	- Education, Language and culture - Social justice, human rights and governance - Sustainable livelihoods - Health and HIV/AIDS
8. Zubo Trust	2009	- Women's empowerment - Livelihoods
9. Twasumpuka FM	2022	- Community journalism

Source: Author 2022.

Local development organisations, such as Basilwizi Trust, Zubo Trust, Amalima Loko Consortium and many others, seek to empower communities through enhancing sustainable livelihoods by way of cross-border trading, the development of life skills and the building of community assets, including dams, community gardens, rehabilitation of solar powered boreholes and irrigation schemes. Besides these local initiatives, there are several development partners operating in Binga district that seek to strengthen people's livelihoods and incomes in various ways. For instance, humanitarian agencies such as Adventist Development and Relief Agency, Caritas Zimbabwe, Save the Children, Red Cross and World Vision support Tonga villagers with cash transfers and food items to improve food security in the district. Nevertheless, because of the consistent presence and depth of poverty in the district, some of the approaches used by the local organisations and development partners need greater scrutiny. This is an important area for further research.

In the end, most livelihood strategies in Binga district are focused on ensuring that people are food secure. Unfortunately, most Tonga people suffer from food insecurity almost every year, though there is some unevenness in this respect. Thus, not all wards suffer from food insecurity. The Lusulu area, which mainly covers Sinamangonde, Kabuba and Lubimbi Wards, is more productive agriculturally because it is in agro-ecological region III, and both cattle ranching and crop production contribute to food security. In other wards where food insecurity prevails, diversification into a range of livelihood options occurs (such as petty trading and accessing wild foods) as a desperate measure to counteract shortfalls in food security, with humanitarian organisations like World Vision also assisting in this way. The fact that Binga remains ranked as one of the least developed districts in the country shows that the standard of living is still very low amongst the Tonga people in the district. People in the district are living precarious lives, characterised by high poverty levels, food insecurity, low incomes and poor living standards.

Conclusion

This chapter has examined the changing livelihoods of the Tonga people in Sikalenge Ward in Binga District over the period circa 1950– 2022. Overall, the livelihood strategies and practices adopted and pursued by the Tonga people in Sikalenge Ward have been mainly influenced by the vulnerability context prevailing at the time. Although the elderly Tonga people bemoan the lost paradise in the Zambezi valley due to the forced relocation in the late fifties, there was an array of intractability factors that exposed them to vulnerabilities that led to precarious living prior to relocation. Similarly, during the post-dam displacement up to 1980, the Tonga people's livelihoods (centred around upland farming, livestock rearing, hunting and fishing) were survivalist in character. Although Tonga villagers diversified their livelihood options after independence in 1980, their ongoing precariousness is apparent from the marked presence of development agents that give food handouts which might lead to a condition of perpetual dependency, thereby pushing them into deeper levels of livelihood unsustainability. In closely analysing the pre-dam, post-dam displacement and post-independence periods, it seems that the recurring motif is the presence of poverty amongst the Tonga in Sikalenge Ward in Binga District.

Notes

1 Professor Elizabeth Colson and Professor Thayer Scudder conducted long-term ethnographic research in the Zambezi/Gwembe Valley on the Zambian side, since 1956, in relation to the impact of the Kariba hydro-electric project on the livelihoods of the Tonga people. They also initiated the establishment of the Gwembe Tonga Research Project (GTRP) in 1956. The GTRP was joined in the 1990s, by Sam Clark, Lisa Cliggett and Rhonda Gillett-Netting, and more recently by Bennett Siamwiza, Allison Hannish, Emma Sitambuli and Joshua Matanzima.

2 Mr. Chamugolya was born in 1948 and was 9 years old when the Tonga people were forcibly relocated. He served in the Rhodesian army as an employee of the settler government, just like other black people across Rhodesia during that time. He also worked in the Rhodesian District Administrator's Office. He survived three fierce clashes with the guerrillas.

3 Mrs. Muleya had two children in 1957. The exact year she was born is not exactly known. Her last-born son told me that she could be around 105 to 110 years old. Amazingly, despite her advanced age, Mrs. Muleya could clearly remember key events before and after relocation.

References

Catholic Commission for Justice and Peace (CCJP). (1992). In Zimbabwe "Gukurahundi in Zimbabwe: A Report on the Disturbances in Matabeleland and the Midlands, 1980–1988".

Colson, E. (1971). *The social consequences of resettlement: the impact of the Kariba resettlement upon the Gwembe Tonga*. Manchester: Manchester University Press.

Dzingirai, V. and Madzudzo, E. (1999). Big men and CAMPFIRE: a comparative study of the role of external actors in conflicts over local resources. *Zambezi*, Vol. 26(1): 77–92.

Hughes, D. (2006). From industrial wasteland to wilderness: how Zimbabwean conservationists redeemed Lake Kariba. *Journal of Southern African Studies [JSAS]*, Vol. 32(4): 807–822.

Hughes, D. (2010). *Whiteness in Zimbabwe: race, landscape, and the problem of belonging*. New York, NY: Palgrave Macmillan.

Mago, S., Nyathi, D. and Hofisi, C. (2015). Non-governmental organisations and rural poverty reduction strategies in Zimbabwe: a case of Binga rural district. *Journal of Governance and Regulation*, Vol. 4(4): 2015.

Manyena, B. (2009). *Disaster resilience in development and humanitarian interventions*. Newcastle upon Tyne, UK: Northumbria University.

Manyena, S. B. (2013). Ethnic identity, agency and development: the case of the Zimbabwean Tonga. In L. Cliggett and V. Bond (eds), *Tonga timeline: appraising sixty years of multidisciplinary research in Zambia and Zimbabwe*. Lusaka: Lembani Trust, pp 26–65.

Manyena, S. B., Maureen, F. and Collins, A. (2008). Disaster resilience and children: managing food security in Binga district in Zimbabwe. *Children, Youth and Environments*, Vol. 18(1): 303–331.

Mashingaidze, T. (2013). Beyond the Kariba Dam induced displacements: the Zimbabwean Tonga's struggles for restitution, 1990S–2000S. *Interactional Journal on Minority and Group Rights*, Vol. 20(2073): 381–404.

Mashingaidze, T. (2020). Risk and Vulnerability in an Untamed Landscape: The Zimbabwean Tonga in the Aftermath of the Kariba Dam Induced Displacements, 1956–1980s.

Matanzima, J. (2020). Large dams: long term impacts on riverine communities and free flowing rivers. *Water International Journal, Taylor & Francis*. doi: 10.1080/14725843.2020.1777839

Matanzima, J. (2021). Thayer Scudder's four stage framework, water resources dispossession and appropriation: the Kariba case. *International Journal of Water Resources Development*. doi:10.1080/07900627.2020.1866505

Matanzima, J. and Saidi, U. (2020). Landscape, belonging & identity in North-West Zimbabwe: a semiotic analysis. *African Identities*. doi: 10.1080/14725843.2020.1777839

McGregor, J. (2008). Patrolling Kariba's waters: state authority, fishing and the border economy. *Journal of Southern African Studies*, Vol. 34(4): 861–879. doi: 10.1080/03057070802456797

Ndlovu, M. (2016). *The Zambezi river refrain. The story of Basilwizi 2002–2015*. Harare: Basilwizi Trust.

Ngwenya, D. M. (2018). The Gukurahundi Legacy, 35 years Later the Socio-Economic Impact of Gukurahundi. A Paper Presented at the Habakkuk Trust-Think Tank Series (Bulawayo).

Tremmel, M. (1994). *The people of the great river, the Tonga hoped the water would follow them*. Gweru: Mambo Press in association with Silveira.

UNDP. (2010). Millennium Development Goals Status Report Zimbabwe. Harare, Zimbabwe.

World Commission of Dams (WCD). (2000). Dams and Development. World Commission on Dams, 16 November.

ZimStat. (2012). Zimbabwe Population Census 2012 National Report. Government Printers, Harare.

ZimStat. (2017). Poverty, Income, Consumption and Expenditure Survey Report. Government Printers, Harare.

ZIMVAC. (2012). Rural Livelihoods Assessment May 2012 Report. Government of Zimbabwe, Harare.

6

RESOURCE ACCESS, LIVELIHOODS AND BELONGING AMONGST THE TONGA IN MOLA, NYAMINYAMI DISTRICT

Felix Tombindo and Simbarashe Gukurume

Introduction

Notes from one of the days in the field by one of the authors for this chapter provide the following story:

> A considerable number of small nchenje trees with golden coloured nchenje fruits covered the whole landscape view of Munego (Mola ward 4) that was before us. Pierre and I sat under the roof of one of his mother's huts shying away from the scorching sun of Tuesday 13 October 2015. We were resting after walking a journey of approximately 12 kilometres from ward 3 to ward 4. As I gazed through the thicket of those fruit trees, I felt an urge to go and feast on the ripened nchenje fruits. Pierre suggested that it would be better for us to go there later in the day after his mother's return from a dam construction project facilitated by the United Methodist Committee on Relief (UMCOR). At almost sunset, Pierre's mother arrived, and we set on a mission to feast on the nchenje fruits. The fruits were fenced off, which was a recent development and part of a top-down conservancy project meant to protect the "depleting environmental resources from extinction". We entered the fence through an opening cut out of the fence by Mola residents ....
>
> In so doing, we were also partaking in an act of resistance: defying the restricted access to natural resources by NRDC in partnership with a private company. We ate the fruits and crossed over a stream, as Pierre wanted to show me the place where Mola residents (including him) speculated that there were pegs that marked off an area endowed with minerals. We saw the place, and what seemed to be pegs in the ground, without though making any definite conclusion about the existence of minerals. We did not take much time at the site and, as we returned, we realised that there was only one

DOI: 10.4324/9781003278580-7

way of getting in and getting out – the "illegal" opening. This is one of the many everyday acts of resistance and struggle for natural resource access and use that people of Mola engage in for survival.

Field notes after visiting Munego, in Mola ward 4, October 13, 2015

This opening vignette from the field reveals the unending struggle for natural resource access, involving a concerted effort by the Tonga on the Zimbabwean side of Lake Kariba to assert their right to livelihood and belonging in their land of Mola in the Zambezi Valley.

The Zambezi River – the boundary between Zambia and Zimbabwe – was dammed in the 1950s to construct the biggest synthetic lake in Africa at the time – Lake Kariba. On the Zimbabwean side of the lake, colonialists divided the littoral into several protected areas, including a recreational park, safari areas and a national park. A relatively smaller part of the littoral was set aside to allow the displaced people access to the lake mainly for gill-net fishing. The host population (predominantly Tonga people) was then subjected to several alienating natural resource and lake management laws. The restrictive colonial regulations have largely continued in the postcolonial era, putting the livelihoods of Zambezi Valley communities at risk. This chapter discusses the struggle for natural resource access, livelihoods and belonging in Mola, Nyaminyami district. Through micro-ethnography, we analyse a case study of resistance against natural resource enclosure practices (in the form of a conservancy) undertaken by a local rural council and a safari operator – Bulembi Safaris. The chapter argues that Mola, like the rest of the of the Zambezi Valley communities in Zimbabwe, typifies a "marginal frontier", in which the state and powerful conservation and tourist interests frequently displace and restrict local people's rights of access to the lake, leading to increased livelihood vulnerability and precarity.

Context

The Bulembi Safaris director with the permission of Nyaminyami Rural District Council (hereafter NRDC) imposed a conservancy in one of the safari areas close to Mola in 2013. Mola is one of the places to which the Tonga people were relocated, to pave way for the construction of the Kariba dam. Mola, just like other places along the Lake Kariba shoreline, is surrounded by safari and wildlife areas. The people of Mola compete with various users for access to and use of Lake Kariba. Among the rights that the people of Mola have are fishing rights. They are also, in principle, beneficiaries of the Communal Area Management Programme for Indigenous Resources (CAMPFIRE) which places ownership of wildlife in the hands of the community in return for their cooperation in the conservation of wildlife. CAMPFIRE seldom benefits local communities like Mola, however, as it brings more costs than benefits as has been widely documented in the literature on conservation (Dzingirai 1995; Balint and Mashinya 2008; Rihoy et al. 2010). The proposed conservancy was a deviation from CAMPFIRE and was going to infringe on the livelihoods of the people of Mola by closing access to some of their fishing camps. Fencing off the safari area and some of the fishing camps upon which the people of Mola depend for livelihoods led to the people asserting their right to livelihoods by way of active resistance.

CAMPFIRE has a participatory development rhetoric marred by a myriad of flaws. Mola area, bordered by Matusadona National Park, a safari area, and Lake Kariba Recreational Park, has an ongoing CAMPFIRE programme, which was introduced in 1989. For the people of Mola, this is a lease of life because, despite its meagre livelihood contributions, they do count it as a positive move on the part of the government and NRDC. CAMPFIRE is referenced locally as one of the ways through which the community is surviving. Gladys, one of the participants in our field study (see below), for example, noted that the programme of CAMPFIRE is assisting the residents of Mola by promoting access to basic amenities in a context of lack of reliable transport. Through dividends from the CAMPFIRE that it receives from NRDC, the community has managed to buy several valuable assets that include a lorry and a tractor. In this sense, the arrangement entails an exchange value, as it is through the sale of environmental resources by way of tourism and related dividends that the community has the money for the purchase of such assets. Gladys explained:

> Of the few things that we have as Mola area, we can count the contribution of CAMPFIRE dividends that have enabled us to buy a lorry of our own and a tractor. The lorry is handy during crisis periods like situations when there is sick [people] and they must be transported to Siakobvu hospital [which is at the growth point, approximately 40 kilometres away from Mola]. The money for fuel also comes from these CAMPFIRE dividends. The tractor is also used for cultivating the fields although there are less rains here and agriculture is not usually profitable.
>
> *November 11, 2015*

Nyaminyami district, in which Mola is located, is divided into three communal lands, namely, Omay, Kanyati (now Makande) and Gatshe-Gatshe (Sibanda 2001; Mubaya 2008). Omay Communal Land, under which Mola falls, has nine wards. The nine wards, broadly speaking and in terms of contemporary state structures, fall under the jurisdiction of NRDC. In Mola and Nyaminyami district more broadly, the Tonga people constitute the majority ethnic group. Tonga people are the "traditional population of NyamiNyami district" (Mashinya 2007: 14). Of the four chiefs in Omay communal lands, chiefs Mola and Negande are Tonga. Chiefs Msampakaruma and Nebiri are of Shangwe origin. The Shangwe ethnic group constitutes the second dominant ethnic group. There are other ethnic groups (including the Shona), but they are in the minority. Ethnicity is a vital issue for claiming access to resources in, and belonging to, places like Nyaminyami.

The geographical location of Mola in relation to major cities and towns indicates that Mola residents are forgotten "orphans of the empire" (Alexander

2004). Alexander (2004: 194) uses the phrase "orphans of the empire" to describe the identity of white Zimbabweans who chose to "live off Zimbabwe, rather than live in it". In the case of the Tonga of Mola, the Zimbabwean state has in large part not been committed to addressing and overcoming the marginalisation that the Zimbabwean Tonga were subjected to during colonialism; hence the added adjective "forgotten" in our view of the position of Tonga people in Zimbabwe. Theirs is not a choice, but a situation in which they find themselves as orphans of the empire, displaced by the Kariba dam and further alienated through wildlife conservation policies. Dusty roads make travelling to Mola very difficult during the rainy season due to floods. Basic social amenities and services are far from the community, and schools are makeshift, with many studying under trees, while the few schools face a perennial challenge of drawing qualified teachers.

The nearest town (Karoi) to the study area is approximately 250 kilometres away and a rugged un-tarred road links it to Mola. There is a marked difficulty for Mola residents who cannot afford the exorbitant transport costs (see later). They must travel on foot an estimated 40-kilometre journey to reach Siakobvu growth point from where they can board transport to either Karoi about 210 kilometres away or to Gokwe Centre, which is much closer than Karoi. For Mola residents, however, free transport is available for those travelling to Kariba urban by boats provided through the services of the Bumi Hills Hotel. These services have waned since the year 2000, with reasons cited by participants in our study linked to the authoritarian politics of the ruling party, the Zimbabwe African National Union Patriotic Front (ZANU-PF) and the victimisation of Mola area as an opposition party stronghold.

Research Methods

We conducted a three-month long micro-ethnographic study in 2015 in Mola using narrative interviews, informal conversations and participant observation as data collection instruments. Narrative interviews, through generative questions, enabled us to understand the lived experiences and perceptions of Tonga participants regarding resource access, entitlement and belonging in Mola and the Zambezi Valley. A generative or narrative question is one that is prepared before entering the field and it must "generate a story, stimulate the subject to speak" (Scârneci-Domnişoru 2013: 23). Short life histories emerged out of the narrative inquiries, around land and landscape amongst the Mola Tonga.

Participant observation allowed us to become deeply familiar with the chores of the people under study through observation of events as they happened and listening to what they said. We also actively participated in everyday life, for instance, taking part in acts of resisting the conservancy – as discussed later. An integral part of the process of observing was the writing down of notes as the observation took place or writing as soon as each observation day ended.

Informal interviews were carried out with Tonga participants as well as people who were not part of the original research design. While in Mola, further happenings were encountered that made informal conversations of some importance. The informal conversations were conducted with the following: a United Methodist Committee on Relief (UMCOR) employee, our research assistant on various occasions, a colleague who introduced us to Mola and a Mola resident at Siakobvu growth point. In total, 12 Tonga people were interviewed through narrative interviews. Three non-Tonga participants were also interviewed, and these included the UMCOR employee and two Mola residents.

Scupin and Decorse (2009) note that, when cultural anthropologists engage in participant observation, they usually become familiar with information that might, if made public, become harmful to the community or individuals in the community. Hence use has been made of pseudonyms to separate information and data from the respective respondents. All the names that appear in this chapter are pseudonyms. Apart from that, we also sought informed consent from all our interlocutors, who were made fully aware of our research and what it entailed.

We also sought the compliance of gate keepers like the Chief and the police who were domiciled in Mola, and they granted us permission to conduct the study. Interviewing people at the NRDC required permission from the Mashonaland West Province Minister of State and we made sure that we followed all steps required to obtain a letter of approval from the Minister of State's office.

The Conservancy: Struggles for Space and Belonging

The people of Mola failed to understand why a conservancy (for Bulembi Safaris) was being proposed when, in the first place, CAMPFIRE placed ownership of the wild animals and inanimate resources in Mola in their hands. For the people of Mola, the imposition of the conservancy meant that they were being dispossessed once again, just as their forefathers were displaced to pave way for the construction of Lake Kariba. Mola residents thus reflected deeply on this conservancy proposal and linked it to the colonial displacements of the 1950s. In the end, they rejected it vehemently. Thomas, as one of the activists against the conservancy, narrated the beginning of the conservancy conflict in the following manner:

> In 2013, the rural district council came up with idea of erecting a wire [conservancy]. They said they wanted to erect a wire that would separate us from the animals and other natural resources .... *Takabuzya kuti, nimwakali kwaamba kuti banyama mbubesu tukkazyane ambabo lino nimwakubabikka mulubaya bachili besu na?* [We asked them, "you once said these are our animals; now that you are fencing them off from us, are they still ours?"]. They are now taking the animals; the white man who is going to put the wire is going to take them away ... how are we going to survive?
>
> *November 22, 2015*

Besides the fact that they were going to be alienated from much of the resources vital for their livelihoods, the people of Mola also resented that the idea of the conservancy was conceived within the NRDC without the involvement of the people at the grassroots level. As with many development projects that are top-down, the conservancy was susceptible to contestation and failure as the people of Mola were not even consulted. The conservancy question also reveals the position of NRDC with regard to land rights and access to natural resources (including wildlife), which is that these fall within the domain and prerogative of the state. Yet, as anthropologists and others invaluably note, "property is a set of relations between people that varies across societies" (Whitehead 2003: 4426). In this regard, Mola residents consider themselves as the "owners" of the land and the resources, not only because of their ancestral claims but also as part of the promises that were made to them when the CAMPFIRE idea was introduced to them in the late 1980s. Moses expressed his dismay regarding the conservancy issue:

> I have a friend who lives on the other side of the stream that you cross when you are coming here from Thomas' place. He is originally from Malawi. Recently he was laughing at me, saying: "You Tonga people are fools … you always accept everything that comes your way. First you were chased away from the Zambezi, now you are being denied access to resources in your territory". My friend is right. This is how we are treated by the government. They do as they like. They did the same with the issue of the wire [conservancy] …. It began as a rumour, and then people began to ask what really this wire was for? And who was its brainchild? People were unaware of what was taking place. In 2013, influential people [village heads] were taken from ward four. These were taken by McKenzie [present Member of Parliament for Kariba constituency who was working at NRDC in 2013 prior to becoming a legislator] and his brother Butch McKenzie. These village heads from ward 4 were not aware that McKenzie and his friends had already sealed deals with the whites who wanted to come and erect the wire. The headmen were tricked after being told about the advantages of the wire and they agreed and endorsed the wire idea by signing the documents whose contents they were not aware of. After the agreement, the wire was erected in ward four.
>
> *October 14, 2015*

The immediate consequences of the conservancy were felt by Mola people in ward 4. These included being alienated from vital resources such as firewood, fruits and other forest resources in the area that was fenced off. The feasting on the nchenje fruits, as narrated earlier, represents an act of defiance against the erasure of people's livelihoods resources. Not only were the people of Mola barred from setting foot in the fenced off area, but they were also restricted from entering fishing camps and hence gaining access to the fish and lake. Lydia recounted the immediate effects and implications of the conservancy in ward 4 which caught them unaware:

> Immediately after the erection of the wire, there came restrictions for us. These included those pertaining to movement. After six pm, no entrance was allowed in the conservancy. Then people began to ask, "why the

> sudden change and restriction?" We are used to moving freely any time of the day. Further restrictions came concerning the fishing camps. People at Nyakatanda fishing camp were instructed to move to Makuyu fishing camp to leave Nyakatanda vacant. The council wanted to remove one of the fishing camps, but people resisted and refused to move for whatever reason .... We told them, "The fence is yours, but it does not concern us; you know the reasons why you erected it, but it does not affect us".
>
> *November 2, 2015*

The resistance against the conservancy by people in ward 4 came only after they had realised that their territory had been fenced off. Their leaders had been tricked in a ploy in a manner like that experienced by Lobengula, then king of the Ndebele people, who was duped into signing the Rudd Concession of 1888. Immediately after erecting the fence for the conservancy in ward 4, the NRDC and Bulembi Safaris moved on to ward 3 to try and dupe the elders there in the same way, but they were not successful.

Power and Selective Projects in Mola

The resistance of Mola residents particularly those of ward 3 has not gone unpunished. At the time of conducting this study, the NRDC was using its power to oversee and endorse relief projects in the district to impose negative sanctions against the rebels who refused to have part of their area fenced off through the conservancy. The NRDC was doing this through excluding ward 3 from the benefits of these projects. Concurrently, UMCOR (an NGO) was involved in relief projects in the area, and one of their employees indicated that they had been advised by NRDC not to implement their dam construction project in ward 3. In fact, we noticed only one project and that was in ward 4. In the words of the UMCOR employee:

> Ward 3 three has been blacklisted because the NRDC says that the people there are not cooperative. We were directed not to implement projects in ward 3. Except in rare cases and for food aid, ward 3 is usually bypassed. They are suffering the consequences of exercising rights over their territory.
>
> *Informal conversation with an UMCOR employee, November 28, 2015*

As confirmation of the use of power and negative sanctions against the people of Mola, the NRDC and the Zambezi River Authority (ZRA) excluded chief Rare from a dialogue meeting that took place at chief Nebiri's homestead. Initially this meeting had been scheduled for chief Mola's homestead but, under unspecified circumstances and for unclear reasons, it was held at chief Nebiri's place. When I arrived at chief Rare's homestead at the beginning of the fieldwork, he had hinted to me that he was going to host special guests (from Zambia and the surrounding areas) of displaced peoples for the hosting of a *lwiindi*[1] ceremony as well as to deliberate on what was troubling their territory on both sides (Zimbabwe and Zambia) of the lake, especially in the context of the looming drought that was bedevilling the country in 2015. He explained that they were going to share their experiences with regard to what messages each of the communities (from both sides of the lake) had received from *banalyo gundu* (literally, owners of the land, referring to the ancestors) about the emerging dangers of drought and hunger. He also said that they were planning to deliberate with ZRA on compensation and grievances with reference to displaced peoples. This meeting never took place, at least at his homestead. In reflecting on this, and in the process claiming that ZRA has never been committed to the implementation of compensation projects in Mola area, chief Rare put forward the following:

> I am not surprised with what they did; leaving me out of the meeting that took place at chief Nebiri's place. ZRA has always helped people who did not come from the river instead of helping people who came from the river. The only help we received was many years ago when they brought us a small grinding machine that broke down several years ago. This year ZRA and the council have excluded us from the meeting, yet we are part of the people who came from the river. They and the council have stopped helping us with developing our area … look at the roads that we have. We used to be helped by German donors, but these were also blocked because the government said we are involved in partisan politics [referring to the popular support from the area for the opposition Movement for Democratic Change, MDC]. But this is how we must survive; we must work for ourselves.
>
> *November 26, 2015*

Such are the complexities of the nature of landscape and land use in Mola that the contestations end up entangled in broader partisan politics. In the face of powerful state (and corporate) actors, who take advantage of the dry physical landscapes of Mola to impose their own visions of how land and other natural resources must be used, the way of seeing and experiencing land and landscape by Mola residents is significantly challenged and often marginalised. Their resistance ended up intertwining with the politics of belonging situated within the context of the nation.

Situating Belonging within the "Nation"

This is a tale of competing claims over land and natural resources and, as Hammar (2002: 137) highlights, "competing claims over landscape especially those marked by displacement and migration have … to do with cultural politics of identity through which strategies of belonging and exclusion are played out". For Mola residents, crucial are their rights to land-use and access to other inanimate resources. But these are difficult to separate from the cultural politics of identity (and social belonging) as it is through who you are that you gain access to land and its use.

Thomas narrated one of the grievances that Mola ward residents have over the imposition of the conservancy by tracing it back to the history of settlement in the Zambezi and linking all this to the "troublesome" safari operators:

> One thing you must remember is that the river Zambezi used to help people sustain themselves through fishing especially during times of hardships like droughts. But now we face challenges. We have the resources in the area we live but these people do not want us to use them; they say we must keep taking care of the resources such as wildlife and forest resources … but we are not allowed to touch them. It is like in-laws who give their daughter in marriage and instruct the son-in-law to take care of their daughter but not to touch her …. If you go fishing, the safari operators are a surveillance menace curtailing the survival chances available to the people of Mola. They demand some of the catch … up to five kilogrammes of fish … yet they put laws in place that do not allow overfishing. Now recently the council came up with the idea of a conservancy that was going to further restrict us from using resources in our own area and we said no. We could not allow that.
>
> *November 22, 2015*

Zimbabwe's tumultuous land question has become deeply racialised to the extent that writers like Hughes (2010) have labelled the land reform exercise from the year 2000 as "equal parts pogrom and land reform". The pogrom dimension involved, it is argued, an attempt to discursively construct all Euro-Zimbabweans in the country as guilty of land theft and hence unworthy of remaining as landholders. Given this racialised politics of land in Zimbabwe, it was not surprising perhaps for Mola people to view the involvement of Mr Wright (owner of Bulembi Safaris) in the conservancy in a highly sceptical way. Certainly, those interviewed queried why a white man was coming to their territory in the name of conservation. Indeed, people questioned the way in which this top-down conservation project alienated them from their livelihoods, thereby putting their very existence in danger and pushing them deeper into abject poverty.

Gladys, who hails from ward 4, spoke glowingly of the resistance in ward 3 to the conservancy and highlighted that ward 4 was following in the footsteps of ward 3. Delving into partisan politics, she also questioned why white people were being allowed to come into Mola yet, in other areas, they were chased away under fast-track land reform. In her narrative, she implied that the idea of entitlement to land and resources was intricately linked to support for the ruling party, ZANU-PF:

> After residents of ward four had realised that they made a mistake by allowing the conservancy to be erected, council made haste to try and convince ward three to accept the conservancy as well. But in ward three the people were clever, they said "no this is very wrong". Ward 3 residents asked, "Why are these people bringing white people here, the same white people whom they evicted from their farms?" Now they are driving the same people here.

> So what message are they trying to convey to us? Are they saying that this is where white people should reside? *Saka kuno uku hakuna Zanuzve kana zvakadaro?* [does this mean that ZANU-PF does not exist here?].
>
> *November 12, 2015*

It appears that, at least in part, people of Mola rejected the conservancy because white people were being evicted from other parts of the country and hence Mola should also not be considered their place. They simply did not see the rationale of having any dealings with a white-owned company that would alienate them from their resources. In this regard, Thomas added his opinion about the rejection of the conservancy with a racialised tone that had been promoted by the ruling party since 2000. For Thomas, the conservancy and subsequent subordination of Mola's lived-in landscapes (which are the basis for the survival of the people of Mola) would only be acceptable if the land reform exercises of 2000 were to be reversed and all evicted whites were allowed back to occupy the country again:

> When Fabian [pseudonym for wildlife manager at NRDC], McKenzie and Jonasi [a council employee] as well as the District Administrator [DA] came to meet the people, as they had been advised by councillor Siabwanda and the chief to do, they introduced the issue of the conservancy. We started asking them questions. We asked the DA and McKenzie, "DA, do you have a farm?" And he answered, "Yes". "McKenzie, do you have a farm?". He also answered, "Yes". "Where did you get these farms?" They all answered, "Ah we got them from white farmers who were evicted under the Fast-Track Land Reform Programme". We said, "That is fine … so have you seen it fit that this is the area where whites should live? Unless you are saying all whites who were chased away should come back to Zimbabwe, then we will not have any problems accepting Mr Wright and his wire".
>
> *November 22, 2015*

Without addressing the key questions posed by Thomas and Gladys, the proponents of the conservancy were left with no room for any successful resolution of the problems raised by Mola people.

In statements which made clear her reasonable contentment with the present situation in Mola (and given that any hope for betterment of the area by government had vanished), Sphiwe opined that the NRDC and its conservancy partner should simply leave Mola area as it currently exists. Her views linked the present restricted access to natural resources arising from the conservancy with the historical experiences of displacement. She said:

> If the people who want to put a wire in both of our wards got farms from white farmers, let them leave us with our *boma* [territory]. We also do not want to cede any part of it. We have lived for so many decades without any help from the whites and very minimal help from the current government.

> We have lived with these wild animals … now you want to come and put a wire for us. When we came from the Zambezi where they chased away our grandparents, they should have put that wire then, so that we would have known that the fenced area is a no-go area for us. But they realised that we posed no danger to the animals, we were used to them, they left us to live with them. So, they must leave us like that, living with our animals; we are very comfortable with that.
>
> *November 15, 2015*

Nature is "a site of struggle" as environmental sociologist Jacklyn Cock (2007) contends, a struggle that is largely shaped by different conceptions of nature and justice. This reflects the situation regarding the question of the contested conservancy in Mola. For NRDC and other powerful stakeholders like Bulembi Safaris, the protected areas of Mola (as defended by the "wire") are a public good for the purposes of the sustainability of nature and society. Ultimately, though, such areas involve an enclosure movement which in fact commodifies nature in the pursuit of private gain. For Mola residents, nature should in large part remain decommodified and open to all. After all, the Mola people claim that before the fencing of their community, they have always coexited with animals and utilised other natural resources sustainably.

In this respect, the people of Mola claim to have accessed documents containing the proposal for the erection of the conservancy through one of the employees at NRDC whose rural home is Mola. After going through the contents of those documents, Mola residents rejected the whole idea on the basis primarily that it was going to undo even the meagre benefits that the people were obtaining under the old CAMPFIRE arrangements, by reducing the dividends disbursed to the community. This new conservancy was also to infringe on the rights of people to move freely in spaces within the designated "wire" or conservancy. The said conservancy was going to have specific rules to which the people of Mola had to abide, and these include restricted movement of people in the area designated as the conservancy during night hours. Thomas further explained the challenges that the community argued would be brought upon them by the proposed conservancy:

> We do not want the wire here. They thought we did not know about their documents on rules and regulations concerning the wire. We already knew the contents of the documents. One, five per cent of the proceeds after 5 years is what they wanted to give back to the community, which is nothing if we look at it in terms of the development of the community. Two, whatever was going to happen in the conservancy was going to be private and confidential … keeping us in the dark on what would be happening in our own territory. No one was allowed to ask except NRDC and Mr Wright … we said "no, we do not want our resources tampered with". All resources found in Mola must benefit Mola people, the five per cent/95 per cent dividend ratio was

> theirs and nothing like that would be allowed to happen in Mola today or in the future.
>
> *November 22, 2015*

In attempts at pushing through the conservancy, NRDC officials made political threats to remove an independent councillor for ward 3 who – along with his constituency – rejected the conservancy. Sphiwe recalled such threats:

> After the resistance from ward three residents, the likes of Fabian and [other] employees at the rural district council intervened. They made threats to the local people of Mola. They even confronted our councillor, Mr Siabwanda, threatening to oust him from office because they were accusing him of influencing the resistance of the locals against the conservancy. The councillor resisted the threats by urging them to go and meet the people as it is the very people who owned the land, and it is the very same people who voted him into office.
>
> *November 15, 2015*

The struggle against the conservancy turned into a conflict reminiscent of similar struggles worldwide by indigenous peoples against encroachment on their lived-in landscape. Police officers were hired by McKenzie (then Member of Parliament) to intimidate the people of ward 3 into accepting the conservancy proposition. As well, the people of ward 3 were labelled as opposition supporters. Being labelled as an opposition supporter meant being immobilised as a "sell-out" and potentially an enemy of the state. Such a scenario is always followed up with targeted violence and victimisation which the Mola people have experienced for a long time. Thomas narrated the events as follows:

> After we had rejected their idea of putting a wire in our ward, McKenzie politicised the whole issue labelling Mola residents as MDC supporters and giving this as the reason why we resisted the conservancy. At one point he came with armed police officers trying to intimidate us. We said "no", we are not going to negotiate about the wire with guns and we boycotted the meeting. From that day we felt that we might lose the case and so we engaged human rights lawyers. The lawyers told us that if people say they do not want a proposed project in their area, they will not be arrested for that; it is their right to say no. So, the wire issue was rejected, and we told them to go and introduce it in another area, but not in Mola area.
>
> *November 22, 2015*

Mola residents articulated a view which at least implicitly expressed support for fast-track land reform. As Thomas argued:

> After a lot of misunderstandings and threats, we ended up telling them that if they wanted the wire so much, they must go to farms that they got from

> the land reform programme, take Mr Wright with them and have him fence off their farms. After they did this, we would offer them a chance to come to us so that we would sell them elephants, a male and female, buffaloes, a male and female, and all the other animal species that he [Mr Wright] might want to conserve; … then, they would have to take these to the fenced farms and breed them there.
>
> *November 22, 2015*

But, at the same time, Mola people were being labelled as part of the opposition conspiracy against the ruling party and thus – like all MDC supporters – they were viewed as falling outside of the realm of the Zimbabwean nation. The fact that Mola is a known MDC area served to justify such a label. Of course, Mola people had always felt excluded from the state-driven nation-building project, well before the emergence of the MDC.

As part of the strategies for resisting the conservancy and claiming entitlement to use of the resources in their territory, people of Mola ended up questioning the territorial belonging of the people who were advocating the erection of the conservancy in their territory. They focused on the people of chief Negande, as some of the workers at NRDC fall under Negande. In this regard, Thomas made the following argument:

> We also gave them a second alternative [besides Mr Wright building his conservancy on fast-track farms] …. Two of the most vocal [council] employees who were supporting the wire come from Negande … Jonasi and Fabian …. We told them that since their area, Negande, is depleted of animals because of poaching, we could as well sell them these male and female species of the animals they wanted so that they would go and erect the wire there and breed the animals there.
>
> *November 22, 2015*

The District Administrator (DA) was also at the centre of controversy as he appeared to have given the nod for the conservancy to be placed in the Mola area.

Thus, in taking matters perhaps to the extreme, some respondents questioned the territorial placement of employees who work at the NRDC and the DA's office. They argued that the people of Mola were not being employed in posts in local government, yet Mola had candidates suitably qualified for such positions. In fact, Mola people claimed that the only employee who hailed from Mola was the one who had tipped off ward 3 residents to resist the conservancy, after he had revealed the contents of the conservancy documents including the constitution that would govern the conservancy.

In the end, the Tonga people of Mola argued that the NRDC and DA were sabotaging development in the Mola area because these people (of the NRDC and DA) did not originate from Mola and simply wanted to extract resources from the area. In this light, Mola people also attributed the high incidences of poaching in the area to non-Tonga speaking peoples who are not concerned about the welfare of the people who live in Mola. In these narratives, people from Negande who were earlier categorised by Mola people as part of the displaced Tonga are now labelled as opportunistic Shangwe people who want to take advantage of the resources in Mola. This shows that belonging is a social construct that changes with circumstances, as do processes of inclusion and exclusion which are central to belonging narratives and practices.

Conclusion

This chapter discussed the struggles for natural resources access and entitlement in Mola in the context of an imposed conservancy by the rural council and a safari operator. Findings reveal the contested nature of landscape as land use in Mola and point to the politicised forms of landscape and environmental resource use in Mola. Landscape, memory and belonging narratives in Mola, as they do so often elsewhere (Wolmer 2005; 2007), actively turn into a politically volatile question imbued with broader questions of national belonging, entitlement and land rights. People of Mola construct notions of belonging as attachment and entitlement to a place and its resources through their historical association with place and, in so doing, they draw upon the history of displacement of their forefathers from the Zambezi River when the Kariba dam was constructed. These natural resource enclosure practices under the guise of conservation have broader ramifications as Mola people tend to question the central state with regard to the citizenship status of the displaced Tonga in general. Although the Tonga of Mola engage in everyday forms of resistance such as those highlighted in this chapter, they remain vulnerable to further enclosure practices by conservation NGOs. For instance, at the time of preparing this chapter in 2022, the same Mola community is at the centre of a struggle to ward off efforts at re-introducing the conservancy, this time by a different conservation NGO called African Parks. As such, Mola, like the rest of the Zambezi Valley communities in Zimbabwe, typifies a "marginal frontier", in which the state and powerful conservation and tourist interests frequently displace and restrict local people's rights of access to the lake, leading to increased livelihood vulnerability and precarity.

Note

1 This is a traditional ceremony in which the Tonga of Mola thank the ancestors for their taking care of them, including providing them with good harvests. At this ceremony, they also pour out petitions regarding problems that they may be facing.

References

Alexander, K. (2004). Orphans of the empire: an analysis of the identity of white identity and ideology construction in Zimbabwe. In B. Raftopoulos and T. Savage (eds),

Zimbabwe: injustice and political reconciliation, pp. 193–212. Cape Town: Institute for Justice and Reconciliation.

Balint, P. J. and Mashinya, J. (2008). CAMPFIRE through the lens of the commons literature: Nyaminyami rural district in post–2000 Zimbabwe. *Journal of Southern African Studies*, Vol. 34(1): 127–143.

Cock, J. (2007). *The war against ourselves: nature, power, and justice*. Johannesburg: Wits University Press.

Dzingirai, V. (1995). Take back your campfire a study of local level perceptions to electric fencing in the framework of Binga's campfire programme. CASS occasional paper – NRM Series. Harare: Centre for Applied Social Sciences.

Hammar, A. J. (2002). The articulation of modes of belonging: competing land claims in Zimbabwe's Northwest. In K. Juul and C. Lund (eds), *Negotiating property in Africa*, pp. 211–246. Portsmouth: Heinemann.

Hughes, D. M. (2010). *Whiteness in Zimbabwe: race, landscape and the problem of belonging*. New York: Palgrave Macmillan.

Mashinya, J. (2007). Participation and devolution in Zimbabwe's campfire program: findings from local projects in Mahenye and Nyami-Nyami. A PhD Thesis submitted to the Faculty of the Graduate School of the University of Maryland, College Park.

Mubaya, C. P. (2008). Community-Based Natural Resources Management (CBNRN) in Distress: Experiences from Omay Communal Lands, Zimbabwe. Conference: Governing Shared Resources: Connecting Local Experience to Global Challenges, Twelfth Biennial Conference of the International Association for the Study of Commons. July 14–18, 2008.

Rihoy, L. Chirozva, C. and Anstey, S. (2010). People are not happy: crisis, adaptation and resilience in Zimbabwe's CAMPFIRE programme. In F. Nelson (ed), *Conservation rights, conservation and contested land*. London: Routledge, pp 174–201.

Scârneci-Domnişoru, F. (2013). Narrative technique of interviewing. *Bulletin of the Transilvania University of Braşov Series VII: Social Sciences*, Vol. 6(55): 21–28.

Scupin, R. and Decorse, D. (2009). *Anthropology: a global perspective* (6th edition). Delhi: PHI Learning Private Limited.

Sibanda, B. (2001). *Wildlife and communities at the crossroads: is Zimbabwe's campfire the way forward?* Harare: SAPES Books.

Whitehead, J. (2003). Space, place and primitive accumulation in Narmada Valley and beyond. *Economic and Political Weekly*, Vol. 38(40): 4224–4230.

Wolmer, W. (2005). Wilderness gained, wilderness lost: wildlife management and land occupations in Zimbabwe's South East Lowveld. *Journal of Historical Geography*, 31(2005): 260–280. Institute of Development Studies, University of Sussex, Brighton BN 1 3PH, UK.

Wolmer, W. (2007). *From wilderness to farm invasions. Conservation and development in Zimbabwe's South East Lowveld*. Harare: Weaver Press.

PART II

Health, Hunger and Livelihoods

7

FOOD INSECURITY, LIVELIHOOD-DIVERSIFICATION STRATEGIES AND GENDER AMONG THE TONGA OF BINGA DISTRICT

Jennifer Muderedzi

Introduction

Persistent hunger and malnutrition is a problem affecting millions of people globally, the majority of whom are women and girls. Food and nutrition insecurity is a political, economic and environmental issue but, most importantly, it is a gender issue: stark gender inequalities are both a cause and an outcome of unjust food access, consumption and production (Brody 2015). Despite women being the key figures in agricultural production and food security on a worldwide basis, gender inequality is holding back progress towards ending hunger and poverty and creating sustainable food systems (Nelson et al. 2013). This is inconsistent with the right to adequate food as highlighted in the United Nations' (UN) Sustainable Development Goal 2 (SDG 2) which speaks about ending hunger, achieving food security, improving nutrition and promoting sustainable agriculture (UN 2015). Eradicating hunger and achieving food security thus remains a challenge, more so in the wake of the Covid-19 crisis. Further, within the international agricultural development agenda, women are increasingly identified as key to the eradication of global hunger (FAO 2011).

Viable livelihood strategies depend on access to assets such as financial, social, natural, physical and human capital. The more and diverse assets possessed by particular households, the less vulnerable they are to various shocks and trends. Overall, though, rural livelihood strategies are heavily reliant on the natural resource base. Challenges such as poor rains, human-wildlife conflict, unfair pricing mechanisms, high input prices, lack of access to markets, land tenure insecurity, limited availability of agricultural extension services, poor irrigation systems and animal diseases contribute to limiting adequate access to food security in Africa (Chingarande et al. 2020), including Zimbabwe.

Research has shown that improvements in household food security and nutrition are associated with women's enhanced access to income and their role in household

DOI: 10.4324/9781003278580-9

decisions on expenditure, as women tend to spend a significantly higher proportion of household income than men on food for the family (Hyder et al. 2005). Rightfully, there is a growing recognition in development policies that women's role is essential to food and nutrition security, with these policies tending to focus on increasing women's productive and economic capacity. This is, however, only a partial solution as it fails to address the entrenched gender-specific inequalities that prevent many women and girls from living a fulfilled life free from hunger, poverty and discrimination (Brody 2015).

To illustrate the challenges faced by rural women in Zimbabwe, the following is taken from a daily tabloid MyZimbabwe News (2021):

> A 61 years old gogo (grandmother) from Binga dies (hungry) after falling from a tree while gathering wild fruits. She died after falling from a busika mpapanyuka tree. She lost balance, fell down, was rushed to a clinic where she was pronounced dead.

Busika is a wild fruit that Tonga communities in some parts of Binga District collect for consumption as well as for selling to travellers. It has a sour taste and is eaten on its own, cooked in porridge or made into a soft drink. Wild fruits serve as a safety net permitting people to survive when crops fail, and wild fruit gathering is one of the roles played by Tonga women to sustain their families. This forms part of a broader repertoire of livelihood diversification undertaken by Tonga households in Binga including cross-border trade, migration, informal trading and sex work, which reduces the number of household members able to work in the fields. In this context, this chapter explores livelihood-diversification strategies for survival purposes among the food-deficient Tonga of Binga with a specific focus on gender.

Context

Food and nutritional security is described as follows:

> When all people at all times have physical, social and economic access to food which is safe and consumed in sufficient quantity and quality to meet their dietary needs and food preferences and is supported by an environment of adequate sanitation, health services and care allowing for a healthy and active life.
>
> *Committee on World Food Security 2012: 5; see also FAO 1996*

Food insecurity is a complex problem with direct and underlying causes that involve many economic sectors and contextual factors. In this context, Zimbabwe is currently experiencing food insecurity and deteriorating household-level nutrition, particularly in some parts of the country's low-lying areas. The situation for rural villagers has been exacerbated further by the devaluation of the local currency, the Covid-19 pandemic and poor harvests recorded in recent agricultural seasons (IFRC 2021). According to an analysis of food security in Zimbabwe over a period of five years, the number of food insecure people increased from 2.6 million in the 2015–2016 agricultural season to 5.5 million in both the 2018–2019 and 2019–2020 seasons (SADC 2019: 7). The number of people compelled to activate crisis-level and negative coping strategies also increased dramatically by the end of August 2021 (WFP 2021).

The problem of food insecurity in rural areas has two dimensions. One dimension is the inability of households to produce all their food requirements because of lack of access to, and the diminishing quality of, productive resources combined with an unfavourable or highly variable production environment. The other problem relates to the inability to acquire food via the market because of inadequate household incomes and unreliable markets that deliver food at very high prices (FFSSA 2003). Therefore, when households encounter food access challenges, they cope by either changing livelihood-consumption patterns or employing livelihood-diversification strategies to somehow increase food access. The extent of food insecurity is often variegated at local level in rural spaces, and cultural arrangements around gender might have an effect in this respect (Ncube 2016).

Research Site and Methods

The research took place in all 21 wards that make up Binga District. The district is located in Matabeleland North Province where more than 80% of the population lives below the poverty line and where food insecurity threatens the everyday life of whole communities. The district not only has limited access to food but also comprises a complex context in which malnutrition feeds a vicious cycle made up of poor diets, lack of incomes to diversify diets, the need to find immediate solutions to feed households and the consequent involvement in activities, often negative, to supplement household income (COSV 2014), including leading to HIV amongst women through sex work. In fact, Tonga women in Binga are generally tasked with the responsibility to cater for the food requirements of their families and children, a burden in such poverty-stricken communities.

This chapter emanates from a larger study on vulnerability, disability and structural violence among the Tonga of Binga in Zimbabwe (Muderedzi et al. 2020). The research was undertaken over an extended period, between 2005 and 2014. Informants were purposively sampled, with a particular focus on Tonga families with disabled children (from birth to 13 years) residing in Binga. While the main focus of the larger study was on the ways in which society addresses and deals with disability, the centrality of issues about HIV and AIDS (specifically for women) emerged during data collection. Informants consisted of 53 caregivers (33 females and 20 males) of disabled children and 4 health professionals (2 females and 2 males) from the Opportunistic Infections (OI) clinic at the district hospital.

The study was conducted in chiTonga using a triangulation of qualitative data collection methods: besides in-depth interviews with the caregivers and professionals, the research entailed 10 focus group discussions (including 1 with the health professionals) and participant observation in 20 households, as well as field notes and pertinent primary documentation. Focus group discussions were used for both data collection and verifying data authenticity after initial data analysis of the interviews to ensure the reliability of the identified themes. Field notes and other data were incorporated to add more clarity and validity to the data collection process. The interviews and focus group discussions were all audiotaped. Data were transcribed verbatim and translated into English. Transcripts were read several times and factors that were associated with food insecurity, gender inequality and HIV and AIDS were identified. The data were labelled through open coding, using conceptual categories to develop the codes (Silverman 2013).

Livelihoods, Gender and Food Insecurity

Tonga livelihood strategies and activities in Binga are complex, diverse and heavily reliant on the natural resource base such as through cultivation, herding, hunting, gathering, wage labouring, hawking and artisanal work such as weaving and carving. These activities do not generate and enhance household-based assets and sustainable livelihoods over the long term and rarely go beyond meeting the most basic and immediate consumption requirements at household level. The Tonga have no resources to improve capabilities and, hence, they tend to survive in an ongoing vulnerability context marked by shocks and negative trends, including in relation to climate change.

As with rural Zimbabwe generally, Tonga women have less access than Tonga men to productive resources and opportunities in Binga, and the gender gap is found in relation to many assets, inputs and services, land, livestock, labour, education, extension and financial services and technology (SOFA 2011). The characteristics of Binga District, particularly its size, remoteness, lack of resources, history, culture and politics have a unique influence on gender roles and relations that create and perpetuate gender inequalities. Among the Tonga, patriarchy is a significant factor in defining power relations between genders. A man is seen as the head of household, powerful and demanding respect – he accumulates wealth through his family, owns and controls assets such as land, cattle and farming equipment and may be married to multiple women. As well, decisions such as children's education are made by the father, with educational advance favouring boys over girls.

Tonga men are valued for their capacity to do hard work such as the clearing and ploughing of fields, with farming as a household commitment dominated and controlled by men. They are in charge specifically of the drought-resistant crops such as sorghum, rapoko and millet. They also have decision-making powers regarding the sale of large livestock, leaving women cut off from this revenue source. Tonga men living near a river try to make a living from small-scale fishing as they cannot afford the recommended fishing rigs and nets as well as government fishing licences that are beyond their financial reach. In some parts of the district, men often carry out illegal hunting and sell the dried meat for cash or barter trade for grain. Men also produce wood-carved products such as "Tonga stools", door carvings and other small carvings which are popular with tourists. When asked whether the income generated by men became part of the household economy, the Tonga women stated:

> Men raise more money than us. They earn their money and drink beer with their friends and girlfriends. They tell us to make our own money and look after our children. They like socialising.
>
> *Female informants, interview 17 November 2013*

Gender inequality is evidenced everywhere, including by women bearing the burden of looking after the household. They are generally responsible for food selection and preparation, and care and feeding of children and, therefore, they spend much of their income on food for the household. This is even though women do not have the same access and control as men over productive resources including finances. Additionally, women carry out much of the back-breaking field activities, such as clearing bushes, ploughing, weeding, harvesting and storing the grains in the granaries. However, the grains harvested are normally just enough to feed Tonga households for four months or less (May–August) every year, depending on the rains. After the grains are finished, women walk long distances to extended families to beg for food or to neighbouring villages to buy or barter trade.

Hence, women's work is "double full-time" as, besides their directly productive work (for instance in the fields), they are responsible for food provision and maintaining their households inclusive of caring for the elderly and the sick. They walk approximately four hours each day to fetch water from open wells or boreholes as well as gathering firewood. Water is collected twice a day, in the morning and late afternoon. Consumption of contaminated water during the rainy season as well as the dry season, which at times leads to cholera, and the presence of salty water in some areas lead women to an impossible situation in fetching the cleanest water. Women with disabled children who could not be left at the homestead have the extra burden of carrying a 20-litre bucket of water as well as a baby on the back. During my fieldwork, I tried to replicate this several times and found it almost literally back-breaking. With some Tonga research subjects, I would leave the homestead around 05:00 and return 07:00 in the morning, totally exhausted. During the dry season, injuries were reported when the women competed with animals at the waterholes. Lack of suitable bath water resulted in eye and skin infections for infants and poor hygiene led to diarrhoeal diseases. Water scarcity resulted in very dire circumstances, as indicated in this quotation:

> The river beds are dry. These days we are having to walk very far for the water. We use it for cooking and drinking only.
>
> *Female informants, interview 2 December 2013*

Meanwhile, Tonga women engaged in different activities depending in which part of the district they lived. Those near a river engaged in gardening and fishing on a small scale, using *mazubo* (traditional hand-woven reed baskets) for catching fish which they would dry and sell for cash. This enabled them to purchase maize or other grains, and pay for their children's education, clothes and healthcare. The problem with these activities related to stray elephants destroying the gardens and crocodile attacks causing death or disability. In other areas, women engaged in poultry rearing, basket weaving (*nsangwa*) and wild fruits (*busika*) collection and selling, while those residing near Binga town centre engaged in cross-border trading and tuck shops to strengthen their economic base. Such activities enhanced their livelihoods and contributed to poverty reduction. However, Tonga women lament the lack of nutritious food for their sometimes malnourished sick infants, especially disabled children with chewing and swallowing problems who need starch in the form of rice and porridge as well as legumes for proteins and vitamins. It was common to hear informants with disabled children stating:

> I need food to improve my child´s health status so that he is able to sit and walk like other children.
>
> *16 year old woman, 4th wife of polygamous man with two children, interview 2 December 2005*

> In the end, my child died from hunger. There was no food to feed him.
>
> *32 year old woman, 5th wife of polygamous man with 5 children, interview 10 October 2005*

At the same time, in enacting their agency, Tonga women typically rely upon their cultural and ecological knowledge in an attempt to sustain both themselves and their families. In particular, older females use their traditional knowledge, experience and expertise to adjust to ecological climatic changes, and they pass on this knowledge to younger females. For example, after harvesting their sorghum crop, sorghum seed for the following planting season is mixed with sand and stored away. This is meant to deter consumption because of dire food insecurity before the next planting season; otherwise no seeds would be available for planting. Older women also accompany young girls to the forest, showing them the edible fruits, leaves, bark and roots to gather for consumption. As a result, young people, especially females, were well versed in famine foods and their preparation, thereby passing on indigenous knowledge from generation to generation. The significance of resilience is taught and normalised within Tonga communities' daily lives more widely, with tales of past epidemics hopefully building resilience in the younger generations.

Food Insecurity and HIV

Zimbabwe's HIV prevalence among adults is 12.9%, including 15.3% for women and 10.2% for men, with Matabeleland North Province having the second highest prevalence at 14.9% (ZIMPHIA 2020: 2). During the time of research, HIV and AIDS services for the whole district relied on one OI clinic at the district hospital, with a few primary clinics accessing Antiretroviral (ARV) medications when available. Unfortunately, these services were not accessible to remote communities resulting in the lack of HIV knowledge, testing and treatment. More women than men (3:1) take the HIV test, resulting in more women knowing their HIV status (Muderedzi et al. 2017). Unlike men who are afraid of taking the test in fear of a positive result, female informants took the test numerous times in anticipation of a positive result. As two women stated:

> I have been tested three times now, first by the Voluntary Counselling and Testing (VCT) people and twice at the hospital when I brought my sick child to be treated.
>
> *Quoted in Muderedzi et al. 2019: 1139*

> HIV is one of those things that happens in life. It is not a crisis.
>
> *Quoted in Muderedzi et al. 2019: 1139*

Such statements were also confirmed by the healthcare workers at the hospital's OI clinic as well as non-governmental organisation (NGO) workers in the district.

One of the food resilience strategies existing among the Tonga of Binga was the acquisition of an HIV-positive result in order to receive food aid from the few NGOs operating in the district. Sadly, women were at the forefront of this negative coping strategy. They would walk long distances (as far as 50 kilometres) through dense forests and scotching heat, risking their lives in the process (from wild animal attacks) in order to reach an NGO's Voluntary Counselling and Testing (VCT) vehicle for the test. Some would have swollen feet and ankles due to the long walk or maybe underlying health issues they did not know about. A positive result resulted in ululations for it meant that the woman would go home with food and be on the list for future aid. Those who tested negative went home dejected. Elderly ladies who were household heads could be seen begging for registration for food aid despite not being HIV positive, crying out:

> There is no food at home. What shall I feed my grandchildren with? I can no longer manage to work as before.
>
> *Quoted in Muderedzi et al. 2019: 1139*

When asked why they did not get tested, the men simply shrugged their shoulders and stated:

> We will get tested. *Banakazi batesitilwa kulya* ["women get tested in order to access food aid"].
>
> *Quoted in Muderedzi et al. 2019: 1139*

The women did not dispute this, highlighting:

> We have children, grandchildren and orphans to feed at home.
>
> *Interview 8 June 2013*

Healthcare workers reiterated that men were reluctant to take the test until such time as when they become ill with AIDS. This applied to the few who managed to access health centres, as the majority got sick and died at home. Polygyny, marriages between elderly men and young girls, early marriages, promiscuity and the practice of widow inheritance are still common amongst the Tonga in Binga and are likely associated with the risk of HIV infections.

The fishing industry in Siachilaba and Sinamatelele (both in Binga) attracted fish traders from outside the district, resulting in a "fish for sex" trade in the local fishing camps. The fishing communities were highly susceptible to HIV and AIDS due to factors such as fishermen staying away from home for long periods without their spouses and having access to a cash income, while women were readily available for commercial sex. Women were noted for travelling long distances to purchase fish for resell or consumption, because of their responsibility for household food consumption. When asked whether or not they were afraid of getting the disease (HIV), most of the female informants stated:

> I am aware of the dangers of the disease, but our families need food to eat. Yes, we sometimes get scared of catching the disease.
>
> *Quoted in Muderedzi et al. 2019: 1138*

> My husband died two years ago. I have to find food and feed my children.
>
> *Interview 10 June 2013*

The HIV and AIDS epidemic among the Tonga of Binga has had a drastic effect on rural development including declining food production and food security due to ill health, disability and death (Muderedzi et al. 2020). Loss of productive household members through death from AIDS or overall deterioration of health as AIDS progressed has affected both males and females, leaving children to work in the fields and resulting in less household food. In the case of households infected and affected by HIV and AIDS, the level of food security was conditioned by the health of household heads, the number and ages of children and the households' relationship with extended families in the district or further away in other nearby districts such as Gokwe. Costs and time incurred in purchasing drugs, special foods and transport to the nearest clinic or district hospital among other expenses affected the household income available for purchasing food for the household.

Food Insecurity and Politics

Binga has been a site of government interventions over a number of decades in the name of rural development and it was supposed to have benefited from post-colonial policies of redress and redistribution. Unfortunately, poverty and food insecurity (including its gendered dimension) still persists and seems to be increasing. Unlike most of the rest of Zimbabwe's countryside, the Tonga suffer from a near absolute lack of social services such as healthcare, education, road infrastructure, clean water and sanitation, with the Binga District's lack of development resulting in perennial food shortages. In fact, the history of the Tonga reflects a series of shocks and persistent, prolonged stresses, though also exhibiting an ability to adapt and get by. If anything, they survive on the back of their own efforts or the efforts of relations (Bond et al. 2013). Those government institutions which access the district seem to focus on the more easily accessible Tonga communities rather than the more isolated ones which are most in need.

Besides government, Matabeleland North Province has developed partners which seek to complement government's development efforts, especially in relation to household-based food security. Overall, several food assistance programmes exist and these are implemented by the government's department of social services, international donors, local NGOs, international NGOs (INGOs) and UN agencies. These diverse bodies use different approaches to food security, including social protection, resilience-building, emergency recovery and long-term development initiatives to promote food security. The modalities used include in-kind, cash/food for assets, cash transfers and vouchers. Twenty years ago, it was noted that: "Almost all the 150 000 people living in Zimbabwe´s western district of Binga are receiving food aid while the community´s farmers anxiously wait for rains to save their life saving crops" (The New Humanitarian 2003: 1). The situation still persists.

This persistence of chronic poverty in Binga District is a paradox, for it is an area endowed with vast natural resources. It is also a paradox as substantial development aid has been poured into the district to fight poverty, particularly since the independence of Zimbabwe in 1980. In this respect, ZVAC (2015) states that, of the 13 million people of Zimbabwe deemed food insecure at the peak of hunger periods, Binga is always one of the worst affected districts. As well, earlier, SCUK (2003–2004) consistently found that between 80% and 90% of Binga's population is trapped in chronic poverty and requires permanent aid in the form of food assistance every year. One of the key challenges in this regard, and indeed a reason for the paradox, is that the Zimbabwean government is known to withdraw food aid from Binga as well as bar NGOs from supplying the Tonga with food handouts, especially during election times. I was in fact forced to stop transporting infant porridge from the district hospital to remote villages during research activities. This was a sad and frustrating time. As one local Tonga person highlighted:

> The government withholds food from us and stops NGOs from giving us food especially during election times.
>
> *Quoted in Muderedzi et al. 2020: 77*

Binga District, as part of a broader trend in Matabeleland North Province, has tended not to be a strident supporter of the ruling ZANU-PF government, particularly after the rise of the Movement for Democratic Change in 1999. Over the years, a number of government ministers have openly stated that the Tonga will never see development until they learn to vote for the ruling party. During the 2005 senatorial election campaign, I witnessed such threats during the visit of the then vice-president to Binga. The vice-president gave a speech full of threats and vitriol.

When asked about the need for urgent intervention around food shortages in Binga, one government minister was quoted as claiming the following in a newspaper article titled "No food before elections" (The Zimbabwean 2005).

> Most of these NGOs play politics with food and they might as well use the food handouts to influence our people to vote for the imperial lapdogs, the Movement for Democratic Change (MDC). We are busy with Senate elections and after that we will look at the situation. But it should not be lost that we have the capacity to feed our own people.

In contrast, Tonga informants made it clear that this was not the case and that, despite their endemic problems, they are being ignored by government.

> Quelea birds destroy our fields every year. We were not threatened by elephants before but now they are everywhere. We no longer bang empty tins to scare them away lest we anger them, but watch as they descend on our fields and graze on our crops; with drought persisting, the number of deaths may increase still more as elephants and humans compete for resources.
>
> *Quoted in Muderedzi et al. 2017: 5*

Overall, the Tonga situation in Binga shows capability deprivation and relative powerlessness to enhance their situation, almost as if they are a defeated people. After all, what is possible after the only thing you have left has just been destroyed? This took place in the village of Dombwe during my fieldwork and I observed its effects. The villagers' gardens had been destroyed by elephants the night before, eating all the vegetables resulting in the villagers facing starvation. The vegetables were going to be their food for the next few weeks before the river dried out. Meanwhile, malnutrition was taking its toll amongst the under-five infants with an increase in co-morbidities such as developmental delays, epilepsy and high infant mortality.

Problematic Food Security Livelihood-Coping Activities

The Tonga households studied resorted to an array of survival list activities which, in effect, were detrimental to good nutrition, food security and general health. They reduced the number of meals consumed when food became scarce. Daily meals were reduced from three to two and then to one and, in extreme cases, informants reported having had a meal every two days. Many informants thus made comments such as the following:

> We now have one meal a day. We no longer have the staple food of maize/sorghum meal but are surviving on wild leaf okra without the starch. We last had something to eat two days ago.
>
> *Quoted in Muderedzi et al. 2017: 5*

As well, the sale of assets to purchase food was a common phenomenon. As a result, only a few Tonga households had significant household assets. Males lamented that they no longer had domestic animals (notably, cattle) and females spoke about their loss of household goods (such as kitchen utensils) as well as chickens. Male informants would state that:

> I used to have cows but not anymore. We sold one to buy medication for my two late children (mainly traditional healer fees), some in exchange for food, and some died from disease and lack of food and water.
>
> *Interview 20 August 2012*

Child labour also exists, with very poor households sending their boys elsewhere to work as cattle herders and girls as housemaids. Tonga mothers in particular expressed their grief, stating:

> How I miss my daughter. I hope she is well. It had to be done.
>
> *40-year-old female, interview 12 November 2013*

Some of these children came back home to die after contracting HIV and AIDS. In this respect, as indicated earlier, sex work existed in the area. Young Tonga females resorted to sex work to raise income for the household. This took place at Binga town centre, along the major road (with long-distance drivers) and at the fishing camps where "fish for sex" took place. When asked about the dangers of catching HIV, one young female informant indicated:

> One needs to survive. I have my own children to care for as well as orphans from my sister.
>
> *Interview 20 April 2012*

Further, parents married off young girls against their consent to older men in return for food. One married-off informant noted:

> There was not enough food at home. Now my husband looks after me and my co-wives.
>
> *Interview 5 October 2006*

Cooking and consumption of unconventional foods, such as boiled ash, takes place as well. This was carried out in extreme situations and household members admitted to not getting any nutritional value from this, as it only kept hunger at bay.

Also significant as a source of food were forest foods, inclusive of wild vegetables, fruits, leaves, barks and roots from some trees (for example, the moringa tree that provides leaves as a vegetable); as well, insects and rodents have become a source of food. At times, I accompanied some informants on forest expeditions and noted the dangers associated with these activities, such as falling from trees and breaking limbs or even death. Snake bites resulted in limb amputations, disability, blindness or death. Malaria was rife during the rainy season as local Tonga people would catch different types of insects in the evenings.

Though all Binga households and individuals were subject to food insecurity at some time and at some level, those suffering the most from food insufficiency were children from six months to five years (who were prone to malnutrition), child-headed households, households headed by the elderly who were taking care of orphans and the elderly without family support as their children had died from AIDS. Historically, strong family ties (beyond the household) had been the best social insurance against starvation in Zimbabwe but, because of AIDS, drought and the deteriorating economic situation, most of the well-established coping strategies involving extended-family safety nets and local support networks are increasingly under pressure and disappearing.

In examining food security and vulnerability amongst the Tonga in Binga, it becomes necessary to focus on the social, political, economic and ecological barriers they encounter and the strategies they use to try to overcome them. Clearly, the capabilities, assets and activities required for sustainable living are wholly deficient for the Tonga, leading to their vulnerability to shocks and negative trends (both economic and ecological) and the curtailing of livelihood opportunities. The government is still not seen by the Tonga as playing its part in empowering their communities. Hence, multiple livelihood challenges remain, such as erratic rains, inadequate farming inputs, roaming elephants and the lack of draught power, technical knowledge, seeds and fertiliser. The ready availability of water sources such as dams and boreholes would be invaluable to Tonga villagers, yet the elderly men and women (the "River Tonga" who were displaced from the Zambezi River decades ago) stress that:

> If there had been no dam, we would not be suffering like this. We want our water to follow us.
>
> *Interview 10 September 2005*

Conclusion

This chapter has examined the specific day-to-day challenges faced in Binga District by Tonga women in constructing household-based livelihoods, with a particular focus on food insecurity. These challenges include HIV and AIDS, local politics and domestic labour. In seeking to overcome these challenges and enhance their food security, Tonga women engage in a fluctuating livelihood portfolio involving livelihood diversification, with some livelihood activities (such as sex work) characterised by serious risks.

The story about water not following them is a lamentation about the loss of access to the waters of the Zambezi. Livelihoods and food security prior to the construction of the Kariba Dam changed to insecurity and impoverishment after their forced resettlement. Before the Kariba Dam displacement, rights to land and property for Tonga women had reduced the risk of poverty. The "River Tonga" women also stated that "the water went with the land", meaning that the landscape and waterscape were inextricably intertwined in the Zambezi Valley. They had lost access to water and land because of the removal, thereby undercutting their livelihoods. Aspects of their matrilineal culture lost over the years, such as fishing in shallow waters, owning land and the responsibility of growing crops, have to be restored because this will increase female access to resources and food security.

Overall, this chapter demonstrates that the current lack of access to resources has been critical to forcing females to adopt poor coping strategies. Without access to technology, finance, productive land, education and healthcare, Tonga women specifically are compelled to turn to problematic livelihood-coping practices which may be of benefit in the short term but have no long-lasting positive effect or outcome in relation to building household-level food security. These practices include not only sex work and early marriage, but also the seeming celebration of an HIV-positive status because it allows for access to food aid packages. Indeed, informants at times stated that "AIDS has come with food" as if, by sanitising the process, contracting HIV was a blessing.

References

Bond, V., Cliggett, L., and Siamwiza, B. (2013). Tonga identity in process. In L. Cliggett and V. Bond (eds), *Tonga timeline: appraising sixty years of multidisciplinary research in Zambia and Zimbabwe*, xiii–xxxviii. Lusaka-Zambia: Lembani Trust.

Brody, A. (2015). *Gender and food security; an overview: in brief BRIDGE development-gender*. Sussex: Institute of Development Studies.

Chingarande, D., Matondi, P., Mugano, G., Chagwiza, G., and Hungwe, M. (2020). *Zimbabwe food security desk research: matabeleland north province*. Washington, DC: Research Technical Assistance Centre.

Committee on World Food Security. (2012). *Global strategic framework for food security and nutrition*. Rome: United Nations.

COSV. (2014). Food security and fighting poverty in Hwange and Binga districts. COSV-Milano.

FAO. (1996). Rome declaration on food security; World food summit: 13–17 November.

FAO. (2011). Notes on livestock, food security, and gender equity. FAO Animal Production and Health Working Paper No. 3, Rome.

FFSSA. (2003). Mudimu, G. Zimbabwe food security issues paper: for Forum for Food Security in Southern Africa.

Hyder, A.A., Maman, S., Nyoni, J.E., Khasiani, S.A., Teoh, N., Premji, Z., and Sohani, S. (2005). The pervasive triad of food security, gender inequity and women´s health: exploratory research from Sub-Saharan Africa. *African Health Sciences*, Vol. 5(4): 328–334. doi:10.5555/afhs.2005.5.4.328

IFRC. (2021). Emergency Plan Action (EPA) Zimbabwe: Food insecurity: DREF Operation n´MDRZW016.
Muderedzi, J., Eide, A. H., Braathen, S. H., and Stray-Pedersen, B. (2017). Exploring structural violence in the context of disability and poverty in Zimbabwe. *African Journal of Disability*, Vol. 6(0): a274. https://doi.org/10.4102/ajod.v6i0.274
Muderedzi, J., Eide, A. H., Braathen, S. H., and Stray-Pedersen, B. (2019). Exploring the relationship between food insecurity, gender roles and HIV/AIDS among Tonga carers of disabled children of Binga in Zimbabwe. *Sexuality and Culture*, Vol. 23(4): 1131–1146.
Muderedzi, J., Eide, A. H., Braathen, S. H., and Stray-Pedersen, B. (2020). Vulnerable groups and structural violence; Case of the Tonga people of Binga in Zimbabwe: Coping of families with disabled children. Unpublished PhD Thesis-University of Oslo.
MyZimbabwe News. (2021). Mpofu, M. 02-09-2021. "A grandmother dies from falling down a tree while gathering wild fruits in Binga": Newsprint-Harare.
Nelson, S., Chaudhury M., and Tranberg, H. (2013). *Training guide: gender and climate change research in agriculture and food security for rural development*. Rome, Italia: FAO.
Ncube, V. (2016). HIV/AIDS in rural Tonga culture. *Theological Studies*, Vol. 72(1): 1–7.
SADC. (2019). Synthesis Report on the state of food and nutrition security and vulnerability in Southern Africa (01–04 July 2019).
SCUK (2003–2004). Report on Household Economy Assessments.
Silverman, D. (2013). *Doing qualitative research*. 4th edition. London: Sage Publications.
SOFA Report. (2011). "Women in Agriculture: Closing the gender gap for development". Wikigender. org/wiki/the-sofa-report-2011
The New Humanitarian. (2003). Binga families depending on food aid, farmers waiting for the rain. IRIN News.
The Zimbabwean. (2005). No food before elections-Mugabe: Newsprint-Harare.
UN (2015). Sustainable Developmental Goals. https://sdgs.un.org
WFP. (2021). Zimbabwe-Food security and markets monitoring report. Zimbabwe Vulnerability Assessment Committee. Harare: WFP.
ZIMPHIA. (2020). Zimbabwe Population-Based HIV Impact Assessment. Summary Sheet.
ZVAC (2015). Rural Livelihoods Assessment. Harare: ZVAC.

8

DISPLACEMENT AND LIVELIHOOD VULNERABILITY AMONG THE TONGA WOMEN OF BINGA, 1958–1980

Codelia Govha Dhodho

Introduction

Binga District in the Zambezi Valley in Zimbabwe is endowed with natural resources, but the people live in abject poverty in what is one of the poorest and least developed parts of the country. Making up most of the population in the district, the Tonga are among the most marginalised ethnic groups in the country despite the natural resource base (Mundia 2010). There is a lack of basic infrastructural development and the people suffer from chronic food and water shortages (McGregor 2009). This chapter traces the hunger and poverty of Tonga people from the time they were displaced from the Zambezi River following the construction of the Kariba Dam in the late 1950s up to 1980 when the nation attained independence. The Tonga were resettled in barren land infested with tsetse flies, malaria and marauding game without compensation, and the colonial government did not assist them in livelihood restoration. Food production became a challenge after involuntary displacement and resettlement in a drought-prone area. It is crucial to identify factors which affected farming and contributed to perennial food insecurity and impoverishment from a gendered perspective, as women were mainly responsible for crop production.

In tracing the impact of displacement on livelihoods of the Tonga, this study thus examines how forced displacement affected farming as a major livelihood for women. It analyses how marginalisation by the colonial government disempowered the Tonga in relation to accessing fertile land from the lakeshore and water for irrigation, as well as fishing and wildlife resources in the region. This entails discussing how discriminatory colonial policies in hunting and fishing impoverished women by decimating their livelihoods regarding food production. National media drew international attention to Binga by publicising the district's leading role in hunger and underdevelopment during the 1982/1983 nationwide drought (McGregor

DOI: 10.4324/9781003278580-10

2009). The district became so poor that 90 per cent of the people required food aid every year, and hence there is a need to understand the causes of perennial food shortages among the Tonga (Mundia 2010). With reference to the colonial period, this chapter hence considers how crop failure posed a major hinderance to food security; and how prohibition to hunt and loss of fishing grounds affected food supply and access. It argues that, although women faced formidable challenges and lived precarious lives, they found ways of coping and adapting without external assistance because of their agency and indigenous knowledge systems.

Context

The Tonga became impoverished after being forcibly torn from the Zambezi River and dumped on dry and barren land on the Zambezi Plateau where they soon failed to make a living. Before the construction of the Kariba Dam, they inhabited both banks of the middle Zambezi River and its tributaries and called themselves "the river people" (*Balonga*) (Waters 2020). They had lived there for centuries where there was fertile alluvial soil, reliable water supply, abundant wildlife and plenty of fish for food (McGregor 2009). But, the construction of the Kariba Dam destroyed the river system upon which they had depended for their livelihoods. About 57,000 people were evicted from the river valley between 1956 and 1958 and were forced to relocate north and south of the river. About 23,000 Tonga people on the south bank were forced to resettle in Binga District of the then Southern Rhodesia, and without compensation (Colson 1971). The colonial government deprived them of the resources from the Lake and they met severe challenges in food production.

Historically, rural women are the most vulnerable population in Zimbabwe because they lack access to land and water necessary for food security and agricultural productivity. To understand the persistence of poverty in Binga up until 1980, the study explores how risks associated with displacement affected men and women's efforts to secure a livelihood. A gendered perspective of displacement of the Tonga is not common, yet there is a need to recognise the complexity and nuances of men and women's roles in livelihoods. This helps to understand the specificities of women's marginalisation in rural communities and of minority women (like Tonga women) in particular. Both Tonga men and women lost economic autonomy via the forced relocation, but women suffered the most as they had fewer livelihood opportunities. Additionally, the impact of food insecurity on women was greater than for men because the former were responsible for caring for children. The Tonga are largely a matrilineal society and they trace inheritance and succession from the maternal side of the family. Due to this practice (called *luzubo*), descent was recognised through women, and children belonged to the lineage of their mother (Scudder 2005). Generally, the woman was responsible for feeding her children as most men had polygamous marriages and left the provision of food to women (Khozi and Yon 2005).

The Tonga became vulnerable to chronic food shortages after resettlement, with the Native Affairs Department reporting that every year became a challenge and a battle for survival for them (Muyambi 1981). There were successive droughts from the second year of forced resettlement and the Tonga suffered so much that they could hardly afford or access one meal a day. There were droughts in 1959, 1963, 1965, 1966, 1968, 1978 and 1980–1983, and colonial authorities had to bring food into the valley from other districts for sale to the Tonga (Muyambi 1981). There was neither humanitarian assistance nor food aid issued to the people during these dry periods because of prevailing racism in colonial Southern Rhodesia. The Tonga people barely had sources of cash, hence they used their livestock to purchase or barter for grain. Able-bodied men had to engage in migrant labour to earn money but they spent their entire income buying grain in times of drought without any savings accumulating (Weinrich 1977).

Colson and Scudder ethnographically explored the social consequences of displacement from the Zambezi River, focusing mainly though on the Gwembe Tonga of Northern Rhodesia (Colson 1960; Scudder 1962; Colson 1971). They argued that resettlement on the south (Southern Rhodesian) bank was not properly planned and the Tonga were not only forcibly evicted but also dumped into the wilderness which was arid and inhabitable without compensation. Weinrich's ethnographical work supplements Colson and Scudder's studies as she traces the experiences of the Tonga of Zimbabwe since resettlement (Weinrich 1977). Later, McGregor (2009) studied how displacement brought about major economic and political changes for the Tonga of Zimbabwe and she discusses their agency in fighting for cultural recognition. Importantly, Manyena argues that the problem of chronic food shortages should be traced to the 1958 displacement and resettlement (Manyena 2009).

This current study benefits from these sources but focuses on how resettlement affected livelihoods from a gendered perspective. It focuses on how women tried to make a living in farming after displacement and explores the challenges which caused long-term food shortages for them. The chapter argues that, although women faced many risks in food production, they used their indigenous knowledge systems to cope and adapt. However, they failed to establish a viable livelihood because of state neglect, thereby becoming impoverished.

The livelihoods framework provides a way to understand the character of Tonga poverty at household level and the linkages between different aspects of their livelihoods. It analyses how poor people operate within a vulnerability context, and how they utilise capabilities and capitals – such as natural and financial assets – to develop livelihood strategies which help them to pursue if not achieve desired livelihood outcomes (Kranz 2001). The framework portrays the vulnerability context as the major challenge affecting poor people's adaptive capacity to pursue sustainable livelihood strategies. Vulnerability is defined as the condition that limits people's capacity to participate, manage, resist or recover from the impact of a threat, shock or crisis (Scoones 1998). Overall, the framework assists in identifying and examining the threats to Tonga women's livelihoods after displacement as well as analysing how these disruptions affected their resilience. The political and economic environment in which people live their lives is responsible for many of their hardships as it often makes them susceptible to poverty.

Criticisms have been raised about the framework. For instance, Morse et al. (2009) argue that the framework fails to fully account for the unequal distribution of resources as well as not conceptualising the lack of assets at household level as both a cause and outcome of poverty. Others claim that the livelihoods framework does not sufficiently acknowledge inequalities of power and conflict of interest at national level (Murray 2001). Considering such points, it is clear that the causes of poverty amongst the Tonga in Binga are complex and multifaceted. In this regard, the Impoverishment Risk and Reconstruction theory (Cernea 2000) assists in shedding light on why the Tonga became poor and remained poor for many years following their eviction from the Zambezi River. This theory proposes a range of risks regarding the deepening of impoverishment often faced by victims of involuntary displacement and provides strategies for how these risks can be prevented. It also puts forward that, if the risks are not properly managed, this can result in long-lasting impoverishment effects amongst the displaced. The Tonga were racially and ethnically inferior at the time of their displacement, and they had no power to claim their resources from the colonial regime (Mashingaidze 2013) – this affected their capabilities in building resilient livelihoods, particularly for Tonga women. As a general tendency, the vulnerability of the communities in Binga was mostly due to state neglect.

Research Methodology

The study employed a qualitative research paradigm to select, interpret and analyse material obtained from both primary and secondary sources. Primary material was collected from archival sources from the National Archives of Zimbabwe, and from reports of hunters and explorers who encountered the Tonga before colonisation. Oral testimonies though provided most of the information for this study. Empirical data was collected in January and December 2020 using in-depth interviews to access aspects of historical experiences which are absent from written works, and to counter the myths and biases of colonial officials. Thirteen key informants were purposively selected for in-depth interviews in the Sikalenge and Binga chiefdoms in Binga District. These included five women and three men whose age ranged from 74 to 92 years who provided narratives of their experiences after displacement. Two women and three men who were born in Binga during the colonial period were also interviewed to capture different views. Semi-structured interviews were conducted as well with two Rural District Officers, one Game Ranger and an officer from the Ministry of Agriculture, to gather information on the viability of livelihoods in the district.

Pre-Displacement Livelihoods

Scholars contend that the Tonga were at the margins of national politics up until 1980, and this limited their access to power and resources (Manyena 2009; Mashingaidze 2013; McGregor 2009). Post 1958, they failed to build sustainable livelihoods in agriculture because they lost their best land which was inundated by the formation of the Kariba Dam.

Before displacement, Tonga women were the backbone of food production in farming, while men contributed by hunting and fishing (Colson 1977). Crop production sustained families and communities because the Zambezi, like the Nile, flooded annually and the floodwater left rich alluvial soil where the Tonga prepared dry season gardens just above the riverbanks. Each homestead had a riverbank garden where they grew crops at least twice a year to extend the farming season beyond the short summer rains. Both men and women owned these permanent alluvial gardens which were inherited by children from parents (Reynolds and Cousins 1993). As a largely matrilineal society which traced inheritance and succession from the maternal side of the family, a man usually provided for his sister's children as the nephews would inherit his name. Generally, as indicated, a woman was responsible for feeding her family because children belonged to the mother.

Ellis emphasises that land is essential for subsistence and any shortage of quality land threatens livelihoods (Ellis 2002). The Tonga were betrayed constantly by the colonial government which forcibly evicted them from their best land without compensation. Soon after displacement, the local District Officer reported that Tonga women complained about their loss of rights to virgin land as the land tenure system was now vested in the state (NAZ File S2929/5/1, 1965). Land was a symbol of wealth and a source of livelihood, hence women had considerable power in Tonga society which they lost after displacement. The women were discontented as they had to depend upon men to clear land for them after resettlement in the mopani woodlands of the Zambezi Plateau. Clearing the forest for preparation of fields required more time and tools (such as axes) which most women did not possess. Deprivation of fertile land thus increased vulnerability and poverty in Binga as it affected self-sufficiency of families during the early years after forced resettlement when they could not plant crops on time.

Before resettlement, there was risk of famine in the hot and arid Zambezi Valley, but the Tonga were largely self-sufficient because they depended on the perennial water from the Zambezi for irrigating their crops. When The Native Commissioner Gielgud first encountered them in 1898, he reported that they were "living in a country where the slightest effort will produce rich crops ... in fact they can raise three crops a year" (NAZ File NB6/1/4/2, 1898). Women drew upon their indigenous knowledge systems to maximise on yields on the limited space close to the water from the perennial river. They mainly produced maize (*zibopwe*) and sorghum (*nzembwe*) as the main staples which were intercropped with beans, cowpeas, cucumbers, melons and Turkish tobacco. A harvest was certain because they planted specifically selected seeds to mature early and produced high yields with less moisture. For instance, a variety of maize (*kaile*) which matured in 60 days was planted twice a year to maintain food security (Scudder 1971) According to Harding (1905), a continuous supply of food throughout the year was obtainable by sowing seed in successive rows as the floods subsided. A river garden had maize at the highest point which was fully ripe, while near the water level other maize plants had just germinated. Small lagoons were also sown with maize as soon as the water evaporated in the dry season, and islands which only appeared when the river was low were utilised as well for crop cultivation. However, it became increasingly difficult to grow maize which required more rainfall and better soils after resettlement on the plateau, and this affected nutrition and food security.

Farming before displacement further provided a source of cash for women as they traded green maize, tobacco and marijuana. Tonga men used to carry sacks of green maize cobs to Gokwe for sale for cash during the 1920s as women remained behind taking care of the gardens and the children. Although transport was a major obstacle to trade, the people also carried green maize on donkey backs to mines at Wankie and Kamativi, and they earned cash for payment of state-tax as well as for purchase of consumer goods (Weinrich 1977). Tobacco and marijuana were the primary export crops from the valley to the plateau (Reynolds 1968) and had a long-standing role in the regional exchange economy. Middlemen from Mashonaland bought tobacco and marijuana from the Tonga and became major suppliers of the products to miners in Wankie Colliery and Kamativi in Southern Rhodesia, the Copperbelt in Northern Rhodesia and in South Africa. The valley was inaccessible to the police; therefore, it was difficult for the colonial authorities to effectively enforce the law that banned the growing and selling of marijuana amongst the Tonga. While men invested the money obtained from the sale of tobacco and marijuana in livestock, women bought consumer goods such as clothes, blankets, beads and grain (Weinrich 1977).

When the floods from the Zambezi receded, the Tonga usually devoted the first planting season which started in December to food crops for subsistence. The main tobacco and marijuana crop were planted in winter and harvested from August to September (Reynolds 1968). The Turkish variety was drought resistant and adapted to the environment, so that it needed less cultivation than maize and sorghum. The personal use of tobacco (*polya*) and cannabis (*lubange*) by both men and women was of great political, economic and cultural significance among the Tonga communities. Because of their matrilineality or *luzubo*, the women had a greater degree of autonomy compared to women from patriarchal societies (Weinrich 1977). Tonga women smoked tobacco in their calabash (*inchelwa*) pipes which were manufactured with ingenuity to filter tobacco fumes in water and ash. This was a cultural and social activity from early adolescence until death, hence the demand for tobacco was high (Reynolds 1968). Sometimes women smoked tobacco mixed with marijuana.

Post-Displacement Reconstruction of Lives

Scudder and Colson's Four Stage Framework identifies four stages of a successful resettlement process which relate to the behavioural or psychological tendencies of the people affected over a period of two generations. The four stages are the planning and recruitment phase, transition phase, development phase, and handing-over or incorporation phase (Scudder 2005). People may face physical and mental stress after displacement and resettlement, but they may eventually adapt to the new environment. Matanzima (2022) uses this framework to understand the long-term impact of resettlement among the Tonga and argues that they failed to reach the transition phase because of lack of access to resources from Lake Kariba.

Forced resettlement robbed the Tonga women of rich alluvial soils on the banks of the Zambezi River which sustained their livelihood. The arid and infertile plateau of Binga was not suitable to produce both food and cash crops. The colonial authorities continued to prohibit the production of cannabis but the District Commissioner allowed both men and women to continue smoking marijuana for cultural and medicinal purposes (McGregor 2009). Because growing of cannabis remained criminalised, they continued to grow it illegally in secret. Interviews with villagers in chief Binga's area revealed that women would grow cannabis in the middle of their millet and sorghum fields and some men owned bigger fields in the forests and in mountains which were inaccessible to the police. The Tonga had strong social networks for ongoing trading of the crop, thereby defying the government. Nevertheless, when they could not meet the demands for tobacco for local use, both men and women had to buy the product from the Shangwe of Mafungautsi (in Gokwe), therefore losing income.

Involuntary displacement imposed conditions of vulnerability regarding crop failure upon the Tonga, who failed to build sustainable livelihoods in farming. They were neglected by the colonial government although they had given up their homes and livelihoods for national development, notably, for power generation. When their land was inundated by the Kariba reservoir, they were moved to an unassigned area where crop cultivation was difficult because of loose sandy soils which were nutrient deficient. The settler government had designated the Zambezi Valley as unassigned land under the Land Apportionment Act of 1931 because of the prevalence of malaria and tsetse fly. The Native Affairs Department even reported that about 9,000 people were resettled in Lubu Valley, where less than 8 per cent of the land was considered suitable for agriculture (Nesham 1961). Following the loss of alluvial soils, which had sustained agriculture by intensive cultivation, the Tonga adopted slash-and-burn farming as the major method of growing food because they lived in small villages in a vast land full of mopani forests.

Adaptation to the Zambezi Plateau was a challenge because of the nutrient-deficient soils, so they practised a form of land rotation whereby they cleared a piece of land which was utilised until its fertility diminished after five to ten years (because they could not afford inorganic fertilisers). A new field could produce high yields of sorghum for three to six years, after which it was abandoned to lie fallow for five to ten years. Men helped in the arduous task of cutting down trees and burning them, but the tree stumps were not removed because they needed them to develop more shoots, which could be burnt again to produce fertiliser for the soil. The women also had to gather elephant dung and goat manure for fertiliser. Despite this slash-and-burn technique being a mitigating factor to the risks involved in farming in the harsh environment, it was not sustainable because of increased demands for labour. As well, the colonial authorities accused the Tonga of deforestation and land degradation but the latter regarded slash-and-burn farming as a sophisticated and appropriate method for taming a new environment. Periodic cutting down of trees cleared the game-infested forests and destroyed the habitats of dangerous wildlife which threatened their lives and destroyed their crops.

Although farming conditions changed dramatically after resettlement and tremendously reduced the amount of food produced, Tonga women worked hard to maintain food security, sometimes drawing from their indigenous knowledge systems. Farming was left primarily to women and children because of the absence of cattle and use of the plough, although men assisted in the clearing of land for the establishment of a field (Tremmel 1994). The women became focused on developing ways to survive in the hostile climate following loss of their alluvial gardens. As the cultivation of maize became impossible, they adopted drought tolerant crops such as sorghum (*maila*) and bulrush millet (*nzembwe*). They intercropped these staple crops with groundnuts (*mandongo*), cucurbits (*myuungu*) and sesame (*bwengo*) to improve the chances of a harvest in case of drought. They practised staggered planting to reduce the risk of losing out completely in the event of protracted absence of rain during the season. They sometimes planted a sorghum crop during the early rains but, when it did not germinate well, they would plant a second crop in the same field to fill in the gaps when more rains came. A field could have two or more different sizes of the same crop mixed with other varieties of crops. By combining different heights, root depths and maturity periods, crops planted during different periods complemented each other in the use of sunlight.

The social, institutional and political organisation of a society can assist or impede livelihoods resilience. The Tonga were denied access to resources and support because of who they were, in the eyes of the colonial state. They thus lacked the financial capital required to apply significant inputs into their cropping system on the barren land to make it more productive. Their main self-mobilised resource became the trees which provided ash for potash to fertilise the soil, which lacked sufficient humus, calcium and phosphorous essential for plant growth. Despite this ingenuity and effort to reduce risks and reconstruct livelihoods beyond displacement, the colonial authorities criticised their coping strategies and blamed the people for having "little use of modern ideas and their lands and villages are full of tree stumps" (NAZ File S2827/2/2/2/2, 1955). This condemnation of indigenous knowledge systems stemmed from the skewed belief that a good farmer is one who left no tree standing in the field and who grew one crop in a field; the rest were weeds which needed to be cleared.

Impoverishment is the most widespread effect of involuntary displacement, particularly without rehabilitation and development programmes (Cernea 2000). McGregor (2009) blames Cockcroft (the District Commissioner) for obstructing development in Binga, arguing that the people should be left to evolve on their own. The Native Affairs Department did not assist them with agricultural extension workers who could teach them new soil management systems. Some colonial officials even acknowledged the government's failures in improving livelihoods options in Binga. When assessing the area's development needs in 1966, the District Administrator C. J. K. Latham noted that: "I would make a special plea for the Tonga. They are a people living in a vacuum, bridged by seventy years of development elsewhere in the country" (NAZ File S2929/1/1, 1966). The colonial authorities had condemned the region as a place where farming was not sustainable as a livelihood basis, because of many risks. They acknowledged that "[t]he problems of agriculture in the district are so formidable that it is difficult to see how any progress is to be made" (NAZ File S2827/2/2/3/3, 1959).

Although they were aware of multiple problems intrinsic to the district, the Rhodesian government nevertheless blamed the Tonga for their vulnerability to crop failure. It also ridiculed them as people with an extremely limited knowledge of agriculture, comparing them with other Africans in ecologically better districts such as Marandellas or Mazowe. One Native Commissioner reported that "[t]he great bulk of the African is as backward in his agricultural methods as he was thirty years ago. Compulsion will make him mend his ways" (NAZ File S1618/1951–1953). White farmers depended upon the use of animal traction for increasing crop yields, and they criticised the Tonga for their continued reliance on the traditional hoe and digging stick in agriculture, instead of adopting the modern plough, for which they had insufficient cattle.

In this light, the continued presence of tsetse fly in the district as late as 1982 placed the people at a tremendous disadvantage in building resilience. In Zambia, resettlement was accompanied by a major programme to control tsetse fly, which made it possible for the Gwembe Tonga to keep cattle and diversify livelihoods (Colson 1971). The Government of Southern Rhodesia failed to control tsetse fly after resettlement which killed numerous cattle, sheep and goats in the district of Binga. In 1973 alone, about 750 cattle were killed by tsetse in Siansali, and this explains why as late as 1974 there were only 20 ploughs in the whole district (Weinrich 1977). Lack of draught power increased labour demands associated with initial digging and weeding by women. Use of oxen traction for cultivating virgin land would have increased productivity and harvests. Cattle were also an important store of capital as they could be exchanged for grain during famine.

The Tonga existed in a colonial national political economy where there were marginalised subjects who were politically invisible, and this constrained their strategies for making a living. They had no access to power because race was the key guide for the construction of oppressive policies by the settler regime. Drawing water from Lake Kariba for irrigation would have solved the problem of crop failure due to drought, but the potential use of Kariba water for irrigation was not even investigated as part of the project of construction of the dam. Several irrigation schemes could have been established around the Lake, and the amount of water extracted by these irrigation schemes would be so low as to have any impact on power generation. Allocating chiefdoms, some portion of irrigated lands on the lakeshore would supplement dry land farming and enable cash crop cultivation. The district also abounded in wildlife, which had the potential of diversifying livelihoods by providing income, jobs and food for the Tonga. However, on racial grounds, the colonial authorities denied the Tonga access to this important resource, which became a curse to the people because of the risk it posed to farming.

Crop Destruction by Wildlife

Besides facing the risks of erratic rainfall and poor soils in limiting the prospects of a good harvest, the Tonga met formidable challenges around marauding elephants which plundered their crops at night. When they were evicted from the banks of the Zambezi River following the construction of the Kariba Dam in 1957 and 1958, they were resettled in a wilderness where they had to coexist with dangerous game. Women claimed that they did not have major problems with elephants feeding on their crops before displacement because "most elephants stayed near the mountains. When they did come into our villages they would be killed by our hunters" (Tremmel 1994: 19). Large game was mostly found in less densely populated areas in thick bushes that were far away from the villages along the river. When the animals came to plunder crops during the farming season, hunting intensified to defend the harvest. However, all hunting became illegal after resettlement and anyone who killed elephants that destroyed crops were arrested for poaching by the Department of Parks and Wildlife Management.

At the turn of the twentieth century, the explorer Colin Harding documented how the Tonga used their indigenous knowledge systems in hunting, an activity which was fundamental to their lives. He noted that there were men "who lived by the gun", hunting using muskets, and he saw heads of animals hung on trees and skins of big game on roof tops displayed as achievements of the hunters (Harding 1905). Hunting and fishing formed the basis of male livelihoods, and these skills were passed down through countless generations (Harding 1905). As a source of meat, hunting for the Tonga was as prominent as cattle keeping was for the Shona. The Tonga killed big game for meat to support the subsistence of communities particularly during famines, but the colonial government jeopardised this livelihood pursuit by the criminalisation of hunting. Up until the 1950s, this caused significant conflict between the government and the Tonga, who regarded the animals as their traditional heritage. However, after displacement, they lost the self-sufficiency which characterised their past, as all hunting and fishing on the Lake were prohibited. This became a major source of resentment, notably for men, because they had been robbed of their role as providers of protein. Most young men had to migrate to towns, farms and mines as migrant labourers, leaving women with the main burden of taking care of crops, livestock and children. The banning of fishing and hunting led to shortages of protein and malnutrition among children, pregnant and breastfeeding women.

The government designated Matusadona and Chete Safari areas as well as Chizarira National Park for wildlife and had erected fences to keep the animals away from local communities. However, the Tonga claimed that elephants and buffalos always broke down these fences and roamed through their villages searching for food from the green fields of sorghum. Hunters were prohibited from killing these animals to safeguard their lives and crops, hence people were compelled to guard their fields and scare them away. Guarding of crops from February to May became a challenge for women who had to reckon with the elephants by screaming and beating noisy gongs from their *busanza* shelters built on stilts, setting fires on the edges of fields, as well as waving burning sorghum stalks. These methods were not highly effective because sometimes the elephants ignored them and destroyed their crops. Men and boys would also sleep in the fields on some nights. After suffering from frequent famines caused by destruction of crops by elephants, the people of Simuchembu chiefdom sought government permission to trap and kill these wild animals, but they were denied permission (NAZ File S2929/5/1, 1965).

Baboons, wild pigs and birds also jeopardised the harvest. This forced women and children to guard their fields during the day as well as scare birds from the time the first sorghum seeds appeared up to the time of harvesting (Tremmel 1994). Most women tried cultivating maize because it did not attract birds, but the crop did not do well due to sparse rainfall and hot summer temperatures. Although sometimes they lost crops to these predators, women did not give up on farming because of this setback. They had to spend the day banging iron pots to chase away quelea birds which could destroy the whole harvest and result in hunger. Men assisted by setting snares for the birds and made many elaborate scarecrow devices across the fields, though sometimes they were not effective enough to drive away the flocks of hungry birds from the green sorghum seeds (Reynolds 1968). Monkeys and baboons were particularly bold and destructive raiders during the day and could destroy crops. For example, Weinrich (1977) reported that the crop of 1976 was destroyed by monkeys and birds and this was the major cause of hunger in that year. The Tonga people suffered frequent famine caused by these crop pests; for instance, the year 1985 is remembered as *Nzala Ya Buyuni* (The starvation/year of quelea birds). After three years of drought caused mainly by low rainfall, quelea birds consumed much of the grain in the good season of 1984–85, and this was followed by *Nzala Ya Kubula Kwamvula* (The starvation/year of no rain) (Reynolds and Cousins 1993). Therefore, famine in the region was either caused by drought or by destruction of crops by birds and wild animals. As a result, the Tonga were not able to become self-sufficient in food. When the harvest failed to sustain them, women resorted to living on wild foods gathered from the forest, while men illegally killed game.

Loss of Fishing Rights

Exclusion from sharing in the Lake's economic benefits prevented the Tonga from building sustainable livelihoods after resettlement. When the dam was constructed, there were no provisions to share revenues generated from the sale of electricity, tourism or commercial fisheries with those who sacrificed their homes and land for the creation of the reservoir. Both men and women were marginalised as they were pushed to the periphery of the fishing industry because they had no voice nor power to demand their entitlements. In this regard, Manyena et al. (2016)

write about the marginalisation of fishermen but do not mention the role of women in fishing during the pre-resettlement period. There was gender parity in fishing which was a major source of livelihood for both men and women. Fishing by women and children contributed to family nutrition as they used nets and baskets in small inlets when the floods receded from the Zambezi and its tributaries.

The Rhodesian government established fishing camps which were far away from resettlement areas, and only men were allowed at these fishing camps. Few men could leave their families to reside in these camps and women did not have any access to fishing resources from the Lake. The temporary shelters at the fishing camps did not accommodate families as the colonial government did not want African settlements close to the Lake, which was designated as a European Area according to the Land Apportionment Act. Permanent villages for the Tonga along the lakeshore would have diversified their livelihoods as they would be able to combine commercial fishing and farming. The Gwembe Tonga of Zambia were trained to fish and were assisted with finances to buy fishing equipment. In 1962, there were over 2,000 local fishermen who used the proceeds to purchase cattle and ploughs (Matanzima 2022). Those in Southern Rhodesia thus lost a major source of livelihood, but women were most affected and this contributed to food shortages.

Tonga men's roles in hunting and fishing were affected detrimentally by resettlement. The *Kapenta* fish industry which developed in the 1970s was very profitable but was dominated by Europeans because it was capital-intensive. The Europeans employed Tonga men to clean fish, rigs and nets, but more jobs could have been created if the fisheries had invested in processing and canning of fish. The resources from the Lake could have transformed the lives of the people had it not been for the racist policies which pushed the Tonga to the periphery. In the meantime, women experienced significant pressure because of the loss of men's livelihood roles. They had to find new ways of increasing food production to supplement fish and game meat. Previously, hunting and fishing had complemented agricultural produce and saved lives during famines. Now women had to cultivate more crops and this increased the labour demands for cultivation and guarding fields against baboons and elephants.

Marginalisation of the Tonga

There were few employment opportunities in Binga district because of lack of investment in possible industries, and the migrant labour system privileged young men. The colonial government lacked political will to assist the Tonga in restoration and diversification of livelihoods. When compared to other indigenous people, there is a misconception about the Tonga as less motivated, less agriculturally inclined and even less intelligent. This stereotyping began with David Livingstone who encountered and described them in the 1850s as "the most primitive tribe" in Central Africa (Livingstone 1865). This attitude, which Msindo (2012) calls "othering", continued during the colonial era and contributed to their losses during the process of displacement as the colonial authorities did not consult them. This is consistent with what McGregor (2009) pointed out, namely, that the Tonga "were a neglected people, cast as inferior and labelled primitive and ignorant". They were a relatively small group of voiceless rural people in a remote corner of the country where the economic choices and development policies of the government were influenced by white political interests. They were simply told to leave their homes without compensation to pave way for the dam. The formidable challenges which they faced in making sustainable livelihoods after displacement and the subsequent impoverishment also contributed to this stereotyping. Manyena (2009) contends that it is marginalisation that generated demeaning, stereotypical myths and prejudices which portrayed the Tonga as dangerous, deformed and primitive. Because of their exceptional levels of poverty and backwardness, stigmatising stereotypes further excluded them from politics (McGregor 2009).

Marginalisation is one of the worst and widespread outcomes of displacement, and the Tonga were aware that the stereotypes affected their access to resources and opportunities in the country, as the government despised them and focused on the "advancement" of Shona and Ndebele people. They lacked rural livelihood opportunities, and those who migrated to towns and cities in search of better opportunities were hindered from getting employed because of their marginalised and despised status. Employment opportunities raise standards of living by diversifying incomes and increasing resilience. The district also lacked basic social services and infrastructure necessary for sustaining livelihoods. There were no roads and the district was largely inaccessible when the country attained independence from Great Britain in 1980. There were few healthcare facilities, and these could not meet the needs of people who suffered tremendously from malaria and sleeping sickness. Illiteracy was high in Binga because the colonial government failed to establish schools in the district due of its location on the periphery. Education is key to livelihoods but there were no government schools in Binga at independence and the few missionary schools did not offer a complete primary education.

The colonial government had promised to "sink numerous boreholes and wells and fit them with pumps" as well as to build "numerous dams and weirs" during the time of displacement but all this did not materialise (Nesham 1961). In 1967, the District Officer (Latham) reported that, if boreholes were not sunk in most resettlement areas, they were going to become uninhabitable – but, nothing was done to bring water from the Lake to the Tonga communities (NAZ File S2929/5/1, 1965). Loss of water had a far greater impact on women than men. Women and girls had to walk more than 10 kilometres carrying heavy containers of water every day. In chief Sikalenge's chiefdom, life was tough for women as they could not bathe every day because of lack of access to water for domestic use. Kitchen utensils were reused before they were washed, and this posed a health hazard. Tremmel (1994) concurs with this as he recorded oral testimonies from the Tonga which emphasised shortage of water as a major challenge to their well-being.

Conclusion

The construction of the Kariba Dam benefited the Southern Rhodesian and Northern Rhodesian manufacturing and mining firms through the production of cheap hydroelectric power, but at a great cost to the Tonga's economic, cultural and social systems. For the Tonga in Southern Rhodesia in particular, they lost their homes, alluvial gardens and access to water from the Zambezi River; and they were resettled in a barren and arid land infested with wildlife where crop cultivation was a challenge. Loss of these crucial livelihood capitals jeopardised farming and increased vulnerability. Women lost their food security status and became vulnerable to crop failure as they failed to provide for their families' food needs. There was need to diversify their livelihoods as survival became precarious as they were denied access to wildlife, fish, tourism and revenue generated from electricity. Overall, the colonial government neglected and ignored them. This confirms the fears of Cernea (2000) that, if the risks of development-induced displacement are not properly managed in a timely manner, it can result in long-lasting impoverishing effects on people, leading to what is known as "new poverty" or "secondary poverty". Further, in terms of the Four Stage Framework of Resettlement, it becomes clear that the conditions of existence of the Tonga until this day fall far short of the development phase because of marginalisation.

This study provides insights into the challenges faced by the Tonga as they attempted to reconstruct their livelihoods after forced displacement. It demonstrates women's agency and resilience amidst insecurity which was compounded by marginalisation after their forced displacement from the Zambezi. They faced food insecurity but, interestingly, they survived recurrent episodes of drought without any assistance, as there was not yet any Non-Governmental Organisation in the region to assist them. Their agency helped them to cope under the most difficult of circumstances, drawing upon and using their indigenous knowledge systems. They managed to survive in this dry region of Binga though they lived near the margins of bare existence.

Funding

This research was partly funded by the Rhodes University African Studies Centre through its funding from the German Research Foundation under the German's Excellent Strategy, Funding Number EXC2052/1.

References

Cernea, M. M. (2000). Risks, safeguards and restructuring: a model for population displacement and resettlement. In M. A. Cernea (ed), *Risk and reconstruction: experience of resettlers and refugees.* Washington, D.C.: The World Bank, pp 11–55.

Colson, E. (1960). *Human problems of Kariba VI social organisation of the Gwembe Tonga, Manchester University Press, London.* Manchester: Manchester University Press.

Colson, E. (1971). *Kariba studies IV: the social consequenses of the Kariba resettlement: the impact of the Kariba resettlement among the Gwembe Tonga.* Manchester: Manchester University Press.

Ellis, F. (2002). Household strategies and rural livelihood diversification overseas development institute papers. www.odi.org>publications

Harding, C. (1905). *In the remotest barotseland. Being an account of a journey of over 8000 miles through the wildest and remotest parts of Lewanika's empire.* London: Hurst and Blackett Limited.

Khozi, M. and Yon, P. (2005). *Our gods never helped us again …, the Tonga people describe resettlement and its aftermath.* London: Panos Southern Africa.

Kranz, L. (2001). *The sustainable approach to poverty reduction. An introduction.* Stockholm: SIDA Division for Policy and Socio-Economic Analysis.

Livingstone, D. (1865). *Narrative of an expedition to the Zambesi and its tributaries and the discovery of Lake Shirwa and Nyassa. 1858–1864.* London: John Murray.

Manyena, B., Collins, A. E., Mudimba, F., and Madimba, D. (2016). Reducing mrginalisation of fishermen through participatory action research in the Zambezi Valley, Zimbabwe. *International Journal of African Development,* Vol. 3(2): 5–22.

Manyena, S. B. (2009). Disaster Resilience in Development and Humanitarian Interventions, Doctoral Thesis. Northumbria: University of Northumbria.

Mashingaidze, T. M. (2013). Beyond the Kariba Dam induced displacements: the Zimbabwean Tonga's struggles for restitution, 1990s–2000s. *International Journal on Minority and Group Rights,* Vol. 20: 381–404.

Matanzima, J. (2022). Thayer Scudder's four stage framework, water resources dispossession and appropriation: the Kariba Case. International Journal of Water Resources Development, Vol. 38: 322–345.

McGregor, J. (2009). *Crossing the Zambezi: the politics of landscape on a Central African Frontier.* Oxford: James Currey.

Morse, S., McNamara, N., and Acholo, M. (2009). Sustainable Livelihood Approach: A Critical Analysis of Theory and Practice. Geographical Paper No. 189, University of Reading.

Msindo, E. (2012). *Ethnicity in Zimbabwe: transformations in Kalanga and Ndebele societies, 1860–1990.* USA: University of Rochester Press.

Mundia, D. (2010). *Sustainable development support for a poverty free Zambezi Valley, strategic plan, 2010–2015.* Binga: Basilwizi Trust.

Murray, C. (2001). Livelihoods Research: Some Conceptual and Methodological Issues. Background Paper 5.

Muyambi, R. K. (1980). Some Tonga notes. The Rhodesian Ministry of Internal Affairs Annual Report NADA VXII (2):137–139.

NAZ File NB6/1/4/2 Native Commissioner's Report to Chief Native Commissioner, 1898.

NAZ File S1618/1951–1953 Native Commissioners Quarterly Reports, Urungwe.

NAZ File S2827/2/2/2/2 Correspondence on Anti-Malaria Spraying and Tsetse Control, Internal Affairs, 1955.

NAZ File S2827/2/2/3/3 Correspondence, Tsetse Control, Internal Affairs, 1959.

NAZ File S2929/1/1 C.J.K. Latham, Report on the Delineation of Tribal Communities in The Binga District of Rhodesia, 1966.

NAZ File S2929/5/1, C.J.K. Latham, Report on the Delineation of Tribal Communities in The Binga District of Rhodesia, 1965.

Nesham, W. (1961). Kariba resettlement. *The Rhodesian ministry of Internal affairs annual.* Vol. 38. Salisbury: NADA, pp 21–26.

Reynolds, B. (1968). *Kariba studies Volume III. The material culture of the peoples of the Gwembe Valley.* Manchester: Manchester University Press.

Reynolds, P. and Cousins, C. (1993). *Lwaano Lwanyika, Tonga book of the Earth.* London: Panos Publications.
Scoones, I. (1998). *Sustainable rural livelihoods: a framework for analysis.* Brighton: IDS Working Paper.
Scudder, T. (1962). *The ecology of the Gwembe Tonga.* Manchester: Manchester University Press.
Scudder, T. (1971). Gathering Among African Woodland Savanna Cultivators: A Case Study: The Gwembe Tonga, Zambian Papers, No.5. Zambia: University of Zambia Institute for African Studies.
Scudder, T. (2005). *The future of large dams: dealing with social. Environmental, institutional and political costs.* London: Earthscan.
Tremmel, M. (1994). *The people of the great river, Silveira house social series no.8.* Gwelo: Mambo Press.
Waters, J. (2020). *Kariba. Legacy of a vision.* Harare: Zunj Publishing House.
Weinrich, A. (1977). *The Tonga people of the Southern shore of Lake Kariba.* Gwelo: Mambo Press.

9

THE ROLE OF TRADITIONAL AND SPIRITUAL BIRTH ATTENDANTS IN MATERNAL HEALTH CARE AMONGST TONGA WOMEN OF BINGA

A Livelihood Strategy or Maternal Health Service?

Lizzy Zinyemba

Introduction

Zimbabwe's healthcare system has been entangled in a deep political and economic crisis over an extended period. The health delivery system in Zimbabwe has drastically deteriorated in the past two decades, with a clear decrease in the sheer coverage of health services (Choguya 2014). Zimbabwe is far from attaining the recommended World Health Organisation (WHO) minimum threshold in terms of the sheer number of healthcare workers (WHO 2016). In districts nationwide, on average, there are only two doctors with at most two qualified nurses at every primary healthcare centre (UNDP 2018). The healthcare system in Zimbabwe is thus characterised by severe shortages of skilled health professionals, in part because of a massive exodus of skilled hospital staff, with national strikes being the order of the day for doctors and nurses. As well, drugs and essential equipment are always in short supply, making it difficult for healthcare workers to adequately perform their duties (WHO 2015). The healthcare system has suffered from a lack of maintenance with 65% of public hospitals being in a dilapidated state (UN 2013), yet there has been a marked increase in hospital fees. The dire economic situation in Zimbabwe not only affects the character of social (including health) services but also has a detrimental economic impact on social service users who can only afford under-resourced public hospitals (Guzha et al. 2018).

It is this under-funded health-care system within which most women seek to attain their maternal health care in urban and rural Zimbabwe. However, the gap between rural and urban disparities in healthcare provision has also increased, intensifying the need for maternal health care in most rural areas. There exists a rise in

DOI: 10.4324/9781003278580-11

maternal mortality, and many pregnant rural women now feel compelled to resort to traditional medical practices that were prevalent before colonialism and into the colonial period. Pregnant women are left with no choice in their quest for maternal health care but to seek the services offered in their local communities by traditional and spiritual birth attendants.

These claims are relevant to all rural spaces in contemporary Zimbabwe, inclusive of the Tonga people of Binga District located in the north-western region of the country. The area where they live is primarily in agro-ecological region V which is characterised by hot, dry and arid weather conditions. Prior to the late 1950s, Tonga livelihoods were centred on the Zambezi River. The Kariba Dam construction and the ensuing lake (Lake Kariba) led to their displacement to Binga and elsewhere. Nevertheless, after displacement, they continued in large part to live a separate existence, preserving in many ways their Tonga beliefs and practices (Gambahaya and Muhwati 2010; Mashingaidze 2013).

In this light, this chapter examines maternal health care and the role of traditional and spiritual birth attendants amongst the Tonga in Binga. This includes assessing whether the current role of these attendants is being practised within the long-established boundaries of altruistic behaviour (as a deeply rooted cultural practice) or whether it has become, at least in addition, a livelihood strategy meant to address the current economic challenges in Zimbabwe. It also entails examining the motivations behind the provision of maternal health services by traditional and spiritual birth attendants. In terms of the distinction between the two types of attendants, traditional birth attendants make use of traditional maternal healthcare services, while spiritual birth attendants focus on spiritual maternal health services.

Context

Colonial Zimbabwe adopted a healthcare system based on racial lines and hence it favoured the white settler minority (Gilmurray et al. 1979). Post independence, the Zimbabwean state sought to address the racial imbalances in health care (Kaseke 1995), but the structural adjustment programme in the 1990s undercut many of the earlier advances from the 1980s. The post-2000 crisis has tended to exacerbate the health problems, including in rural areas. The majority of the Zimbabwean populace resides in rural areas and challenges around availability, accessibility and affordability of healthcare services have tended to impede health access in these areas. This is certainly the case amongst the Tonga.

Historically, prior to colonialism, health was provided by traditional healers, with traditional birth attendants included in this category. Spiritual birth attendants during this era did not exist as the Christian faith was only introduced during the colonial period. The custodians of traditional health care had a wide range of roles in the provision of health (Chavhunduka 1994; Chukwuma et al. 2019). Further, the local community was responsible for validating the practice of traditional healers, thereby legitimising their qualifications. Choguya (2014) defines traditional birth attendants as women who assisted pregnant women during pregnancy, delivery and after birth. The service offered by these attendants was purely altruistic with women's maternal-health needs prioritised. They possessed empirical medical knowledge which was developed through trial and error, experimentation and systematic observation over a long period (Gelfand 1976). This knowledge was passed on from one individual healer to another through apprenticeship programmes, with the graduates of this healthcare knowledge system being well-informed about the medicinal properties of local flora and fauna. The role of traditional healers and traditional birth attendants specifically in health delivery continued to be crucial among indigenous people (including the Tonga) throughout the colonial era and into the post-colonial era in Zimbabwe.

In recent decades, there has been a move towards promoting and instituting community-based birth attendants. For instance, in the 1970s, the WHO advocated for a community-based healthcare system to address the serious problem of maternal mortality. In the case of Zimbabwe, this resulted in the official training of many existing traditional birth attendants in order to supposedly improve access to (and the quality of) maternal health care in rural areas (Choguya 2014). This training entailed "modern" biomedical models of health. These attendants became known as trained traditional birth attendants and those not trained remained as traditional birth attendants. The Government of Zimbabwe formerly recognised trained traditional birth attendants as providers of maternal health care in rural communities.

Research, however, shows that despite implementing this community-based healthcare system, there was no significant decrease in the level of maternal mortality rates (Choguya 2014). In Zimbabwe, the training of these birth attendants was in fact problematic for local communities because of the use of the biomedical models that did not take into account the key cultural aspects of the work of traditional birth attendants, namely, the realisation of their cultural duties like giving pregnant women traditional medicines for quick delivery as well as for pregnancy complications as a result of witchcraft. Because of the shortcomings of the "modern" community-based healthcare system, there was a further shift in the 1990s to the use of more skilled birth health personnel like nurses and doctors as well as institutional delivery rather than home deliveries (Choguya 2015).

The shift in policy did not undermine totally the community-based maternal healthcare structures and the clientele base of the trained and untrained traditional birth attendants in most rural communities. In rural Zimbabwe (including amongst the Tonga), pregnant women continue to date to make use of traditional birth attendants and trained traditional birth attendants because of the unavailability and inadequacy of resources in institutional care facilities. Rural women also simply prefer these birth attendants, as they offer flexible payment terms and do not have negative attitudes like nurses (Dodzo et al. 2016; Mhlanga et al. 2017). In Zimbabwe, half of the births are still assisted by trained and untrained traditional birth attendants, while almost all pregnant women are checked by these birth attendants before delivery (Choguya 2014). Earlier studies by Waite (2000) and Chavhunduka (2001) demonstrate that traditional health care has stood the test of time in Zimbabwe, with rural villagers not abandoning their traditional medicines for European bio-medicine, in part because the latter does not address the spiritual problems that are linked to illness. In African societies generally, there is no disease without a spiritual connection or explanation.

Generally, the use of traditional health care and medicines during pregnancy and birth is still common amongst rural Zimbabweans. Spiritual birth attendants have also been reported by many scholars (Dodzo et al. 2016; Ohaja et al. 2019) to be on the rise in sub-Saharan Africa. Similar to traditional birth attendants, spiritual birth attendants likewise assist during pregnancy, delivery and after birth. Traditional birth attendants and spiritual birth attendants are mainly women who incorporate cultural values and ethics into their health practices. Dodzo et al. (2016) show that spiritual birth attendants are people who have spiritual powers. Their practice, though, is linked to a Christian church normally of the Apostolic Sect in the case of Zimbabwe. The introduction and salience of spiritual birth attendants is evidence of a blended dimension to the provision of maternal health care amongst those who have adopted Christianity.

Adatara et al. (2019) and Shimpuku et al. (2021) note that the main roles of both trained and untrained traditional birth attendants in rural communities currently are to: conduct home deliveries; provide health education to women on the care of their pregnancy; advise women on best nutrition during pregnancy and after delivery; advise on breastfeeding practices; arrange the means of transport and accompany pregnant women to health facilities during delivery; provide natural family planning to women and offer psychological support and counselling. Both trained and untrained traditional birth attendants provide traditional medicines to pregnant women and newborn children as reported by scholars like Shewamene et al. (2017), Mudonhi and Nunu (2021) and Mawoza et al. (2019). The main reasons for making use of traditional medicines are for the treatment of pregnancy-related ailments, to facilitate childbirth, to avoid prolonged labour and to avoid tears and stitches. Mudonhi and Nunu (2021) conclude that the use of traditional medicines is in fact associated with lesser chances of experiencing maternal complications. Panganai et al. (2021) also argue that women use traditional medicines during pregnancy as it is part of their cultural beliefs and because of previous pregnancy experiences.

In the past, traditional birth attendants were paid in kind for the services they offered. They reportedly found joy in assisting community members and felt that the children whom they assisted were their grandchildren (Mhlanga et al. 2017). Recently, this has changed because of the post-2000 economic crises in Zimbabwe, which has resulted in traditional (and spiritual) birth attendants attaching a fee to the service offered during maternal health care. Hence, there appears to be a shift in the role that traditional and spiritual birth attendants provide in maternal health care in rural Zimbabwe, and in the kind of transaction it entails. This chapter examines changes occurring in terms of the gratuity offered to traditional and spiritual birth attendants, with specific reference to the Tonga in Binga District.

Research Site and Methods

The study was conducted in Ward 1 of Binga District in the 18 villages under Chief Sinakatenge and 11 villages under Chief Sinamusanga. Binga District was selected because it has one of the highest maternal mortality rates in Zimbabwe (Zimstat 2012). The research employed a qualitative research design making use of 24 focus group discussions and 21 key informant interviews as data collection methods. The data collection process was carried out in 2019. Respondents for the focus group discussions were conveniently sampled in Binga District (which has a total population of 75,356 females and 63,736 males) (Zimstat 2012). Two cohorts were developed by dividing the participants by sex and age, namely, the young reproductive age group, the middle aged and the elderly as well as male and female groups. There were 12 focus groups but 24 focus group discussions as each group met twice, with 6 female focus groups and 6 male focus groups. Each group consisted of between 6 and 12 people. Men were sampled for the focus group discussions as they contribute economically, socially and reproductively to maternal health care. The purposive sampling technique was used to select 21 key informants, including traditional birth attendants, spiritual birth attendants, nurses, village health workers, religious healthcare workers, elders and healthcare staff at Binga hospital and all the clinics in the district.

Ethical clearance was acquired from responsible authorities in Binga to conduct the study. Each participant who participated in the study also filled in a detailed consent form. The consent form explained to the respondent (before participating in the study) the nature of the objectives, risks and benefits of the study. The researcher also observed strict confidentiality, anonymity and voluntary participation during the entire data collection process.

Role of Traditional Birth Attendants in the Provision of Maternal Health Care

In rural Binga, traditional birth attendants perform a significant role in the provision of maternal health care. The study discovered that most Tonga women delay visiting the clinic or hospital or have at least one prenatal care visit by a birth attendant before going to the clinic/hospital. They prefer their pregnancies to be monitored in the community by traditional birth attendants or trained traditional birth attendants. These attendants are considered important in protecting the pregnancy from witchcraft which was reported to result in stillbirths, or deaths of the neonate or the pregnant woman. The attendants provided "traditional" treatments to pregnant women for several other purposes, such as positioning the foetus, changing the sex of the foetus, treatment for pregnancy-related ailments and instant delivery. Pregnant women were also reported to be given traditional medicines to drink during delivery (see below) for a safe maternal health outcome. One female interviewee alluded that:

> It is within the Tonga culture to take traditional medicines while pregnant for a successful pregnancy outcome. We are expected to take the different

> traditional medicines as the pregnancy progresses. Failure to take most of the traditional medicines will limit the chances of one delivering a healthy child.
>
> *Middle aged female respondent, Tuesday 11 June 2019*

In return for their service, the birth attendants are given foodstuffs like chicken, grains, peanuts and vegetables. If the pregnant woman does not have foodstuffs then they are expected to assist the attendants with household chores. If the pregnant woman was advanced in pregnancy, she would ensure that family members assisted the birth attendant in this regard. One respondent had this to say:

> Both the trained and untrained traditional birth attendants play a very important role in the protection of my pregnancy. Not everyone will be happy to see you being blessed with a child. I also make sure that my pregnancy is monitored by the traditional birth attendant so that my pregnancy is covered spiritually. I also provide for my traditional birth attendant in cash or kind so that she happily provides her services.
>
> *Young female respondent, 17 July 2019*

The gift of appreciation would ensure that the birth attendants will always be on the lookout for any pregnancy complications that might befall the pregnant woman and continuously provide her with traditional medicines. The transaction between the pregnant women and birth attendants would ensure regular visits and check-ups.

Birth attendants sought to give pregnant women knowledge on how to take care of their pregnancies in the villages. In circulating and passing on "traditional" Tonga knowledge about pregnancy to pregnant women, they ensured that women adhered to well-established Tonga values and norms. In counselling sessions, Tonga taboos were taught to pregnant women, normally without any expectation of payment or reciprocation. When probed further as to why this particular service had no price tag, the key informants (traditional birth attendants, trained traditional birth attendants and community elders) reported that it was meant to attract pregnant women to make use of birth attendants' broader services during pregnancy and delivery. It also enabled the passing on of Tonga culture from one generation to the next generation. One respondent from the focus group discussions highlighted:

> If you are not sure of how to take care of your pregnancy, traditional birth attendants or the trained traditional birth attendants are readily available to offer their knowledge on how best pregnant women can take care of themselves.
>
> *Elderly female respondent, 18 September 2019*

Another Tonga informant added:

> Once the traditional birth attendants gave you their knowledge on pregnancy they would monitor if you are adhering to the Tonga beliefs and practices.
>
> *Female trained birth attend, 19 July 2019*

Further, the birth attendants have the responsibility of accompanying pregnant women to the clinic. The nurses at the local clinic opposed the idea and practice of home deliveries so they caution the birth attendants who performed home deliveries. Typically, the attendants accompany the women to the clinic to ensure that they give the latter traditional medicines if any complications arise during labour. One key informant reported that:

> We accompany our clients to the clinic to make sure that they have a safe delivery. At the clinic, we will be monitoring how the pregnancy is progressing allowing the nurses to do their part while we also do our part.
>
> *Trained traditional birth attendant, 17 July 2019*

Despite the cautioning from the local nurses not to assist pregnant women during delivery, it became clear that some birth attendants continued to perform home deliveries. Most birth attendants reported that they were incidences when pregnant women came to them with pregnancies that were almost due for delivery, and that this left them with no option but to assist in the delivery. One respondent highlighted that:

> Home deliveries were common as one cannot predict when the delivery is going to occur. In some cases, labour pains can start in the evening and there is usually no transport to ferry you to the clinic. This forces you to be assisted by traditional birth attendants.
>
> *Young woman, 27 June 2019*

Unlike in the past when their predecessors did not expect to receive any remuneration for delivering a baby, the current attendants all expected a form of gratuity for assisting in delivery, with some birth attendants charging a goat for this service.

Intriguingly, traditional birth attendants (both untrained and trained) are central to the naming of newborn children. However, the birth attendant's name was only used in the community and it is not the official name. It does appear, based on the fieldwork, that this form of appreciation increased the fame of the birth attendants and resulted in many clients coming to them for maternal health services. This in turn increased the gratuities of the attendants as their clientele base increased. One Tonga man noted that:

> My child is popularly known as "Tupou"; he was named after the traditional birth attendant who assisted my wife to successfully deliver my first child after 6 miscarriages. A lot of people with the problem of miscarriages find their way to her.
>
> *Middle aged man, 7 June 2019*

The traditional birth attendants also bathe the newborn child after delivery. The interviewed elders reported that this was a sign of respecting the birth attendants for the role that they would have played in the delivery process. It also accorded the attendants the opportunity to use their traditional medicines on the newborn child so that the child is protected from any evil. An elderly Tonga woman put it this way:

> Traditional birth attendants or trained traditional birth attendants bathe the newborn child so that they finish their role of making sure that the newborn child drinks all the traditional medicines required for the protection of the child as he grows.
>
> *Elderly Tonga woman, 1 August 2019*

The research also revealed that birth attendants are supposed to be the first ones to cut the hair of the newborn child. Soon after this, they would smear some "traditional" medicines on the head of the child. It was only after this took place that family members have the right to cut the child's hair. In return for practicing this role, it was expected that, as the child grew, he or she would frequently be sent to the birth attendant with gifts from the child's family. One male respondent in a focus group discussion indicated that:

> The hair that the child would have been born with is removed by the birth attendants. This is done to ensure that the attendants will always benefit from the child as they grow.
>
> *Young male respondent, 1 August 2019*

Additionally, the birth attendants imparted postnatal care knowledge, like good breastfeeding practices, proper hygienic practices and the general upkeep of the child. This imparting of knowledge further ensures the observation of Tonga taboos and practices about raising children. For this role, the birth attendants are not paid, but they acquire further respect in the local community. This role also reaffirms the special bond between the birth attendant and her clients, thereby helping her to at least maintain her clientele base. Another focus group respondent added that:

> The Tonga culture needs to be maintained. It is the role of the birth attendants to make sure that all the traditional beliefs and practices surrounding child-rearing are adhered to.
>
> *Middle aged man, 17 July 2019*

In support, another Tonga respondent had this to say:

> Traditional birth attendants have a lot of knowledge on good child care practices and they are trusted in the community as they have several children whom they have assisted during their infancy stage to date.
>
> *Elderly man, 7 June 2019*

Role of Spiritual Birth Attendants in the Provision of Maternal Health Care

In rural Binga, spiritual birth attendants were likewise involved in the provision of maternal healthcare services. Tonga women, whether Christian or not, might interact with both traditional and spiritual attendants, as their overriding concern is a good maternal health outcome. As in the case of traditional birth attendants, most Tonga women delay accessing prenatal care services at local clinics/hospitals as they prefer to receive pregnancy check-ups from spiritual birth attendants in the community. In providing their services, these birth attendants are said to prevent women from experiencing pregnancy-related complications resulting from witchcraft. The attendants made use of prayers and spiritual artefacts to protect the pregnancy from evil intentions and attacks. One female informant indicated that:

> For religious people like me, I prefer having my pregnancies being checked by spiritual birth attendants as their services are in-line with my religious beliefs.
> *Young female respondent, 27 June 2019*

In support of this, another Tonga villager added:

> When one is pregnant, you need to have your pregnancy checked so that you become aware of what is happening to you and the child spiritually.
> *Middle aged woman, 11 June 2019*

The attendants provide women with religious artefacts like red string that they are required to tie around their waist to protect the pregnancy from miscarriages. One respondent had this to say:

> When pregnant, you visit your spiritual birth attendant so that she would give you a string to tie around your waist; as long as you have that string around your waist, nothing will happen to your pregnancy.
> *Young woman, 15 June 2019*

The attendants disseminated church doctrines to the pregnant women to ensure that they were familiar with how best to take care of their pregnancy. The key informants in the study emphasised that the attendants listened to the Holy Spirit when it came to advising pregnant women. This spiritual counselling is given for free. When probing why this was the case, I was informed that the service encouraged pregnant women to attend church services. One key informant (a spiritual birth attendant) reported that:

> We do not take orders from anyone even the nurses; we assist pregnant women as God would have directed us in the spiritual realm.
> *Spiritual birth attendant, 27 June 2019*

In Binga, spiritual birth attendants assisted pregnant women during delivery. There is a stipulated form of gratuity offered for assisting in delivery. The interviewed spiritual birth attendants noted that they should be given Vaseline, a bar of soap and clothing material, as stipulated by the Apostolic Sect's rules and regulations. One respondent hence claimed:

> All the spiritual birth attendants from our church are given a bar of soap to wash their hands and clothes after delivery, clothing material for them to put on, and Vaseline to smear on their hands after the delivery. We, however, give them some groceries on top of the stipulated items. The groceries are given as one is pushed by the Holy Spirit on how to thank the spiritual birth attendant.
>
> *Middle aged woman, 15 July 2019*

As well, the spiritual birth attendants have the role of foretelling the sex of the child before delivery. In return for this, the attendants received forms of appreciation from the pregnant women, such as groceries. One female Tonga villager thus highlighted:

> I was foretold about my child's sex by the spiritual birth attendant and it made my life easy when it came to buying preparatory clothing for my baby.
>
> *Young female respondent, 27 June 2019*

In addition, the attendants are involved in naming newborn babies, seven days after the child's birth, with the children named after angels' names. When probed on this, the Tonga informants indicated that the reason behind this practice was that the child should be given his or her guardian angel's name so that the guardian angel will always protect the child. As one villager put it:

> At our church, the spiritual birth attendant names the children after a guardian angel that is identified by the prophet.
>
> *Young male respondent, 17 July 2019*

A further role performed by the spiritual birth attendants is that of bringing the newborn child from the mother's house to be presented to the priest as stipulated in the Bible in Leviticus Chapter 12. It is only after the child has been presented to the priest that other community members are allowed to visit to see the child. Presenting the child to the church leaders was reported to be a prestigious event as it resulted in church members respecting and having confidence in the spiritual birth attendant. The church leader develops deep faith and trust in the spiritual attendant. One Apostolic Sect church leader reported that:

> The role of being a spiritual birth attendant is a gift from God and should be done in line with the church doctrine. As a church, we promote spiritual

> birth attendants that normally have successful home deliveries. When a spiritual birth attendant presents a newborn child to me it is a sign that she is listening and paying attention in detail to all that the angel of birth will be telling her.
>
> *Apostolic Sect church leader, 19 July 2019*

Some spiritual birth attendants perform home deliveries, and this is not frowned upon by church leaders – as being a birth attendant is a gift received at church.

Finally, spiritual attendants impart postnatal care knowledge to their female clients on how to look after the newborn child, breastfeeding and necessary hygienic practices. In imparting their knowledge, the attendants receive further respect in the local Tonga community. One female respondent from a focus group discussion highlighted that:

> We are taught by senior women at women's services on how best to look after our children.
>
> *Young female respondent, 15 June 2019*

Reflections

The main roles of traditional birth attendants have not changed significantly over time. Panganai et al. (2021) thus argue that traditional birth attendants (both trained and untrained) have continue with their practices during pregnancy, birth and after birth as embedded in people's local cultural arrangements. Despite the fact that many traditional attendants received biomedical training to assist pregnant women during delivery (Choguya 2014), these birth attendants still encourage the use of "traditional" medicines and adherence to long-standing taboos. However, a significant change has taken place over time, namely, that traditional birth attendants are now charging for their maternal health service, unlike their predecessors who provided the service for free.

One of the most cited weaknesses of mainstream "modern" medicines is their inability to address the spiritual aspect of health. For local Tonga people, the biomedical model cannot explain issues of miscarriages as a result of witchcraft as well as pregnancy-related illness due to the improper use of traditional medicines. This study is in line with arguments by Shewamene et al. (2017), Mudonhi and Nunu (2021) and Mawoza et al. (2019) who report that pregnant women in rural African spaces often make use of traditional medicines for the protection of their pregnancies from witchcraft, a protection which is not offered within the conventional healthcare system. Because the traditional and spiritual birth attendants are the only healthcare practitioners who offer solutions to spiritually and culturally related maternal health problems, there is a growing tendency for charges to be raised by birth attendants for their specific services.

Zimbabwe's economic situation over the past three decades has resulted in the ongoing deterioration of maternal healthcare services, as well as a decline in livelihood circumstances and possibilities. This has also contributed to shifting the dispositions of traditional birth attendants away from their altruistic behaviour to remuneration-based services (Mhlanga et al. 2017). Spiritual birth attendants, who perform almost similar roles to traditional birth attendants (Ohaja et al. 2019), also tend to engage in financial transactions in providing maternal health care (Mawoza et al. 2019). There are variations in charges for specific tasks. For instance, a successful delivery requires a high price for the service offered, while other roles (like bathing the newborn child) require no remuneration and are meant to create a bond for future pregnancies with the female client. In this respect, it cannot be ignored that pregnant Tonga women have limited choices in rural areas when it comes to maternal health care, including in terms of availability and accessibility.

The presence and use of traditional birth attendants and spiritual birth attendants in rural Zimbabwe (including in Binga District) does not imply that the biomedical model, as practised in rural spaces, is totally frowned upon or ignored by pregnant women. As has been the case for a long time (Chavhunduka 2001), there is a dual healthcare system in rural Zimbabwe. For maternal health care, Tonga women make use of more than one healthcare system in their endeavour for a successful maternal healthcare outcome, including navigating their way through both the so-called modern and spiritual-traditional systems (with deliveries mainly occurring now in clinics/hospitals) (Zimbabwe Demographic and Health Survey 2015).

Conclusion

The main objective of this chapter was to offer an analysis of the role of traditional and spiritual birth attendants in maternal health care amongst Tonga women in Binga District, with a specific emphasis on the motivations of these different types of birth attendants in providing their maternal health services. It is clear that these birth attendants perform a diverse array of roles, including in both the prenatal and postnatal phases, and at times being directly involved in the delivery of babies. In the past, birth attendants typically provided their maternal health services free of charge. However, today, it is quite clear that forms of gratuities are expected by the attendants and indeed offered by women and their families. However, it is not the case that all services require some form of payment. Some roles are associated with bringing fame to the spiritual and traditional birth attendant, and hence such roles indirectly increase the birth attendants' clientele base thereby increasing their source of revenue. Roles with no price tags are, in effect, meant to lure clients to the birth attendant. Overall, being a birth attendant has become a livelihood strategy for many Tonga women in Binga.

Tonga women continue to be appreciative of both traditional and spiritual birth attendants, but there is a possibility that pregnant women at times may be subject to exploitative practices by birth attendants, and hence some sort of monitoring of their work is required. There is a need for a standardised register of traditional and spiritual birth attendants offering maternal healthcare services in particular communities. This will reduce the number of possibly self-proclaimed traditional and spiritual birth attendants who manipulate women who are in search of maternal health care. There is a need for vibrant community structures that monitor the maternal healthcare service being offered by these birth attendants.

References

Adatara, P., Strumpher, J., and Ricks, E. (2019). A qualitative study on rural women's experiences relating to the utilisation of birth care provided by skilled birth attendants in the rural areas of Bongo District in the Upper East region of Ghana. *BMC Pregnancy and Childbirth*, Vol. 19(1): 1–8.

Chavhunduka, G. L. (2001). Dialogue between civilizations: the African religion in Zimbabwe today. *Occasional Paper*, Vol. 1(2001) (pdf).

Chavhunduka, L. (1994). *Dialogue among civilization African religion in Zimbabwe today*. Harare: University of Zimbabwe publications.

Choguya, N. Z. (2014). Traditional birth attendants and policy ambivalence in Zimbabwe. *Journal of Anthropology*. doi: 10.1155/2014/750240

Choguya, N. Z. (2015). Traditional and skilled birth attendants in Zimbabwe: a situational analysis and some policy considerations. *Journal of Anthropology*, Vol. 2015. Hindawi Publishing Corporation. http://dx.doi.org/10.1155/2015/215909. Accessed 11. 07. 2018.

Chukwuma, A., Mbachu, C., and McConnell, M. (2019). The impact of monetary incentives on referrals by traditional birth attendants for postnatal care in Nigeria. *BMC Pregnancy Childbirth*. https://doi.org/10.1186/s12884-019-2313-8

Dodzo, M. K., Mhloyi, M., Moyo, S., and Dodzo-Masawi, M. (2016). Praying until death: apostolicism, delays and maternal mortality in Zimbabwe. *PLOS*, Vol. 11(8): e0160170. doi: 101371/journal.pone.0160170

Gambahaya, Z., and Muhwati, T. (2010). Tonga orature as a historical record: an Afro-centric exegesis of the dialectics between African human factor agency and the European enslavement of place. *Journal of Black Studies*, Vol. 41(2). https://jbs.sagepub.com

Gelfand, M. (1976). *A service to the sick: a history of the health services for Africans in Southern Rhodesia (1890–1953)*. Gweru: Mambo Press.

Gilmurray, J., Riddell, R., and Sanders, D. (1979). *The economy, the health sector, and child health in Zimbabwe since independence*. Gweru: Mambo Press.

Guzha, T., Magwali, T. L., Mateveke, B., Chirehwa, M., Nyandoro, G., and Munjanja, S. P. (2018). Assessment of quality of obstetric care in Zimbabwe using the standard primipara. *BMC Pregnancy and Childbirth Journal*, Vol. 18(1). https://doi.org/10.1186/s12884-018-1863-5. Accessed 27. 08. 2019.

Kaseke, E. (1995). Social policy and development. *Journal of Social Development in Africa*. Harare: School of Social Work, Vol. 6(3): 33–45.

Mashingaidze, T. M. (2013). Beyond the Kariba Dam induced displacements: the Zimbabwean Tonga's struggles for restitution, 1990s–2000s. *International Journal on Minority and Group Rights*. Brill.com/ijgr

Mawoza, T., Nhachi, C., and Magwali, T. (2019). Prevalence of traditional medicine use during pregnancy, at labour, and for postpartum care in a rural area in Zimbabwe. *Clinics in a Mother and Child Health*, Vol. 16(2). https://doi.org/10.24105/2090-7214.16.321

Mhlanga, M., Zvinavashe, M., Gwanzura, L., and Stray-Pederson, B. (2017). Factors associated with maternal and child health services uptake and their association with health outcomes in Mashonaland East, Zimbabwe. *Clinics Mother and Child Health*, Vol. 14(3): 1–7.

Mudonhi, N., and Nunu, W. N. (2021). Traditional medicine utilisation and maternal complications during antenatal care among women in Bululima, Plumtree, Zimbabwe.

Maternal Health Neonatal and Perinatal, Vol. 7(9). httpd://doi.org/10.1186/s40748-021-00130-w

Ohaja, M., Murphy-Lawless, J., and Dunlea, M. (2019). Religion and spirituality in pregnancy and birth: the views of birth practitioners in Southeast Nigeria. *Religions*, Vol. 10(2): 82.

Panganai, T., Shoko, T., and Mufunda, E. (2021). *Forces behind the use of herbs during pregnancy by Zimbabwean women: a case of Gweru*. doi: 10.4236/jbm.2021.95005

Shewamene, Z., Dune, T., and Smith, C. A. (2017). The use of traditional medicine in maternity care among African women in Africa and the diaspora: a systematic review. *BMC Complementary and Alternative Medicine*. https://doi.org/10.1186/s12906-017-1886-x. Accessed on 19. 11. 2021.

Shimpuku, Y., Madeni, F. E., and Shimoda, K. (2021). Perceived differences on the role of traditional birth attendants in rural Tanzania: a qualitative study. *BMC Pregnancy Childbirth*, Vol. 21: 137. https://doi.org/10.1186/s12884-021-03611-0

UNDP (2018) *UNDP fact sheet*. Geneva: UNDP.

United Nations (2013). *Maternal mortality in Zimbabwe*. Geneva: United Nations.

Waite, G. (2000). Traditional medicine and the quest for national identity in Zimbabwe. *Zambezia*. Harare: University of Zimbabwe. www.researchgate.net. Accessed 07. 07. 2017.

WHO (2015). *Maternal health care practice in Zimbabwe*. Geneva: WHO.

WHO (2016). Global strategy for women's, children's adolescents health 2016–2030. Available online: www.who.int/life-course/partenrs/globalstartegy/globalstrategy-2016-2030/en/. Accessed on 10. 10. 2020.

Zimbabwe Demographic and Health Survey (ZDHS). (2015). *Maternal health services in Zimbabwe: determinants of use and related financial barriers from 2015–2016 survey data*. Harare: Zimbabwe.

Zimbabwe National Statistics Agency (2012). Census National Report. Government of Zimbabwe. Harare.

PART III

Water, Borders and Livelihoods

10

OF DAMS, CONSERVANCIES AND CHANGING LIVELIHOODS

The Case of Tonga People of Binga

Ivan Marowa and Joshua Matanzima

Introduction

This chapter investigates the contestations between the state and society in relation to accessing and managing the Kariba Dam waterscape. It analyses how the Zimbabwean state's control of Lake Kariba has been viewed and criticised by the Tonga following their alienation from the Zambezi River landscape and its resources. It also examines how this alienation has shaped the Tonga's agency, politics and economics in their new home in Binga district.

The Tonga hold two claims to the Zambezi waters: firstly, they lay claims predicated on the historical relationship they had with the Zambezi from time immemorial and, secondly, they assert claims to the Kariba Dam because they bore the costs of its creation as they were uprooted from the Zambezi River in 1956–57. Since their forced movement in 1956–57, the Tonga have been denied access to the Lake by both the colonial and post-colonial governments, which have allocated much of the Lake's littoral and waterscape to conservancies, fisheries and tourist industries. Much of the Zambezi River including the Kariba Dam has been appropriated by the central government to the detriment of the Tonga who lost homes, graves and key landscape features that had spiritual significance. This exclusion has seen them receiving no compensation, let alone accessing the socio-economic benefits of the dam such as electricity and water.

The only positive issue that came out of the engineering of Kariba Dam for the Tonga was the promise made by the colonial government that "the water would follow them" (Tremmel 1994); a promise, however, that has remained a pipe-dream to this day. Instead, as McGregor (2008, 2003b) has rightly observed, Kariba and Victoria Falls were turned into a "playground for white settlers" during the colonial period, while also representing the triumph of colonial science over local tradition and beliefs. Licences or permits were introduced by the colonial state for those

DOI: 10.4324/9781003278580-13

interested in engaging in any kind of business activity in and around Lake Kariba. Unfortunately, until now, the Tonga have not been given priority in this regard, including even permit exemptions to owning fisheries, as a gesture of recognising what they lost in the dam process, especially their homes, ancestral graves and cultural heritage (Marowa 2010; Tremmel 1994). Though we highlight that the Tonga have largely been mistreated by the state, we also argue that they have found ways of dealing with life outside the cultural and socio-economic world of the Zambezi Valley and its river landscape.

This chapter argues that in spite of being restricted by government regulations from accessing the Kariba waterscape, the Tonga have developed tactics to address the many restrictions placed on their lives and livelihoods, which include disrespecting the prohibitions imposed on the use of the Lake and its littoral. Some pressure groups concerned with the welfare of marginalised communities have also come to the side of the Tonga to assist them in engaging the authorities in light of the loss and suffering caused by forced displacement. Forced movement is not what pains the Tonga the most; rather, it is the memories of past interactions with the river and loss of the sacred sites and graves of their ancestors which were submerged by the Kariba waters. Against such frustrations, some Tonga men engage in illegal cross-border trading and others in opposition politics, while women have resorted to riverbed cultivation for family subsistence and income generation, a practice pursued along the banks of the Zambezi River. Apart from calling for compensation and restitution, the Tonga have been instrumental in forming local organisations such as the Binga Development Association (BIDA) and Basilwizi Trust to advocate for Tonga development.

The imported modernisation and neo-liberal and developmental state models that have been used by both the colonial and post-colonial administrations in governing Lake Kariba have not considered the historicity and centrality of water to the socio-cultural livelihoods of the Tonga. These methods of governance have worsened the plight of the Tonga who occupy a very dry agro-ecological zone with low-agricultural potential. In this regard, the appropriation of land and construction of dams like Kariba (which exclude or bar the local or surrounding communities from accessing resources therein) have long-term impacts on the socio-economic livelihoods and political orientation of the concerned people.

As Kariba was being built, emphasis was placed on,

> The importance of dam and irrigation schemes for European-dominated industry, agriculture and settlement, and equally for recreation and white aesthetic sensibilities for pristine wilderness, wildlife and watery shorelines was recognised by both federal and territorial governments, feeding into and out of longstanding "Euro-African" attempts to construct belonging and a claim to land.
>
> *Fontein 2015: 173*

This white-centred perception disregarded African opposition and the socio-cultural cost of uprooting Africans from a place that was their home for several centuries and where their essence of existence was embedded and drew its socio-historical meaning.

Research Methods

Using secondary data and ethnographic research conducted in Binga between September and October 2017, this chapter analyses the Tonga's agency through exploiting their environment and taking advantage of minimal control by the state over resources and the ensuing lack of necessary infrastructure to better their lives after forced removal. It uses case studies of the chiefdoms of Sinakatenge and Siamupa to illustrate the agency of the people, discussing the human-environment relationship and analysing the Tonga's interaction with conservancies in the area.

The research involved lengthy stays in the field in the respective chiefdoms. Semi- structured interviews, Focus Group Discussions and participant observation were the data gathering tools utilised. In total, 45 interviews sessions were carried out with people across generations, including 20 first generation resettlers (FGRs), 20 second generation resettlers (SGRs) and 5 local youths. FGRs are those born before the Kariba resettlement; and SGRs are those born after resettlement. The interview sessions lasted approximately 45–60 minutes. As well, two Focus Group Discussions (FGDs) were conducted – one with the FGRs and the other with the SGRs. Both FGDs comprised men and women: the group with FGRs had 4 women and 5 men, and the group with the SGRs had 3 women and 2 men. The FGDs lasted between 70 and 80 minutes. The researchers asked questions about Tonga displacement, resource access and agency. Participant observation included visiting Lake Kariba, the riverine fields and local stores in the quest to better understand the current economic activities of the Tonga people and their agency.

Context: Harnessing the Zambezi Waters and the Fate of the Tonga

Construction of Kariba Dam was a flagship project under the auspices of the Central African Federation, which was born in 1953. It was "an ambitious hydro-electric project that transformed the landscape and ecology of the Zambezi River beyond recognition, creating a vast man-made lake – the largest in the world at the time" (McGregor 2009: 1). Its creation "answered a deep European longing for water in inland, semi-arid Africa" and, within three years (1956–58), Kariba's waters had flooded 5,500 square kilometres to create one of the largest man-made dams and lakes (Hughes 2006: 823). Kariba's generated electricity transformed critical economic sectors such as agriculture and industry. It also gave a new face to white settlers' social life and activities in then Rhodesia.

The decision to build Kariba Dam was premised on a genuine desire to bring socio-economic development to the Federation, but mainly to Southern Rhodesia. Lake Kariba was envisaged to boost the fishing industry, the production of electricity, agricultural irrigation schemes and tourism, while also bringing about the emergence of a tourist and border town, and the creation of employment and community formation. No doubt, all that came to fruition and the greatest beneficiaries of Kariba Dam were industries and plantations that required electricity and irrigation, respectively, across the country.

Nevertheless, this renowned colonial development had its antithesis which ignored the needs of African ethnic groups that had lived in the Zambezi Valley landscape for several centuries occupying the Kariba Gorge and surrounding areas. The decision also affected other ethnic groups that occupied the Chirundu and Mana Pools areas of the Zambezi Valley, several hundreds of kilometres away from Kariba Gorge (which included Chiefs Mudzimu and Dandawa and their people). This 1955 decision, which placed Southern Rhodesia on the world map, continues to cause problems by even creating life-threatening situations, particularly when the Kariba Dam floodgates are opened to maintain the requisite water levels in order to keep the dam walls from weakening and breaking. The opening of the gates results in the flooding of the Zambezi River, thereby affecting people downstream in Dande and surrounding areas whose homes are destroyed, and livestock and human life endangered and lost each and every year.

Consequently, the construction of the dam on Kariba Gorge caused the massive dislocation of more than 57,000 Tonga who had occupied the margins of the Zambezi Valley for many centuries (Howarth 1961; Colson 1971; Scudder 2005; Tischler 2013). As Colson (1971: 1) has rightly observed, "massive technological development hurts". This was exactly what happened not only to the Tonga, but also to other chiefdoms around Kariba Gorge and downstream the Zambezi River, whose areas fell under the threat of massive flooding. This associated social effect was not given due cognisance by planners and politicians, certainly not ahead of the related socio-economic benefits and advancements that would accrue officially from the Kariba hydroelectric project and Lake.

Before the Kariba project was envisaged and implemented, nothing was articulated regarding the socio-economic status of the Tonga, at least not under the now widely conceived and held perceptions of "impoverishment" or "marginalisation". Subsequently, studies on development-induced displacements have emphasised the impoverishment discourse in relation to local people who have endured internal displacements (Scudder 1993; Alexander 2006; Abbute 2009; McGregor 2009; Turton 2009; Pradhan 2009). Resultantly, the argument has found strong grounding following the creation of the dam, absence of compensation and lack of direct benefit and interaction of the Tonga with the human-made dam landscape. This act of succumbing to force, giving up land which was inundated with their rich history and ancestral graves surely deserved attention by the Southern Rhodesia government, as was done by the Northern Rhodesia government to the Tonga on the northern shores of the Zambezi River.

Here was a clear case of state power over its subjects, a situation which has continued to this day even with the present government that was founded on nationalist ideals. What happened with Kariba Dam and the subsequent removal of local inhabitants created a struggle over memory in which the Tonga found themselves being pushed into forced forgetting. The power was exercised firstly through state coercion and, secondly, by not allowing the Tonga to access and exploit the Kariba Dam (McGregor 2009; Scudder 2005; Colson 1971; Howarth 1961), socio-political moves that relegated the history of the local Tonga inhabitants which then became superseded by a modern history.

Historical memories inscribed and embedded in specific places and landscapes, according to Bollig (2009), carry a profound political statement vis-à-vis neighbours and the government. He argues that landscape is used as a medium to present specific political messages to members of the community as well as political actors beyond that community (Bollig 2009). Thus, the local Tonga were tricked into moving through a promise that "their water would follow them", but up to this day the promise has not been fulfilled and they continue to suffer an acute shortage of water. Indeed, the colonial state used water as a bargaining mechanism to persuade the Tonga to move because they knew that the latter's social life, livelihood and social history revolved and was attached to the Zambezi River and its waters. In the end, the move entailed hidden coercion and the way it was used has been perceived as responsible for shaping the Tonga's patterns of resistance and compliance to both the colonial and post-colonial governments (McGregor 2009; Marowa 2010).

Non-Governmental Organisations (NGOs), opposition political parties and activists have used the idea of absence of compensation and perceived "marginalisation" of the Tonga as their trump cards to court them against the state. Any narrative though that gives such prominence to external influence tends to present the Tonga as people who lack agency and who have not adapted to their new situation and environment; yet, that thinking mispresents what is obtaining on the ground in north-western Zimbabwe, as this chapter seeks to show.

According to Cliggett (2005: 58) "before the building of the dam, the Zambezi River flowed through the lowest points of the Valley and offered valuable bottomland for river basin agriculture, on which the valley Tonga relied for their primary subsistence", an observation also made by McGregor (2003a). The magnitude of riverine cultivation drastically changed upon removal because the plateau country to where they were resettled had small rivers (such as Tyuunga and Semwa) which prevented them from practising riverine agriculture at the scale they did along the Zambezi River. It is no secret that the Tonga like the Dandawa, Mudzimu and Nyamhunga chiefdoms were moved to very dry lands with poor agricultural potential mostly falling within agro-ecological regions III and IV. Fishing in the Zambezi was an important activity, but the removal placed them away from an abundant water body to small rivers and streams that dry up, and hold less fish, and, thus, they could not practise artisanal fishing throughout the year. Undoubtedly, this change exposed the evictees to hunger, poverty and malnutrition at a large scale as they had to learn and develop new livelihood practices that suited the plateau environment. Apart from developing a relationship with the new environment, the resettled people found themselves faced with new operational conditions that included local government reforms, conservation policies and wildlife restrictions which were introduced by the colonial government, and these greatly hindered and slowed the process of change and adaptation.

We argue that though these restrictions and policies were meant to protect wild animals from human encroachment and stop the Tonga from "misusing" and "damaging" the environment, the Tonga have over the years adapted to this new environment. They have also manipulated the remote presence of the state and its agencies to eke a living in Sinakatenge and Siamupa where they now live. In this context, the chapter does not focus (though it mentions in passing) the negative effects of forced movement after more than sixty years of removal from the Zambezi River. Rather, it focuses on how the Tonga have adapted to the change and are interacting with conservancies and the Department of National Parks and Wildlife Management (DNPWM) to improve their situation.

Governing the Waters, Conservation Policies and Restrictions

Water is a very important resource and a central non-human agent in the making of history and in stirring conflicts and tensions. In order to avoid conflicts between Northern and Southern Rhodesia (now Zambia and Zimbabwe, respectively) following the filling up of Lake Kariba, the respective governments were given rights to independently govern their waters. Whereas the Tonga on the northern shore of Lake Kariba were given increased access through irrigation and unrestricted fishing rights, the same did not happen to the Tonga on the southern shore whose interaction with, and access to, the Lake's littoral were curtailed. They were moved and resettled far away from the lakeshore on the arid plateau above the valley. Nonetheless, they were granted access to a few fishing camps via the permit system that allowed for small-scale gillnet fishing in the shallow waters, but angling (operated by whites) was the major activity.

Matters changed following Zambia's independence in 1964 as crossing of both the river and Lake became forbidden in the interests of state security (McGregor 2003a) due to the rising fear of guerrilla and nationalist activities that were being planned and executed from their bases located in Zambia. During the 1960s and 1970s, the Tonga resisted and fought alienation from their land and resources by supporting nationalist parties especially the Zimbabwe African People's Union (ZAPU) (McGregor 2003a). From 1964 onwards, trained guerrillas in exile began infiltrating Zimbabwe (then Rhodesia) by crossing the Zambezi River. Resultantly, restrictions in accessing the river and Lake became tighter and the Tonga found themselves further alienated and losing even the limited space they had been promised for interacting with the Lake through fishing permits. Being forbidden to cross the river had repercussions for the Tonga, especially ferrymen because they ceased to enjoy their trade (as crossing was restricted to the official posts of Kariba, Chirundu and Victoria Falls which many of them could not reach). Crossing at any undesignated and unauthorised point endangered the traveller's life as the Rhodesian forces would open fire without hesitation if a traveller was suspected to be a guerrilla.

The lakeshore was reserved for tourist and conservationist uses, which in turn restricted local communities from accessing it, thereby resulting in further evictions (McGregor 2003a). These further evictions occurred when land close to the Lake or river was purchased by a white person for conservation purposes, culminating in local populations being pushed further inland. Lake Kariba thus had several ripple effects of which establishment of conservancies was one of them, leading to pushing African ethnic groups further away from the lakeshores and the river. A Tonga fisherman who was interviewed by McGregor (2008: 867) pointed out that

> we are not recognised as legitimate users of the lake ... (we are) forced to move from camp to camp as the camps are sold by the council officers. We black men will be forced off ... as the lake is purchased by the white man.

Enlarged substantially by the tourism industry, the littoral's new presence and use turned Kariba into a white space. The Tonga, already physically removed from the southern shore, lost their place in its history (Hughes 2010).

As Kariba and Victoria Falls were turned into white play grounds, little room, if any, was left for the Tonga and others who occupied the Zambezi River to make a living from and to exploit the littoral as before, and to use it as a religious site, a most important function of the river to the people's way of life (Hughes 2010; McGregor 2003b). Similarly, when Kyle Dam in Masvingo was constructed in 1960, it resulted in the removal of people from Chinango and Nyangani who occupied the northern edges of the then Mtilikwe reserve before the areas became flooded (Fontein 2015). That move marked another appropriation of land by the colonial government which displaced African occupants and moved them away from the new benefits and developments associated with the harnessed water. Completion of Kyle Dam led to the expansion of wildlife and recreational facilities in the following decades after 1960 and, coupled with other ancillary developments, culminated in the Europeanisation of Mutirikwi's landscape (Fontein 2015).

The construction of Lake Kariba kick-started a process of place-making and meaning-making which superseded claims by, and the history associated with, the Tonga. McGregor (2003b) notes how the white government celebrated the triumph of white colonial science over (and the taming of) the Zambezi River and, in turning it into a white-ground, rewrote the history of the Zambezi landscape by silencing that of the Tonga. Hughes (2010) has rightly observed that developments at Kariba caused the whites to rename and rebrand nature, hotels and conservation companies in their language (i.e. English), a move which further strengthened their ownership and "artificial" entitlement to the Lake. He went further to argue that:

> To appropriate the landscape symbolically, one had to do more than evacuate blacks from it. Government trucks had moved the Tonga physically. Spatial and temporal scales associated with exploration pushed them metaphorically to the margins. But these tropes did not automatically replace blacks with whites as "river people", hence something more (like English naming)

> was needed to cement the replacement of blacks with whites as the "river people".
>
> *Hughes 2010: 58*

European names replaced and effaced the Native analogue and, from the settler's perspective, these new names re-categorised the topography, breaking it into units and features that made earlier (Tonga) meanings unrecognisable, thereby setting in motion a process of new meaning-making by erasing and replacing those of the former inhabitants. Islands, bays and other features that carried local names were renamed, in most cases, after "famous" European people. The naming and branding of such sites and aspects of the Lake were for marketing and consumption (Hughes 2010), and the Tonga's legendary and religious figures lost their place in the new naming process.

Post-independent Zimbabwe has not addressed at all the Tonga's concern of denied access to their former waters. The Lake has remained a recreational park run by and serving mainly the interests of whites and government. Conservancies that run and control certain sections of the landscape surrounding Lake Kariba have also remained intact and largely white-owned. Despite the de-racialisation of laws and regulations after Zimbabwe's independence, there are still notable continuities in the Lake's control and operation regime. Nyikahadzoi (cited in McGregor 2008: 865) argues that conservationist interests continued to grow stronger as tourism boomed, and indeed white-owned companies continue to dominate both the *kapenta* fish business and trade in other fish species, despite an explicit and politicised "indigenisation" programme in the 1990s and 2000s. A few permits in the fishing industry were offered to black fishing cooperatives, but the majority of those who got permits and started fishing companies were the Shona and the Ndebele at the expense of the Tonga. Marowa (2010) notes that this has angered the latter due to government's skewed orientation in approving and allocating fishing permits. In this light, Mpofu (cited by Marowa 2010: 181) highlights that the Tonga once threatened to invade part of Lake Kariba (in October 2004) "if the government did not intervene in the allocation of fishing permits which only favoured a few people who were coming from outside the district".

All the conservancies, fishing industries and boat cruse companies have gained momentum because of the harnessed water at Kariba Gorge. The Tonga have suffered twice, firstly by failing to gain access and fishing permits to the Lake and, secondly, by not benefiting from the revenue raised from the fishing industry and conservancies to create development in their areas. Road infrastructure and communication networks in much of north-western Zimbabwe, especially in Binga and Nyaminyami rural districts, are poor and degraded, while schools and clinics are poorly constructed and in a sorry state with no electricity and sometimes no water due to dysfunctional or dried-up boreholes. Such a situation has left Binga as one of the most poorly served districts in Zimbabwe, with its people reduced to depending on food handouts from the government and NGOs. The Tonga's situation is not unique and isolated but mirrors what is obtaining in the wider waterscape politics of the world. For instance, in the Mekong region, the waterscape there has provided investment opportunities for private gain to powerful players that typically include local/national politicians, bureaucracies, firms and funding partners, while the local population is suffering and under siege (Molle et al. 2010).

The DNPWM oversees the interaction between human society and wildlife and conservancies in Zimbabwe. All aspects of gillnet fishing in Kariba and elsewhere in the country are regulated by the government through the DNPWM which has demarcated fishing grounds and closed areas, located temporary fishing camps, controlled the number of permits, methods of fishing and net sizes, monitored catches and prohibited permanent homes and lakeshore agriculture (Bourdillon, cited in McGregor 2008: 865). Gillnetters caught breaking the rules are subjected to draconian punishment that includes imprisonment and the confiscation of boats and nets (McGregor 2008). Narratives from local people state that the DNPWM also operates a "shoot to kill" policy against wildlife poachers. Thus, white conservation and DNPWM regulations greatly limit the Tonga from accessing the Lake's resources, the very people who consider the Lake as their own resource as they bore the costs of its creation back in 1956–57.

Those places where the Tonga are allowed to fish lack good fish species and stocks. Many of the best fishing grounds are closed to fishing either because they are designated breeding grounds or they are next to islands and shorelines reserved for conservation and "wilderness" tourism (McGregor 2008). The Lake is not open to the Tonga for such socio-economic activities as cultivation, irrigation, animal husbandry and domestic purposes.

Tonga's Agency and Response to Exclusion from Kariba Dam

The Tonga like other ethnic groups such as those in Insiza in Matabeleland, Mutambara and Nyanyadzi in Manicaland (Alexander 2006) and the Dandawa Korekore in Hurungwe (Marowa 2014) have endured forced displacement and suffered marginalisation due to racial colonial policies on land and development-related eviction (McGregor 2003b). However, a focus on this alone has outlived its usefulness and its continued use inhibits an examination of the Tonga's agency in dealing with their socio-economic exclusion from the Kariba waters. In being excluded from fully accessing the Lake and its littoral resources as compared to whites and other ethnic groups, the Tonga have not been mere "passive" recipients of alienation from river resources found in Lake Kariba; indeed, they have not lacked agency. Here, we examine and emphasise the various ways by which both Tonga men and women have engaged with the state in order to deal with their circumstances.

Politics and Landscape Claims

The Tonga have been very vocal in meetings, public hearings and election campaigns with authorities over issues of water management and restrictions around accessing forests and environmental resources. Mashingaidze (2013: 381) argues that, starting from the 1990s, "local minority people's rights conscious activists assembled and circulated discourses of entitlement to natural resources within Binga District and the Zambezi Valley at large". These activists aligned themselves with emerging global discourses which expose the effects of dams on indigenous people's rights, using such spaces to echo their concerns of marginalisation on both international and local platforms.

Despite having spent more than sixty years away from the Zambezi River and Valley after forced removal, the issue of the Lake has remained, to borrow McGregor's phrase (2009), "unfinished business" for the Tonga. Apart from engaging the state over their grievances and situation, they have also made use of local resources at their disposal for their own subsistence and sustenance, particularly where government control and restrictions are minimal or next to non-existent. In extreme cases, some Tonga have engaged in poaching and illegal cross-border trading across the Lake and river (McGregor 2008). Since the government has created bottlenecks in allocation of fishing permits, the Tonga have resorted to illegal hunting and fishing as a means to protest the continued denial to access the Lake. These illegal activities, as viewed in the eyes of the state, are perceived by the Tonga as a way of maintaining socio-historical connections to the Zambezi River and for their socio-economic survival. In spite of the state's and its relevant departments' view of Tonga activities as illegal, the latter do not perceive them as such because they still hold and believe they are a "river people" and rightful owners of the Lake (McGregor 2008: 862). This Tonga-state tension has existed since the time of the liberation struggle against the colonial government and now, in the post-colonial setting, the tension has not subsided.

In post-colonial Zimbabwe, Tonga agency has continued to rise and has been driven by various local institutions such as the Binga Rural District Council (BRDC), Basilwizi Trust and BIDA. For example, in 1981, BRDC drafted the Lusumpuko plan which was a radical plan aimed at transforming Binga so that it could be at the same level of development as other districts in Zimbabwe (Manyena 2013). McGregor (2009) notes that the plan was comprehensive: it advocated for major developments in the transport and fishing industries around the Lake, including fish canning and freezing plants, boat and net manufacture, fresh-water prawn fishing and aquaculture. Such a radical plan meant engaging in competition with the already established white businesses that were in operation. Plans to have a fair share in the Lake were considered a threat to the state's interest as it had acquired a massive amount of revenue through the Lake's resources. At times, Binga councillors have passed resolution after resolution to try and increase the number of permits for the Tonga gillnetters and their access to the Lake, campaigned against license fees, protested the eviction and closing of fishing camps in the interest of tourism and conservation and opposed heavy-handed policing efforts, in which whole camps were periodically rounded up and punished indiscriminately (McGregor 2008: 869), but all these efforts have been to no avail.

The Zimbabwean state's failure after 1980 to deal with these unsettled grievances fuelled demands for the recognition of Tonga's rights as well as growing disillusionment and frustration with the ruling ZANU-PF party which pushed them into opposition politics (Marowa 2010). During our research in 2017, we noted that of the 22 wards in Binga district, 21 of them had elected either Movement for Democratic Change (MDC) or independent members as councillors and only 1 (in Luunga ward) was ZANU-PF. One youth in Binga said that "we now vote for MDC because the ZANU PF led government has failed us" (Interview, September 2017). Voting for the opposition shows the Tonga's discontentment with the government as it has failed to resolve their problems; instead, it has further perpetuated them by not giving Tonga people full control of their own waterscape resources in their districts. Land and resources are contentious issues in the world over and access to them have contributed to the emergence of both inter-state and civil wars. Hitchcock (2006) argues that rights to land and natural resources for indigenous people are conflict-ridden issues in many areas of the world. He gives the example of the San's struggles over the Kalahari and its resources against the Botswana state (Hitchcock 2006) which, like that of the Tonga, is embedded in the fight over whose rights over ownership of land and natural resources weigh more than the other.

Conservation programmes have contributed significantly to the alienation of resources along the littoral of Lake Kariba. In this context, governments, whether colonial or post-colonial, have failed to give due recognition to human needs as they have crafted, enacted and imposed measures that protected wild animals which made it appear as if wild animals mattered more than humans. Such measures created a rift between the local population on the one hand and the game-guards and wild animals on the other. For example, in 1996, the Binga District Council created six posts for game-guards whose main task was to guard wildlife from ordinary villagers. Leaders of these scouts were drawn from the National Parks Department and were authorised to shoot suspected poachers.

However, the Tonga's claims to the landscape were not totally effaced in this process. Even though much of the shoreline was made the white man's space through renaming of the landscape and creation of other waterscape features that include the establishment of hotels, lodges, safaris, conservancies and national parks, the Tonga still maintain their claims of ownership of their Lake. As a result of these claims, they want benefits from the Lake's resources, including at least by getting a quota of the fishing permits and also a quota of the revenue from the Lake. This would be channelled towards the development of their communities such as construction of roads, clinics, bridges and schools among other social services and amenities. Memories of past interactions with the river and of being "river people" still retain great significance today for some Tonga. Much of their economic, political and religious life "has ceased to be focused on the river, being inaccessible as a result of government restrictions, landmines (from the guerrilla war) and the waters of the Kariba Dam" (McGregor 2003a: 88). Despite this, and indeed because of it, they demand some access to the river and compensation for infrastructural development in Binga.

Poaching, Illegal Fishing and Informal Cross-Border Trade

Failure to obtain official fishing permits has not hindered the Tonga fishermen from exploiting Lake Kariba. In the face of the state's restrictions through the presence of DNPWM on the fishing grounds, fishermen engage in what they locally refer to as "patrols" which are illegal expeditions along the Lake to place fishing nets in restricted Lake zones. Such illegal activities take the form of trips of several days. McGregor (2008) observes that such "patrols" are common among fishermen of the five fishing camps of Binga (Mala, Masamu, Kalulwe, Simambo and Mujele). Restricted water zones are usually breeding places for fish (including *kapenta*) or have been reserved for conservancy and tourism; hence fishing in these protected areas is highly prohibited. In defending their actions (that are tantamount to trespassing), the Tonga use their memories of past interactions with the river and of broken promises by the government to justify their breaking of the regulations and restrictions to the Lake.

The Tonga also engage in illegal crossing of the Zambezi River, despite this being prohibited because of crocodiles and dangerous wild animals. The DNPWM is responsible for overseeing and regulating activities along the river. The local population has had to rely on both their canoeing skills and their acquired knowledge of the river in crossing it. This crossing of the Zambezi dates way back to the times of Ndebele raids around the 1880s (McGregor 2009) and now the Tonga are hired by people from others parts of Zimbabwe to assist them cross illegally into Zambia and back.

As well as "patrolling", the local Tonga people in Binga have also resorted to poaching as a survival strategy which is done mainly by middle-aged men and boys. The Tonga in the Mola chieftainship (which is adjacent to Sinakatenge) consider the forests and animals surrounding their chiefdom as theirs, which is a direct challenge to the authority and control of DNPWM. In 2015, inhabitants of Mola vehemently resisted the establishment of a conservancy in their territory, which sought to alienate their natural resources through fencing their villages (*The Financial Gazette*, 24 May 2015). This resistance was directly connected to fears of being cheated for a second time by the government, like what happened in 1956 when, despite state promises, they eventually lost their ancestral graves, ritual sites and access to the Zambezi River. Their experiences since 1956 have made the inhabitants of Binga very suspicious of any moves by the state to short-change them, especially in human-environment relations.

There is compelling evidence that the people in Binga engage in poaching. In Sinakatenge, we saw one elder eating wild animal meat and he told us that "I am eating impala meat, we buy it from young boys who hunt and catch impalas using dogs and spears" (Interview, October 2017). Another old woman said that "people are tired of eating *mubhidha* [green vegetables], that's why sometimes young men hunt wild animals and catch birds in restricted forests for subsistence" (Interview, September 2017). The people legitimise their poaching activities by making reference to the broken promises and failures from the controversial Communal Areas

Management Programme for Indigenous Resources (CAMPFIRE) programme which they feel alienated their animals that live along the lakeshore through the establishment of conservancies and national parks. CAMPFIRE was introduced in 1989 in Binga, as a "form of commercial partnership between safari operators and rural communities in wilderness zones along the lake shore" (Dzingirai 1996: 19). Its objective was to create cordial relations between the Tonga and safari operators, in which the latter were to give back a quota of their revenues to the communities for development purposes.

In the first years, it appeared to work properly and to benefit the local population. For instance, by 1992–93, CAMPFIRE had disbursed to the local population of Binga (estimated at 87,000 people) as much as Z$837,000 (US$130,000) in cash as dividends (Dzingirai 1996: 21). However, as time went on especially by the late 1990s, the people of Binga ended up not benefiting at all from the CAMPFIRE programme. The Lake's resources, and the animals and other natural resources bringing in much-needed foreign currency into Zimbabwe, have not helped Binga's cause as it remains one of the poorest districts. As of September–October 2017, chieftaincies in Binga lacked the necessary development infrastructure and basic social amenities. In Sinakatenge, for example, many boreholes were dysfunctional and in disrepair which left the majority of families relying on unsafe and contaminated water fetched from local rivers. The net effect of this has been an increase in deaths related to chronic diseases such as cholera and diarrhoea, and a general spread of waterborne diseases like bilharzia. The local population recalled, for instance, that in 2008 there were about 17 cases of deaths from cholera in Sinakatenge.

In spite of their access and interaction with the Zambezi River being restricted and considered trespassing, the Tonga have learnt to circumvent the regulations by relying on their historical and intimate knowledge of the Zambezi landscape to continue making a living for their families. They have not let their circumstances stand in the way of survival, as they manipulate the state's uncoordinated monitoring and presence in certain parts of the river landscape. Through their agency, they have become innovative in the face of hardships and challenges, rather than merely complaining about their plight. The DNPWM and related law enforcing departments of the state have their own challenges owing to the country's economic woes which have affected these arms of the state from discharging their duties properly. Sometimes their patrol vehicles break down or have no fuel and this creates opportunities for the local Tonga villagers to interact with the Lake, the river, fenced forests and restricted national parks. Thus, they are not deterred at all by the state's presence or by armed safari patrol guards because their knowledge of the landscape and canoeing skills have historically proved to be efficient in the face of adversity and dangerous wild animals.

Women's Agency and the Riverine Resources

The state does not have a clear understanding of what matters most to the Tonga's day-to-day activities, and this has left Sinakatenge villagers (particularly women) with no option than to illegally exploit riverine resources. Women in our study noted how the harsh ecological environment has discouraged tight state control and that the economic challenges facing Zimbabwe since 2000 have also prevented frequent state patrols in enforcing restrictions and environmental regulations. As a result, they have taken advantage of the circumstances to exploit restricted resources and to practise illegal fishing and flood recession agriculture. In this sense, challenges (particularly financial and capacity problems) being faced by the state have given a lifeline to peripheral communities such as in Sinakatenge and Siamupa to engage in subsistence practices and in income generation.

Women in Binga have their own ways of dealing with the "moral economy" of the district. Taking advantage of the state's limited visits in the district and villages, the Tonga women practise *mabbonzye* (riverbed farming) which has become the most important economic activity and established survival strategy for women. *Mabbonzye* is "an innovative way of using scarce natural capital [land and water] and it is a centuries-old farming practice linked to floodplain cultivation that was practiced in the Zambezi Valley before displacement of the Tonga people" (Tombindo 2018: 156–157). In the face of adverse agro-ecological conditions such as poor soils, high temperatures and limited-employment opportunities as well as low income, riverine agriculture has become once again a kind of panacea to the people's daily needs and livelihoods. In Sinakatenge and Siamupa chiefdoms, women practise riverine farming along the Tyuunga and Semwa Rivers, respectively. *Mabbonzye* emanated from people's lived experiences as a mechanism to cope with stressful situations and conditions in the severely hot Zambezi Valley (Tombindo 2018), and the resultant impoverishment caused by forced removal and further alienation from the Zambezi waters.

Tyuunga and Semwa Rivers are very small compared to the Zambezi, but the Tonga women have not let their displaced past connection and experiences affect their ability to fend for their families. These small rivers have exploitable riverine resources that include water, floodplains, fish, sandy soils and reeds, which the women of Sinakatenge have used to their advantage. Reeds are used by those who engage in basketry, water and sandy soil are important in the construction industry (with women supplying these to the industry in return for money or food items) and fish assist in their dietary requirements as well as income generation through selling or barter trade. The economic crisis in Zimbabwe has had an adverse effect on rural dwellers especially women who have to feed their families. Against such challenges, women have taken the risk to confront the state's control head-on because, otherwise, they will see their children suffering from malnutrition and dying from drought and famine.

Conclusion

This chapter accepts, and indeed shows, that the Tonga have had to endure restricted access to the Zambezi River and Valley subsequent to their removal to the plateau landscape of Binga. However, it has been highlighted that the Tonga did not let the state's policies and practices push them deep into a life of misery. They knew that trespassing in state policed and conservancy areas might culminate in arrests and imprisonment, but this has not deterred them from engaging in livelihoods for subsistence purposes. In spite of their blocked access to Kariba Dam and the Zambezi River landscape, the Tonga developed new forms of agency-based activities that are rooted in historical claims to the river landscape and the unfulfilled promise of "water following them".

The Tonga's life and livelihoods before forced movement revolved around the Zambezi waters and a close relationship with both the physical and spiritual environments of the waterscape. Forced movement did not completely destroy that relationship, although it cut off physical contact through strict environmental policies that prohibited unauthorised fishing, hunting and any other activities in state controlled and conservancy territories. The Tonga engage in "illegal" crossings, poaching and "patrolling" as well as riverine agriculture, including in restricted areas. The Tonga do not regard these activities as immoral, though considered illegal from the state's perspective. The failure by the post-colonial state to settle what the Tonga regard as "unfinished business" premised on their grievances of forced movement and "water following them" has made them appear to challenge state power and policies. However, the Tonga are not concerned about what constitutes an illegal activity from the eyes of the state; rather, they are guided by their day-to-day livelihood needs which, ultimately, derive legitimacy from deeply moral claims around their status as "river people".

Funding

The research for this chapter was funded by the University of Zimbabwe to support research on various aspects of Kariba Dam.

References

Abbute, W. (2009). Social impact of resettlement in the Beles Valley. In A. Pankhurst and F. Piguet (eds), *Moving people in Ethiopia: development, displacement and the state*. Suffolk: James Currey, 130–137.

Alexander, J. (2006). *The unsettled land: state-making and the politics of land in Zimbabwe 1893–2003*. Oxford: James Currey.

Bollig, M. (2009). Kinship, ritual and landscape amongst the Himba of Northwest Namibia. In M. Bollig and O. Bubenzer (eds), *African landscapes: interdisciplinary approaches*. New York: Springer, 327–351.

Cliggett, L. (2005). *Grains from grass: aging, gender and famine in rural Africa*. Ithaca: Cornell University Press.

Colson, E. (1971). *The social consequences of resettlement: the impact of the Kariba resettlement upon the Gwembe Tonga*. Manchester: Manchester University Press.

Dzingirai, V. (1996). Every man must resettle where he wants: the politics of settlement in the context of community wildlife management programme in Binga, Zimbabwe. *Zambezia*, Vol. 23(1): 19–30.

Fontein, J. (2015). *Remaking Mutirikwi: landscape, water and belonging in southern Zimbabwe*. Suffolk: James Currey.

Hitchcock, R. (2006). We are the owners of the land: the San struggle for the Kalahari and its resources. In R. K. Hitchcock, B. Megan and I. Kazunobu (eds), *Updating the San: image and reality of an African people in the 21st Century.* Osaka: Senri Ethnological Studies.
Howarth, D. (1961). *The shadow of the dam.* London: Collins.
Hughes, D. M. (2006). White and water: how Euro-Africans made nature at Kariba Dam. *Journal of Southern African Studies*, Vol. 32(4): 823–837.
Hughes, D. M. (2010). *Whiteness in Zimbabwe: race, landscape, and the problem of belonging.* New York: Palgrave Macmillan.
Manyena, S. B. (2013). Ethnic identity, agency and development. In L. Cliggett and V. Bond (eds), *Tonga timeline: appraising sixty years of multidisciplinary research in Zambia and Zimbabwe.* Lusaka: Lembani Trust.
Marowa, I. (2010). The Tonga people of Zimbabwe. Historical memories and contemporary challenges of a minority society. In M. U. Mbanaso and C. J. Korieh (eds), *Minorities and the state in Africa.* New York: Cambria Press, 171–194.
Marowa, I. (2014). Forced Removal and Social Memories in North Western Zimbabwe, c1900–2000, PhD Thesis, University of Bayreuth. https://epub.uni-bayreuth.de/2090/1/Ivan%20Book%20pdf.pdf
Mashingaidze, T. (2013). Beyond the Kariba Dam induced displacements: the Zimbabwean Tonga's struggle for restitution, 1990s–2000s. *International Journal of Minority and Group Rights*, Vol. 20(3): 381–404.
McGregor, J. (2003a). Living with the river: landscape, and memory in the Zambezi Valley, Zimbabwe. In W. Beinart and J. McGregor (eds), *Social history and African environments.* Oxford: James Currey.
McGregor, J. (2003b). The Victoria Falls 1900–1940: landscape, tourism and the geographical imagination. *Journal of Southern African Studies*, Vol. 29(3): 717–737.
McGregor, J. (2008). Patrolling Kariba's waters: state authority, fishing and the border economy. *Journal of Southern African Studies*, Vol. 34(4): 861–879.
McGregor, J. (2009). *Crossing the Zambezi: the politic of the landscape on a Central African Frontier.* Oxford: James Currey.
Molle, F., Foran, T. and Kakonen M. (2010). Contested Mekong waterscapes: where to next? In F. Molle, T. Foran, and M. Kakonen (eds), *Contested waterscapes in the Mekong region: hydropower, livelihoods and governance.* London: Earthscan.
Pradhan, P. (2009). Impact of displacement on the socio-economic life of tribals. In R. C. Pandit (ed), *Development-vs-displacement of tribal people in India: problems and prospects.* Delhi: Abhijeet Publications, 86–94.
Scudder, T. (1993). Development-induced relocation and refugee studies: 37 years of change and continuity among Zambia's Gwembe Tonga. *Journal of Refugee Studies*, Vol. 6(2): 123–152.
Scudder, T. (2005). "The Kariba Case Study" (Working Paper, California Institute of Technology).
Tischler, J. (2013). *Light and power for a multiracial nation: the Kariba scheme in the Central African Federation.* Basingstoke: Palgrave Macmillan.
Tombindo, F. (2018). Livelihoods vulnerability among riverbed farmers in Negande, Nyaminyami District. In M. K. Chiweshe (ed), *The political economy of livelihoods in contemporary Zimbabwe.* London: Routledge.
Tremmel, M. (1994). *The people of the great river: the Tonga hoped the water would follow them.* Gweru: Mambo Press.
Turton, D. (2009). Refugees & forced resettlers: towards a unitary study of forced displacement. In A. Pankhurst and F. Piguet (eds), *Moving people in Ethiopia: development, displacement and the state.* Suffolk: James Currey, 23–34.

11

CHALLENGES FACED BY WOMEN IN SMALL-SCALE FISHING IN SIABUWA, BINGA DISTRICT

Vimbainashe Garaiza

Introduction

Small-scale fishing communities are confronted with serious problems throughout the stages of the fishing cycle that include fish catching, processing, distribution and marketing. This chapter examines the multiple challenges bedevilling small-scale fishing projects in Mujele fishing camp, in the Siabuwa area of Binga District along the Zambezi valley. This case study is examined in the context of Zimbabwe's broader economic crisis characterised by cash shortages, high unemployment rates and soaring inflation. In pursuing this, specific attention is paid to women's involvement in small-scale fishing. The Zambezi Valley is home to the Tonga, often referred to as the "forgotten people", with the Siabuwa area having an estimated population of 50,000 people (Siabuwa Development Trust 2011). Siabuwa has many fishing camps, not only Mujele but also places like Nsengwa, Kalungwizi, Malube, Chibuyu, Tshunga, Nagangara, Vanda and Mweenda (Mutale et al. 2018). Besides large water bodies for fishing, there are also fish ponds constructed by Basilwizi Trust (a non-governmental organisation – NGO).

The Tonga ethnic group make up the majority of the approximately 200,000 people living in rural Binga District in Matabeleland North Province (McCray 2014). Binga District is well known for its inhospitable climatic conditions, making it a drought-prone area (Martens 2010). In this troubling context, the Tonga seek to maintain their identity through activities focusing on history, culture, language and economic practices (Mwinde 2016). The Siabuwa community is located a hundred kilometres from Binga District's centre, and it is where packaging of dried fish and wholesale fish marketing is undertaken. Mujele is the District's largest fishing camp along the Zambezi River and it ensures a regular supply of fish to the markets (Mutale and Chisango 2017). Fishing (known as *kujatabaswii*) is one of the major sources of livelihood for Tonga people (McCray 2014), but they also engage in

DOI: 10.4324/9781003278580-14

weaving baskets and sculpturing, rearing animals like pigs and chickens and vegetable and other gardening.

The regulatory authority managing Mujere fishing camp is the office of the National Parks and Wildlife Management Authority. The Zambezi River is divided into fishing basin grounds by the regulatory authority and, as well, it designates areas which are too dangerous for people to undertake fishing using nets or boats. Beyond demarcating fishing grounds, the Authority prevents cultivation along the river, controls the number of permits and methods of fishing (for example, setting the minimum mesh size for catching fish) and designates areas safe to live while at the camp. This includes prohibiting permanent homes, as even the local Tonga people live in the camps temporarily. The Mujere fishing camp consists of two grounds along the Zambezi. One currently has extensive crocodiles present (Ground number 1) which has led to restrictions over its use. Ground number 2 is used by most local people, including women fishers, who do not have sophisticated equipment for fishing. Ground number 2 has a less record of loss of lives compared to Ground number 1. There is also a committee structure in the camp, namely, a chairman and his committee members. The chairman is responsible for prohibiting the building of permanent housing structures, controlling entry into the fishing camp, and helping Parks and Wildlife Management with necessary information and reports like the day-to-day activity in the camp. The committee members assist with camp security and the writing of the daily reports. The implementation and enforcement of regulations in the fish camp are meant to instil discipline amongst small-scale fishers in order to conserve the natural resource base.

Context

Small-scale fishing is a complex term as it is used differently across the globe. The term small-scale fishing is interchangeably used with such terms as "artisanal", "local", "coastal", "traditional", "small", "subsistence", "non-industrial", "low-tech" and "poor" (Gibson and Sumaila 2017; Basurto and Smith 2019; Biswal 2015). The Food and Agricultural Organisation (FAO) tends to equate "artisanal" with "small-scale", implying the use of small vessels with low levels of technology, traditional fishing methods and a reference to small size (Garcia-Florez et al. 2014). Generally, the working definition of small-scale fishing for this research refers to an activity performed at a community or local level by people living near perennial rivers to acquire a source of food (i.e. fish) or to generate income to meet their basic needs, using minimal capital investment and low-technology fishing gear.

Irrespective of the precise definition, small-scale fishing is one of the most important livelihood options pursued by poor people living in developing countries. Most African nations, and Zimbabwe in particular, rely extensively on crop cultivation to sustain their economy, but climate change has brought forth many difficulties for those who rely exclusively on crop cultivation. This has led to the diversification of livelihoods, including by way of small-scale fishing. In the case of Zimbabwe, this has also involved urban to rural migration, as urban Zimbabweans leave urban spaces in the face of a declining economy to find alternative means of making a living, including by fishing. Fishing is now an important source of income, food, employment and development in rural areas across the world (FAO 2012). According to FAO (2020), 120 million people globally rely on fisheries, with almost 97% of these residing in developing countries. Of all the global food production systems, small-scale fishing is widely considered as imperative with reference to enhancing nutrition and human health, alleviating hunger and poverty, and generating employment (Arthur et al. 2020; Basurto and Smith 2019; Bennett et al. 2018; Kawarazuka and Bene 2010). Besides this, small-scale fishing is regarded at local levels as a way of living, and as embedded in "tradition", history and culture in rural spaces.

Small-scale fishing is faced with many challenges across the African continent which impacts its productivity and sustainability. Declining fish stock is very serious and is the most common issue confronting fishing communities across the world and in the sub-region. For example, the Chambo fish species have declined in Malawi (Hara 2011) and, in Ghana, fish stocks are in crisis and this is causing fishers to migrate to areas where stocks are more plentiful (Kraan 2011). Some of the main reasons cited for stock decline include the increased number of people engaged in fishing, over-exploitation and the use of illegal fishing methods (Bavinck 2011). A decline in fish stocks has direct implications for livelihoods, income and food security for communities involved in fishing. Hence, the Anlo Beach community in Ghana faced multiple constraints which led to depletion of fish and reduced fish productivity, thereby undercutting food security, nutrition and income (Maravanyika et al. 2017). For the inlands of Africa (that is, away from the coastlines), unsustainable fishing activities are also taking place. This is illustrated by Tanzania, where rare and endangered species are harvested by means of unsustainable and illegal methods (for example dynamite fishing), which affect future generations of fishers. In Mozambique, the main problem facing small-scale fishers of Cabo Delgado (a province bordering Tanzania) arises from illegal fishing activities undertaken by migrant fishers from Tanzania, who resort to inappropriate fishing methods such as scuba outfits and mosquito nets (FAO 2008).

Furthermore, another problem encountered in most African fishing communities is deforestation that is contributing, in turn, to desertification. This is clear as well from Anlo Beach in Ghana, which is experiencing high population densities (Maravanyika et al. 2017). In Anlo Beach, some 20% of all mangroves trees have been lost since 1980, and 40% of coral reef systems are considered severely or highly degraded. Mangroves are used as a source of energy for drying fish, and this undermines environmental sustainability. There are energy alternatives to cutting down trees – for example, the use of *tsosto* stoves to cure fish – but these are not being deployed extensively for this purpose. An additional matter is that of poor transport systems which hamper the distribution and marketing of fish, such that rural road systems are almost unusable during the rainy season.

In many sub-Saharan African countries, policymakers tend to view fishing as being exclusively for the poor (for subsistence purposes only) and, since the returns are palpably trivial, there is little potential for development via fishing (Mwenesi 2016) and little reason to invest in these areas. Reflecting this marginalisation, fisheries are largely uncared for in relation to research on water productivity, agricultural water management and, more broadly, rural development and poverty alleviation (Bene 2008). Many national policies simply fail to give fisheries the needed attention, with small-scale fishers typically not involved in policymaking processes in many Africa countries, including Kenya, Mozambique and Zimbabwe. At times, the tourist industry takes priority which leads to allocating sites and islands for tourism development to the exclusion of small-scale fishers (FAO 2008). Lack of governmental support is a major problem for the sector of small-scale fisheries, which remains poorly planned and regulated and inadequately funded, even being neglected in national economic and fisheries statistics (Pomeroy 2015). Because of this, the state's regulatory agencies are sources of uncertainty and challenges for small-scale fishers. Proper regulatory and supportive policies are needed to guide the development processes in fisheries and to address issues caused by environmental threats and market imbalances.

Women and Small-Scale Fishing

Broadly speaking, women are marginalised in rural development initiatives and programmes. Feminists scholars like Boserup (1970) argue that women have been neglected and misrepresented in development initiatives at community levels yet they are crucial for the diversification of the household economy. In this light, men tend to dominate the small-scale fishing industry worldwide. In most African rural communities, there are various dimensions of life underpinned by patriarchal systems which curtail female involvement, and these include: socio-cultural constructions of the motherly myth; religious and cultural antagonism; and poverty, lack of education and absence of supportive institutions for women. Combined, these profoundly undermine the capacity of women to raise their voice and aspire to construct meaningful livelihoods. In the fishing industry, women typically perform supportive roles in the areas of childcare, household upkeep and psycho-social support for male fishers (Kabeer 2011). In ensuring a balanced, equitable and sustainable development of small-scale fishing communities, it is necessary to revalue women and recognise their significance in engaging in fishing more directly and fully (Benett 2005; Neis et al. 2005).

Binga District is one of the least developed districts in Zimbabwe, with women and children most intensely affected by poverty. Women in the district in particular have been excluded from development processes for many decades (Bindawuko Women Fishing Cooperative 2003), resulting in unequal access to the utilisation of local natural and other resources of economic importance. Social exclusion for the Tonga women of Binga is in part attributable to cultural or religious norms and practices that deny women economic and political rights as well as full access to education (Sachs 2005). Boosting Tonga women's participation in diverse livelihood activities that are economically viable and natural resource-based can increase their income and asset basis and help them escape the poverty cycle. In this respect, several cooperatives (for example, the Bindawuko Women Fishing Project) have made central in empowering rural women to venture into the traditionally male-dominated fishing industry (Mago et al. 2015).

Research Site and Methods

The research was carried out in 2017 and 2018 at the Mujele fishing camp in Siabuwa, located in Binga district, along the Zambezi River and it was primarily qualitative in character. There is a paucity of research which considers the lives of informal small-scale fishers in Siabuwa. Situated along the river, the fishing camp is a haphazard settlement where people live in huts made of dagga and poles on rocky spaces. The local Tonga people turn to fishing at Mujele and elsewhere because the area rarely receives regular rainfall for crop cultivation. The fishing camp comprises people who are the descendants of the Tonga villagers who were displaced during the dam wall construction in the late 1950s and their fishing activity performs some role in preserving Tonga identity (McGregor 2008). Many of the Tonga fishers are school dropouts who, because of lack of household income, left school and were not able to subsequently find formal employment. Some of the fishers are informal traders from towns.

A qualitative approach underpinned the fieldwork for this research and this was crucial in identifying and understanding the practices, perspectives and perceptions of the female small-scale fishers. Women are involved in fishing just like men and, in terms of equipment, the majority of women use a spin cast rod and nets. The collection of evidence involved in-depth interviews, key informant interviews and observation methods. Through purposive sampling, 15 women directly involved in small-scale fishery were selected focusing on fish traders, female fishers and also fishermen's wives. Key informants were those very conversant about small-scale fishing in the area, including local members of the Zimbabwe Parks and Wildlife Management team, chairman of the fishing camp and camp committee members. Interview guides were used for conducting the interviews with the women and the key informants. Both Tonga and Shona language were used during the interviews. Whenever there was a chance that the Tonga language would be the medium of communication, I made use of a translator, as I am a Shona speaker. The key informants permitted me to record them verbatim using an audiotape machine.

Participant observation was also crucial for the study. The researcher collected information late in the day and even during the evening when temperatures dropped along the Zambezi River. This enabled witnessing barter trade, whereby women fishers would exchange fish for basic consumables and goods, particularly with urban residents purchasing fish. These observations led to informal conversations as well, during which time I had a translator in case of language barrier challenges. I used audio-taping, a notebook and photographs to document the evidence. During the fieldwork, I was able to establish a close professional relationship with the female fishers, as they openly engaged with me along the shore during the day,

day-end and night, meeting for interviews and allowing for observation of their daily activities. This helped me to understand in some depth the ordinary Tonga women as they went about their small-scale fishing, including how they operate, how they perceive law enforcement efforts and how they interact with each other, as well as their level of organisation. This facilitated the development of an insiders' perspective of the lives and livelihoods of the female fishers of Mujele.

Problems Encountered by Small-Scale Fishers at Mujele

The fishing communities in Siabuwa face serious problems when it comes to their lives and livelihoods along the Zambezi River, including basic infrastructural problems, production and marketing challenges, wildlife-human conflicts and governance issues.

The lack of infrastructure in the Siabuwa area restricts small-scale fishing development in terms of fish handling and storage, and transport facilities, including Mujele fishing camp in particular. One fisher highlighted that the area suffers from significant deficiencies in terms of the condition of the road network, which inhibits the movement of cars. In this regard, another fisher lamented that customers complain that they cannot access the Mujele fishing camp in Siabuwa because the state of the roads is so bad. Physical access in and out of the area, especially to and from Mujele, is problematic as well because of the long distance, thus affecting fish sales. Previous research also discovered that the poor road network hinders fish demand and profits for Tonga fishers (McGregor 2008). Another infrastructural issue relates to water and sanitation. In particular, the outbreak of water-borne diseases at Mujele has been a challenge. The female fishers bemoaned that they (and their children) are the most vulnerable group when it comes to water-borne diseases such as cholera and dysentery. But it was observed that women dump waste materials in the lake's waters, and bathe and wash clothes in the water (even while also drinking it). This has contributed to water pollution in the Mujele fishing camp.

Acquiring fish storage facilities is another major issue. The absence of modern facilities for sanitation, chilling, cold storage and distribution makes it imperative for the artisanal fishers to use indigenous fish preservation methods like smoking, salting and sun-drying as a feasible alternative (Mndeme 1998). In addition, typically, small-scale fishers do not have refrigerators for storage, and they operate where temperatures are extremely high. The lack of refrigerators for handling fish affects deeply the quality of fish that small-scale fishers present to customers. In many cases, the fishers simply do not have the funds available to purchase refrigerators. However, the Mujele fishers claim that they can afford to buy refrigerators, but the government has failed to provide electricity to their community. One fisher spoke about the problems in this respect:

> Small-scale fishing is the last resort to sustain my livelihood. However, due to poverty, my business is not growing because I do not have enough equipment like refrigerators to store large quantities of fish. You are aware that fish is in

> the category of fresh produce, and it easily rots, and most customers want fresh fish. Therefore, lack of equipment affects my business at large.
>
> *Interview, 20/10/2018*

As with the poor road network, storage facility problems affect negatively the fishers' access to markets.

Lack of access to capital, finance and funding mechanisms and credit facilities also act as a serious constraint for most fishing communities like Mujele, as Chuenpagdee (2011) brings to the fore. Hence, capital/credit facilities are a major requirement insofar as small-scale fishers can sustain and expand their production and marketing activities. As one fisher put it very plainly:

> I wish I had access to bank loans and credit to boost my business.
>
> *Interview, 20/10/2018*

The Mujele fishers do not have any substantial collateral for security, hence they fail to apply for and acquire loans vital for operating a business and for growing their operations.

Small-scale fishers also spoke about the unavailability of hard cash for transactions when selling fish. It was highlighted that most customers buy fish using EcoCash (mobile money) – they do this due to the unavailability of hard currency in circulation in Zimbabwe. This concurs with Matenga (2018) who argues that most transactions in Zimbabwe are processed through EcoCash. At the same time, access to the mobile network is at times a problem, including for Tonga communities along the Zambezi River. The liquidity crisis in Zimbabwe is a broader problem for the Tonga, as it has hindered, delayed and even postponed the carrying out of certain cultural practices amongst the Tonga, such as *Masabe* and *Lwiindi*, as these ceremonies require the purchasing of many ritual materials and labour with cash (Saidi 2016; Matanzima and Saidi 2020; Siwila 2015). Besides the cash problem, there is a three-tier pricing system used in the fishing industry, with different prices for transactions when selling fish – for Zimbabwean bond notes, United States dollars and "plastic money" (which includes EcoCash and bank cards). In this light, the small-scale fishers tend to make the least amount of profit when accepting plastic money for fish. Hard cash is preferred amongst the fishers, especially in United States dollars because it is not affected by inflation. This is reaching distressing proportions for the Mujele fishers who strive to obtain cash on an everyday basis.

Wildlife attacks have been a setback in the Mujele fishing camp. McGregor (2005) examined past conflicts between crocodiles and the fishing communities sharing spaces along Lake Kariba, and these conflicts continue. The Tonga community in the Mujele camp shares the water landscape with crocodiles and other life-threatening animals like hippopotamus, and there are fears about the loss of life. The Tonga fishers destroy nests and eggs as a way of trying to control the crocodile population. Mujele fishers are vulnerable to crocodiles and other river wildlife due to the lack of proper equipment (which, in-itself, is a further problem). One small-scale fisher bemoaned the fact that proper nets are very expensive as are the recommended fishing boats, and that local fishers simply cannot afford to buy the more effective types of equipment. They risk their lives by using inferior equipment as it exposes them to crocodiles, elephants, buffalo and hippopotamus when on the water. For instance, *bwaato* is a metal boat used by most fishers, and it is unstable and dangerous to use because it can be easily crushed by hippopotamus. There is also a lack of safety equipment on board and no formal training around safety and security aspects.

Research participants argued that reports about the loss of lives and boats capsizing had become the order of the day. For example, according to one female fisher, more than ten people died in one month alone recently. Another noted:

> My husband doesn't have a boat. We cannot afford to buy a boat; hence we are exposed to crocodiles, hippopotamus, elephants. We use a manmade boat; hence windy waves usually threaten our lives most of the time.
>
> *Interview, 21/10/2018*

Still another spoke about specific incidences regarding crocodiles:

> We used to do fishing using Ground number 1; nowadays we have shifted because of a crocodile that is eating people there. We used to harvest a lot of fish and earned a living [in Ground number 1].
>
> *Interview, 21/10/2018*

There is now a crocodile-vigilance zone in the Ground number 1 area of Mujele fishing camp because of the crocodile attacks on humans. Due to the problems faced in Ground number 1, many fishers are now pursuing their trade in Ground number 2. However, fishers in Ground number 2 are very vigilant there because of the threatening crocodiles they experienced at Ground number 1. During the interviews, the fishers indicated that using the Kariba water source for daily activities like bathing, washing and fishing could lead to being attacked by crocodiles. Local Tonga people are unaware of the sheer number of crocodiles in the area, and hence they live in fear daily. Some crocodiles have been killed by villagers out of fear, or when looking for meat to eat and trying to limit attacks on livestock.

An important matter around vulnerability affecting small-scale fishers in Siabuwa is the governance structure of natural resources management in the area. The governance structure is deeply centralised and hierarchical in character, including for communities along the Zambezi River, such that fishers have found themselves without a voice in the governance of local resources. They lament that the government does not include them in any decisions that affect their livelihoods directly, therefore feeling marginalised and excluded. Because of this, there is significant tension between the Zimbabwe Parks and Wildlife Management Authority and the local fishers. Generally, the fishers are passive recipients of rules and regulations rather than partners in the management process, and they do not always follow the rules and regulations (for example, the use of fishing nets is prohibited but the fishers continue to use them). The Mujele fishers, especially the women, complain that the government was not considering suggestions such as supporting small-scale fishers in decision-making processes in the fishing camps, and they accuse Parks and Wildlife of deploying junior officials with no real decision-making powers to announce or administer new regulations – and, further, that these officials engage in corruption.

Access to resources such as wildlife and fisheries is controlled through a system of government-issued permits and licences. Under the permit system, several options for accessing the fishing sector exist, from commercial companies to small-scale fishers at the subsistence level. The Zimbabwean laws on fisheries are very restrictive, and from a sustainability point of view, this is to preserve aquatic life and guard against depletion of fish. The Mujele fishers understand the importance of the stringent rules regarding fishing in the interest of sustainability and protection of the environment; hence they tend to abide by many of these rules. For instance, Parks and Wildlife does not allow them to catch fish shorter than three inches in length because it is a threat to sustainability in reducing the multiplication of fish. But the female fishers complained about the permit fee for subsistence-level fishing (in which they are involved), as it is difficult to afford the amount. Although fisheries' restrictions are there, some fishers operate without permits. As one fisher said:

> We cannot afford the permit fee so we sometimes resort to fishing during the night. Since fishing improves our livelihood, we greatly depend on it. At the end of day, we usually operate in harsh conditions with the Parks and Wildlife as they take our equipment for fishing.
>
> *Interview, 22/10/2018*

Beyond these systemic problems, there is also competition and conflict over fishing and fishing space within the fishing industry in Siabuwa. There are a number of poachers in the area who engage in overfishing, which threaten the livelihoods of Tonga small-scale fishers. Fishers at Mujele lament that poachers are deeply wasteful in their fishing practices as they harvest fishes of all sizes, which in turn affects the breeding cycle of the various fish species. Small-scale Tonga fishers praised Parks and Wildlife for performing a positive role in protecting the environment from poachers, especially poachers from Zambia. Poaching has resulted in considerable economic loss and depletion of stocks for fishers in Mujele. A woman expressed the following:

> Poachers tend to overexploit our natural resources, using practices that threaten the environment.
>
> *Interview, 24/10/2018*

Though the small-scale Tonga fishers at times fight amongst themselves for space, it normally occurs between the Tonga fishers and others (McGregor 2008). Thus, the conflict is with registered and licensed fishers together with commercial fishers who chase the Tonga fishers away, accusing them of operating illegally and polluting the environment (McGregor 2008). These conflicts reflect the fact that the Zambezi River is still, at least in part, a common pool resource that everyone draws upon and utilises for survival or profit. As one female fisher said during an interview session:

> We usually face challenges with people who do not cherish our natural-based livelihood; they tend to use destructive fishing methods such as nets. Fisheries regulations restrict these practices, … and we have few alternative livelihoods. We used to fish using Ground number 1 but, due to rampant crocodiles, we shifted to Ground number 2. However, nowadays this is overpopulated by people, hence there is a lot of competition over fishing space.
>
> *Interview, 24/10/2018*

Coping Strategies Used by Mujele Small-Scale Fishers

In the face of these multiple challenges, and the stresses that come with these challenges, the study discovered several coping strategies used by small-scale fishers in Siabuwa. In enacting agency, these fishers deploy different tactics and ways of adaptation in trying to circumvent the challenges they face. These tactics include altering their fishing schedule, diversification of livelihoods and barter trade.

It emerged from the research that, given the active presence of the Parks and Wildlife Management Authority, illegal small-scale fishers stay vigilant and increase their awareness of movements in the area to defend themselves from harassment and arrest. Small-scale fishers in Mujele fishing camp engage in what Bayat (2008) calls "quiet non-compliance" or a form of passive resistance without engaging in outright demonstrations. Bayat (2008) also terms such strategies as "modest encroachments", meaning the existence of covert individual survival strategies employed by the poor to sustain their livelihoods. The female fishers, for instance, indicated that they do not harvest fish during environmental agency (Parks and Wildlife) raids. Rather, they stay home and do domestic work to avoid possible maltreatment and repression from this agency's officials. Through fieldwork observations, it became clear that there was an absence of illegal fishers and/or poachers along the Zambezi River during wholesale evictions by Parks and Wildlife. Overall, Parks and Wildlife Management does not have a constitutional right of forcefully evicting fishers, so it engages in joint operations with the Zimbabwe Republic Police to arrest illegal fishers. This entails Parks and Wildlife crafting operation orders with the police in which it recommends specific evictions. The evictions for illegal fishing are meant to protect the local natural resource base and ecosystems.

In this light, small-scale fishers change their working timetable, constructing a schedule whereby they fish when Parks and Wildlife officers are off-duty. The small-scale fishers revealed that Parks and Wildlife officials do not operate during the night and, thus, they flock to the Zambezi River to fish at that time. This was evidenced during the fieldwork, as the fishers deliberately operated during the night to evade the environmentalist raids and harassments taking place during the day. The revised fishing timetable has indeed become the most important coping strategy by small-scale fishers, as they catch most of their fish during the night. A research participant stressed this by saying:

> During Parks and Wildlife raids, I only operate during the night because I discovered that they don't work during the night. Operating during the night is also good since I harvest more fish.
>
> *25/10/2018*

To surmount the challenge of lack of requisite storage facilities (and extremely hot weather) which impinges on the freshness of products, small-scale fishers have devised a strategy of salting fish (which respondents termed "*Tubabikkamumunyo*") and smoking fish (called "*Tubawumpaamulilo*"). These methods preserved fish, thereby safeguarding the quality of fish products, especially during the summer temperatures. Regarding this, one interviewee had this to say:

> I dry fish using salt as a preservation method, and many people like salted fish; hence, it is advantageous.
>
> *25/10/2018*

To overcome the cash and financial crisis and its effects on the operations of small-scale fishing, the women noted that they accept EcoCash as a form of payment for their fish. Thus, instead of cash transactions (which they prefer), the small-scale fishers are compelled to turn to mobile banking in allowing customers to pay using EcoCash. A woman alluded that:

> Regarding the cash crisis in Zimbabwe, I decided to use EcoCash as a payment method.
>
> *24/10/2018*

Apart from mobile banking, some fishers spoke about the utilisation of barter trade whereby they organise with their customers to pay them with basic commodities like cooking oil, soap, mealie meal and sugar. This particular coping strategy seemed to be quite prevalent and also very important for current fishing livelihoods.

The research also established that small-scale fishers diversify livelihoods to gather other sources and forms of income. Thus, women practice cultivating vegetables and tomatoes to circumvent the cash crisis, while men practice carpentry where they make wooden chairs (which they term "*chuuno*") and doors, or they engage in the selling of firewood. They sell these items or products to nearby communities to generate income for their families.

Conclusion

This chapter thematically presented the diverse challenges faced by small-scale fishers, and specifically female fishers, in one fishing camp in Siabuwa, Binga District, as well as the coping strategies pursued in seeking to address these challenges. The female fishers confront challenges around the presence of wildlife (notably crocodiles), competition over fishing space with poachers, restrictive Wildlife and Parks laws and regulations and a cash crisis. These challenges inhibit the capacity of the fishers in Siabuwa to maximise fishing as a viable and sustainable livelihood practice. At the same time, though, they seek to undercut the weight of these challenges by undertaking coping strategies, such as livelihood diversification, drying fish as a preservation method and accepting EcoCash for fish transactions. The small-scale fishing undertaken by Tonga people in Siabuwa undoubtedly pose certain environmental risks for the local ecosystem, insofar as they use methods which disturb fish-spawning and involve over-exploiting the fish stock. Hence, the regulations implemented and enforced by Parks and Wildlife are of some significance in this regard. However, the Zimbabwe government, via Parks and Wildlife, needs to put in place policies and programmes in relation to fishing which also provide an enabling environment for the female fishers in Binga District, to ensure that small-scale fishing is more viable as a livelihood project.

References

Arthur, R. I., Skerritt, J. D., Schuhbauer, A., Ebrahim, N. and Friend, M. R. *Small-scale fisheries and local food systems: transformations, threats and opportunities*. First published: 09 August 2020 https://doi.org/10.1111/faf.12602

Basurto, X., and Smith, H. (2019). Defining small-scale fisheries and examining the role of science in shaping perceptions of who and what counts: a systematic review. *Frontiers in Marine Science*. 7 May 2019. https://doi.org/10.3389/fmars.2019.00236

Bavinck, M. (2011). Wealth, poverty, and immigration: the role of institutions in the fisheries of Tamil Nadu, India. In S. Jentoft and A. Eide (eds), *Poverty mosaics: realities and prospects in small-scale fisheries*, pp. 173–191. Dordrecht : Springer Netherlands.

Bayat, A. (2008). From dangerous classes to quiet rebels. Politics of the urban subaltern in the global south. *International Sociology*, Vol. 15(3): 533–557.

Bene, C. (2008). Contribution of Fishing to Households' Economy- Evidence from Fisher-Farmer Communities in Congo. IIFET 2008 Vietnam Proceedings, 22–25 July Nha Trang, Vietnam

Benett, E. (2005). Gender, fisheries and development. *Marine Policy* ,Vol. 29: 451–459.

Bennett, A., Patil, P., Kleisner, K., Rader, D., Virdin, J. and Basurto, X. (2018). Contribution of Fisheries to Food and Nutrition Security: Current Knowledge, policy, and Research. NI Report.

Bindawuko Women Fishing Cooperative. (2003). https://canoncollins.org/projects/bbindawuko-women-fishing-cooperative-zimbabwe/

Biswal, L. R. (2015). Fishing is more than just a livelihood: Wellbeing and small-scale bag net fisheries governance in Gujarat, India Natural Resources Institute Clayton H. Riddell Faculty of Environment, Earth, and Resources University of Manitoba Winnipeg, Manitoba R3T 2N2 August 2015.

Boserup, E. (1970). *Woman's role in economic development*. London: George Allen & Unwin.

Chuenpagdee, R. (2011). *World small-scale fisheries contemporary visions*. Netherlands: Eburon Delft Academic Publishers, pp 3–16.

FAO. (2008). Report of the FAO Expert Workshop on Climate Change Implications for Fisheries and Aquaculture. FAO Fisheries Report No. 870. Rome, FAO. 32 pp. also available at www.fao.org/docrep/011/i0203e/i0203e00.htm

FAO. (2012). *State of world fisheries and aquaculture 2012*. Rome: United Nations Food and Agriculture Organisation.

FAO. (2020). FAOSTAT. In: FAO [online]. www.fao.org/faostat/en/#data/QC

Garcia-Florez, L., Morales, J., Gaspar, M. B., Castilla, D., Mugerza, E., Berthou, P., Garcia de la Fuente, L., Oliverira, M., Moreno, O., Garcia del Hoyo, J. J., Arregi, L., Vignot, C., Chapela, R., and Murillas, A. (2014). A novel and simple approach to define artisanal fisheries in Europe, *Marine Policy*, Vol. 44: 152–159.

Gibson, D., and Sumaila, U. R. (2017). Determining the degree of "small-scaleness" using fisheries in British Columbia as an example. *Marine Policy*, Vol. 86: 121–126. doi: 10, 1016/ j.marpol.2017.09.015

Hara, M. M. (2011). Community response: decline of the Chambo in Lake Malawi's Southeast Arm. In S. Jentoft and A. Eide (eds), *Poverty mosaics: realities and prospects in small-scale fisheries*, pp. 251–274. Dordrecht: Springer Netherlands.

Kabeer, N. (2011). Citizenship narratives in the face of bad governance: the voices of the working poor in Bangladesh. *Journal of Peasant Studies*, Vol. 38(2): 325–353.

Kawarazuka, N., and Bene, C. (2010). The potential role of small fish species in improving micronutrient deficiencies in developing countries: building evidence. *Public Health Nutrition*, Vol. 14: 1927–1938.

Kraan, M. (2011). Creating Space for Fishermen's Livelihoods. Anlo-Ewe Beach Seine Fishermen's Negotiations for Livelihood Space within Multiple Governance Structures in Ghana, Vol. 19, Leiden: African Studies Centre. PhD thesis, University of Amsterdam and International Development Studies, African Studies Collection

Mago, S., Nyathi, D. and Hofisi, C. (2015). Non-governmental organisations and rural poverty reduction strategies in Zimbabwe: a case of Binga rural district. *Journal of Governance and Regulation*, Vol. 4(4): 59–67.

Maravanyika, M. T., Mills, D. J., Asare, C., and Asiedu, G. A. (2017). Enhancing women's participation in decision-making in artisanal fisheries in the Anlo Beach fishing community, Ghana. *Water Resources and Rural Development*, Vol. 10: 58–75.

Martens, J. (2010). *Complexities of rural in globalised environment: lessons from Binga District, Zimbabwe*. Johannesburg: Rosa Luxemburg Foundation Johannesburg.

Matanzima, J., and Saidi, U. (2020). Landscape, belonging and identity in northwest Zimbabwe: a semiotic analysis. *African Identities*, Vol. 18(1–2): 233–251.

Matenga, L. (2018). Towards sustainable livelihoods: trends and survival strategies used in street vending in Masvingo, Zimbabwe. Masters in Urban Studies in the school of Architecture and planning.

McCray, B. (2014). Zimbabwe's Tonga fishermen cut off from Zambezi lifeline, Binga, 29 September 2014.

McGregor, J. (2005). Crocodile crimes: people versus wildlife and the politics of postcolonial conservation on Lake Kariba, Zimbabwe. *Geoforum*, Vol. 36: 353–369.

McGregor, J. (2008). Patrolling Kariba's waters: state authority, fishing and the border economy. *Journal of Southern African Studies*, Vol. 34(4): 861–879.

Mndeme, Y. E. S. (1998). *Efforts to save the marine environment in Tanzania*. Naga: The WorldFish Centre, Vol. 21(3), pp 10–12.

Mutale, M., and Chisango, T. (2017). Current trends on women's participation in aquaculture/fish farming and future prospects; the Zimbabwean perspective: a case of Siabuwa community in Binga District; Matabeleland North Province, Zimbabwe. *The International Journal of Business Management and Technology*, Vol. 1(1): 51–56.
Mutale, Q., Muchinako, G. and Muzingili, T. (2018). Child protection concerns: situation of girls in fishing camps in Binga, Zimbabwe. *Journal of the Social Sciences*, Vol. 57(1–3): 1–13.
Mwenesi, C. (2016). Factors influencing fish production among small scale farmers in Kenya: A case study of Hamisi Sub-County. A research thesis of Masters of Arts.
Mwinde, M. (2016). A historical Analysis of Politics of Self Inscription and Struggle for National Identity among the BaTonga of middle Zambezi Valley, Binga in Zimbabwe in the 21st Century. Dissertation submitted to the faculty of arts in partial fulfilment of the requirements of Bachelor of Arts in History Honours Degree.
Neis, B., Binkley, M., Gerrard, S. and Maneschy, M. C. (eds). (2005). *Changing tides: gender, fisheries and globalisation, 307*. Nova Scotia: Fernwood Publishing.
Pomeroy, R. S. (2015). Linking science and people: applying socioeconomic and governance science to solve problems and create opportunities in Caribbean fisheries, in Proceedings of the 67th Gulf and Caribbean Fisheries Institute Conference (Barbados).
Sachs, J. (2005). *The End of Poverty: how we can make it happen in our lifetime*. London: The Penguin Press.
Saidi, U. (2016). Cracking the nonverbal code: Analysing cultural artefacts of the BaTonga in Zimbabwe, [Unpublished PhD Thesis] Midlands State University.
Siabuwa Development Trust. (2011). https://zw.linkedin.com/in/siabuwa-development-trust-57883973
Siwila, L. (2015). An encroachment of ecological sacred sites and its threat to the interconnectedness of the sacred rituals: a case study of the Tonga people in the Gwembe Valley. *Journal for the Study of Religion*, Vol. 28(2): 138–152.

12

NEXUS BETWEEN BORDER (IN)SECURITY AND ECONOMIC DEVELOPMENT IN BINGA DISTRICT SINCE 2000

Teverayi Muguti

Introduction

Border security is essential to the territorial integrity of any nation, with ineffective border security possibly leading to a multiplicity of detrimental activities that can disrupt a country's economic, social and political fabric. Smuggling, poaching, border conflicts, terrorism and other transnational organised crimes are some of the common threats to economic development and political security posed by ineffective border management strategies. At the same time, global trade, inter-state cooperation, tourism and transnational socio-economic relations are positive outcomes of effective border management. Globally, borders are subject to significant political controversies and tensions. There are numerous cases in post-colonial Africa of border-related conflicts, insurgencies and terrorist activities, including borders between Nigeria and Benin, Nigeria and Cameroon, Eretria and Ethiopia (in the border town of Badme), North and South Sudan (mainly in Abyei), Tanzania and Malawi (around Lake Malawi), Kenya and Ethiopia (Al-Shabaab infiltration).

Important scholarly work also exists about the nexus between border security and economic development, including about the history, functions, challenges and future projections of borders in Africa. Much of the literature on African border security focuses on issues such as the artificiality of African borders (Asiwaju 1984; Ikome 2012; Englebert et al. 2002), border disputes (Jackson 2006; Yoon 2014; Babatola 2015), illegal cross-border trade (Matanzima 2021) and migration and smuggling (Pophiwa 2010; Daimon 2016). It tends to concentrate less on covering development in borderlands and, when it does, the focus is on questions around displacement, conflict prevention and post-war reconstruction. There are also useful scholarly works that seek to understand the marginalisation of borderland communities in various African countries, showing how state policy and practices usually

DOI: 10.4324/9781003278580-15

neglect the interests of people residing in the border areas (Flynn 1997; Coplan 2010; Mashingaidze 2013; Zeller 2015; Manyena et al. 2016).

In the Zimbabwean case, the Zimbabwe-South Africa border contributes in important ways to cross-national economic transactions, while also being a hotspot for border security crises over a number of years. Because of the scale of these transactions and crises, the Beitbridge border post on the Zimbabwean side of this border has received significant scholarly attention. This chapter turns our attention to the western part of Zimbabwe by focusing on the Zimbabwe-Zambia border, in particular from the year 2000, in relation to the nexus between border (in)security and economic development. It considers this with specific reference to the Tonga borderland communities residing in Binga District. In this way, the study examines the livelihoods of the Tonga people in the Zambezi Valley through the interplay between border security and economic development.

The lives and livelihoods of Tonga borderland communities in Zimbabwe have been examined by various scholars (Chipere-Ngazimbi 2020; Mashingaidze 2020; Marowa et al. 2021), who interrogate for instance the cross-border economic transactions of the Tonga people, advocacy initiatives amongst the Binga Tonga in reclaiming their identities and human-animal conflicts in the Zambezi Valley. While these and other studies provide important insights into the past and present status of the Tonga (including in Binga) and relate broadly to the focus of this chapter, they are not framed specifically in terms of the nexus between border security and economic development – as this chapter seeks to do through a Binga-based case study.

Research Site and Methods

This chapter focuses on Binga District, located in Matabeleland North Province in the northwest of Zimbabwe, along the Zimbabwe-Zambia maritime borderline (Zambezi River) to understand the complexity of the interplay between border (in)security and economic development for the local Tonga people. There are 25 administrative wards in the Binga Rural District Council (BRDC). The district had an official population of 139,092 in 2012 with a projection of 186,942 people for the year 2021 (Zimbabwe National Statistics Agency 2012, Zimbabwe National Statistics Agency 2020). The district's inhabitants are mainly Tonga people, although there are also Shona, Ndebele and Nambya people residing in the area. Major economic resources in the district include Lake Kariba (water and fish), Chizarira and Chete National Parks, wildlife, forestry conservatives and coal reserves. In relation to border security, the district's boundary with Zambia is characterised by several informal crossing points including Simatelele, Mlibizi, Kaani, Sijarira, Chete, Chibuyu and Mujele.

The qualitative research informing this study was conducted from 2018 to 2021 and I used a mixed-methods approach in collecting the data. Semi-structured interviews were done with a total of 52 interviewees including the District Development Coordinator (DDC), the BRDC Chief Executive Officer (CEO), Zimbabwe National Parks and Wildlife Authority (ZIMPARKS) Area Manager and personnel, Lake Navigation personnel, Communal Areas Management Programme for Indigenous Resources (CAMPFIRE) personnel, fishermen, fishing companies and cooperative owners, Zimbabwe Republic Police (ZRP) officers, BRDC councillors, traditional leaders and 33 ordinary Binga residents. Two focus group discussions were also held with fishermen from various private-owned fishing companies and cooperatives at Chilila harbour and Chinzonzo fishing camp (along Lake Kariba) to obtain a fuller appreciation of their operational environment for fishing in Lake Kariba (which contains within it the Zimbabwe-Zambia borderline).

I also made use of pertinent documents, including government publications (Hansards, Gazettes, Acts of Parliament, etc.), and reports from various government offices as empirical sources. Additionally, the study as well draws insights from real-life observations and ethnographic data collected by the author in his decade-long stay in Binga. The various data-sets facilitated a comprehensive and diversified analysis of the intermeshing changes and continuities with respect to border security and economic development for the Tonga in Binga District. For ethical reasons, I do not reveal the real identities of interviewees because of the sensitivity of some of the security issues discussed. Notwithstanding this observance of confidentiality, some people agreed to have their names revealed.

Border Security in Binga District

The interpretation of what border security entails in the district is configured by anecdotal, social, cultural and professional considerations, among other factors. People from diverse backgrounds in the district have different, though not necessarily competing, understandings of the border security concept. For most Binga residents interviewed, border security is mainly concerned with government's efforts at ensuring the safety of humans and goods as they move to and from Zambia. A senior police officer at Binga Police Station argued that border security encompasses in particular monitoring the borderline to ensure that there is no smuggling, entry by evasion, poaching and stock theft by both Zimbabweans and foreigners. In the end, there is not a monolithic conceptualisation of border security throughout the district.

The differences in the interpretation of border security might mean that some activities characterised as compromising border security by the state may not be for communities living along the border. This is more so considering that the Tonga communities on both sides of the border are kith and kin, separated by the Zambezi River border, which was constructed during colonialism by the formation of Northern and Southern Rhodesia. One ordinary resident noted that, before colonialism, families could settle on whichever side of the river they wished, and they would cross the river without asking for permission from any authority. Moving to-and-fro across the Zambezi River is a social and historical norm for the Tonga communities living on the border margins of what are now Zambia and Zimbabwe. Consequently, border controls which inhibit movement across the Zambezi might be labelled in negative ways by Tonga people in Binga.

Binga District is characterised by the lack of border security infrastructure. Apart from the absence of a properly built and fully constituted border post, the maritime borderline with Zambia itself is not clearly demarcated and visible. This presents challenges for the Zimbabwean state in implementing border policies along the borderline. In an interview, an executive member of the Binga District Residents Association (BIDRA) said that:

> The Immigration Department of Zimbabwe was allocated land to construct a border post by the Binga Rural District in 1998; but, 23 years down the line, the border post is yet to be constructed.

People operating in the river rely on identifiable landmarks such as islands and gadgets such as fish finders to estimate whether they have crossed into Zambia's territory or not. A Lake Navigation officer indicated that houseboat operators mostly use Global Positioning System (GPS) devices in combination with the map charts that show the borderline within Lake Kariba. In a separate interview, a fishing company owner revealed that:

> Fishermen in the river use fish finders which detect the depth of a site in the Lake. Hence, when sailing across Lake Kariba towards the Zambian side, when they reach the deepest point in the Zambezi River, it is imagined that they have reached the border.

The middle or centre of the river forms the boundary between Zimbabwe and Zambia, which conforms to international law governing river boundaries (Le Febvre 2014).

Despite this existing law, it is evident that without visible boundary marks, map charts and GPS devices, it is difficult for ordinary Binga residents to locate the Zimbabwe-Zambia boundary in Lake Kariba. The invisibility of the borderline also means that people operating in the river for survival, mainly fishermen from both sides of the border, are vulnerable to being arrested by law enforcement agencies for illegally crossing the border. The lack of border security infrastructure in the district, therefore, not only adversely affects the implementation of effective border security measures – it compromises as well the livelihoods of Tonga villagers in accessing local maritime resources because of their exposure to trans-border crimes and prosecutions. When the livelihoods of the Tonga community are negatively affected by border insecurity, the economic development prospects of the community are likewise undercut.

The monitoring of the border in Binga District is mainly done by the ZRP which oversees the movement of people and goods. In this respect, the police were for some time issuing border passes for the local Tonga villagers travelling to Zambia primarily for social and cultural reasons. Subsequent to the official opening of its temporary offices in Binga District in March 2020, the issuance of border passes was taken over by the Immigration Department. The border passes are in large part issued to local Tonga residents for visiting their relatives on the other side of the border, in such districts as Sinazongwe and Maamba in Zambia. In doing so, they are only allowed to carry limited groceries to and from Zambia. Those who want to carry substantial quantities of goods have to use the Victoria Falls crossing, the nearest border post where there is a fully fledged border post manned by the Zimbabwe Revenue Authority (ZIMRA) and the Immigration Department, where they undertake their normal customs and immigration duties (Binga ZRP 2019). However, the ZRP's Binga Front Harbour is still in use pending the construction of an official Immigration Harbour in the district along Lake Kariba. There remain other illegal crossing points along the river, from Devil's George to Sengwa River, including in the Mlibizi, Simatelele, Binga Centre, Sijarira, Chete, Chibuyu and Mujele areas.

Other stakeholders actively involved in border security are the Lake Navigation Department, the ZIMPARKS, the Forestry Commission, the Judicial Service Commission, the President's Department and the Zimbabwe National Army. Joint patrols along the river are undertaken by the security forces from the various Zimbabwe national security institutions in Binga District, as they monitor activities along the river. But, one police officer revealed that:

> The joint patrols are inconsistent and irregular due to lack of resources such as boats and fuel.

In addition, some critical service characteristics of official border posts (such as health clearance and revenue collection) are not found in the district's current border security mechanisms. Agencies such as ZIMRA, Medicines Control Authority of Zimbabwe, Plant Protection Inspectorate and other government border agencies usually found at fully established border posts in Zimbabwe are not operational in the district.

Bilateral meetings between Zimbabwean and Zambian security services take place at least twice a year to discuss mainly border security issues along the border-line (Binga ZRP 2019). A senior police officer at Binga Police Station indicated that the heads of Binga Police Station (Zimbabwe), Maamba Police Station (Zambia) and Sinazongwe Police Station (Zambia) give each other a daily update on cross-border crimes and other incidences along and in Lake Kariba in their respective areas of jurisdiction. Thus, updates on such crimes as poaching, entry by evasion and smuggling are shared among the three police stations. While many government agencies are involved in monitoring security in the district, the police and ZIMPARKs are visibly the most important regarding the Zimbabwe-Zambia border.

Border security in Binga District also incorporates the safety of humans on transit across the river. All legalised transporters which move people across the river are small-engine fibre boats which are not safe for transporting large numbers of people. An official from the Lake Navigation Department highlighted that canoes are used as well as a mode of transport by most illegal cross-border travellers. He added that canoes are very risky as they can be overturned by animals such as crocodiles and hippos. Further, the border in the district is used by human traffickers to smuggle people from other countries destined for South Africa, where they engage in various illegal activities such as robbery and commercial sex work. In 2017, a Zimbabwean man smuggled 12 Ethiopians from Zambia through Binga en-route to South Africa, but he was later arrested in Gwanda after police investigations. The lack of proper infrastructure at the Binga borderline thus exposes people to danger and encourages illegal human trafficking.

Additionally, the safety of humans in Binga is compromised by armed robberies which usually take place in Lake Kariba and the district's Kaani ward. In a discussion with fishermen who catch *kapenta* in the Lake, usually during the night, reference was made to their exposure to armed robberies from Zambians, who steal boat parts (such as alternators), *kapenta* and other personal belongings. A Zimbabwean policeman noted that the relaxed ammunition policy in Zambia in comparison to Zimbabwe's firearms regulations allows for a relatively higher number of ordinary people in Zambia owning guns. Overall, then, the Zambian-Zimbabwean border in Binga is characterised by cross-border crimes that are harmful to personal security in diverse ways.

Economic Development in Binga District

Like in the case of border security, the concept of economic development in Binga District is interpreted by people in different ways and conditioned by personal, professional, social and cultural backgrounds. A cross section of Binga residents interviewed pointed to the lack of an effective road network, inadequate health and education infrastructure and insufficient cellular network coverage as characteristics showing that Binga District is not yet economically developed in comparison to other districts in Matabeleland North Province and Zimbabwe in general. Other authors have brought this to the fore as well (Matanzima and Saidi 2020; Chipere-Ngazimbi 2020; Mutale 2018). While there are variances in the understanding of economic development in the district, the concept is generally understood as a condition in which most citizens are well fed and free from hunger and starvation, have access to efficient transport and communication services as well as good education and health services and are able to access job opportunities and empowerment projects.

For Mashingaidze (2013), the lack of development in Binga District is attributable ultimately to the colonial government's Kariba Dam-structured displacements and the subsequent failure by the post-colonial government to redress the challenges. The construction of the Kariba Dam between 1955 and 1959 undercut the Tonga people's thriving social and economic practices that were built around the Zambezi River (Muwati 2015). Besides displacing the Tonga without any compensation, the colonial government did not carry out environmental, social and economic impact assessments before the hasty forced relocations of Tonga people to the dry, infertile and tsetse fly infested, but wildlife rich, adjoining upland plateaus. As such, the current development status in Binga is traceable to the failures of both colonial and post-colonial government administrations spanning more than six decades.

Presently, Binga District is dominated by the fishing industry which involves catching mainly *kapenta* and larger fish (such as breams) through gillnetting as well as rod and line fishing. By 2019, the district had about 60 private companies and 30 fishing cooperatives with a total of 157 fishing rigs (fishing vessels) involved in *kapenta* fishing in Lake Kariba (Binga ZIMPARKS 2019). Tourism also forms one of the core economic activities of the area as visitors from other parts of Zimbabwe and foreign countries want to enjoy cultural tourism, trophy hunting and boat cruising in the waters of Lake Kariba (BRDC 2019). As well, the district has wildlife conservancies including the Chizarira National Park, Chete National Park, Sijarira Forestry, Kavila Forestry and Mzola Forestry. These areas contain wildlife such as elephants, buffaloes and rhinos. Overall, these areas contribute economically to the district in terms of tourism, timber and ivory.

At the same time, as Mashingaidze (2013) demonstrates in relation to the colonial period, Europeans monopolised the exploitation of the fishery and tourism businesses around the Kariba waterscape as well as the safari hunting operations in Binga District. Then, after the attainment of the country's independence in 1980, "well-connected Ndebele and Shona peoples gradually substituted Europeans as the major beneficiaries in the exploitation of Zambezi Valley's natural wealth" (Mashingaidze 2013: 382). Current discourses in terms of benefitting from both the fishing industry and tourism are characterised by an outcry from the local Tonga people over the lack of a deliberate government policy to empower them to own fishing and tourism companies.

The district's benefit from wildlife is partly structured through community management of wildlife under the BRDC, through the six CAMPFIRE hunting concessions which have animals such as elephants, lions, buffalos, hippos and crocodiles. These concessions cover a total area of about 7,698 square kilometres and they are situated in areas bordering national parks and forestry areas in the district. In Zimbabwe, generally, CAMPFIRE has been cast as an antidote to the colonial legacy of technocratic and authoritarian development which had undermined local people's control over the environment and criminalised their use of wild animals (Alexander and McGregor 2000). However, in the case of Binga District, just like many other districts in the country, the proceeds of CAMPFIRE are not completely utilised for the benefit of ordinary people in the community due to variegated reasons. There is anecdotal evidence of the benefits in the many wildlife producer communities being manipulated by local elites for their individual advantage (Frost and Bond 2006). In Binga District, CAMPFIRE has been beset with challenges including destruction of crops by animals, a flawed contract system, lack of transparency in the disbursement of dividends, corruption, poaching and lack of community proprietorship over wildlife (Manyena et al. 2013). Thus, the existence of CAMPFIRE projects in the district does not automatically translate into a vibrant economic development base for the borderland communities.

In terms of agriculture, the district is mainly arid and there are deficient crop production activities with the exception of the southern part (Lusulu area) where there is relatively comprehensive grain and cash-crop production compared to the northern parts of the district. Due to the persistent drought and hunger in the district, Binga is characterised by the large-scale presence of Non-Governmental Organisations (NGOs) ranging from 15 to 20 each operational year, mainly involved in food distribution and livelihoods programmes. Binga also has yet-unexploited coal reserves in the Lubu (Ward 11), Lubimbi (Ward 20) and Lusulu areas, giving the district a significant potential for economic development in the event that extraction of such resources commences. Despite all the economic resources, activities and potential, Binga District faces important economic development challenges such as lack of social services (including health), water insecurities and poor road and communication networks.

Border Security and Economic Development in Binga District: The Nexus

There are several overarching ways in which border (in)security and economic development are intertwined in borderland communities in Zimbabwe and perhaps the world over. In this last main section, I analyse the complexities of the linkages between the two variables and how they shape trends in the everyday lives of the Tonga in Binga communities.

Ineffective Border Security Leads to Rampant Pilfering of Resources Out of the Country

The lack of border infrastructure and efficient border security services along the Zimbabwean-Zambian border in the district causes many illegal activities that lead to the outflow of national and local resources. These resources would otherwise be harnessed to contribute meaningfully to both national coffers and community economic development. Poaching, cattle rustling, smuggling of wildlife resources as well as theft of private property by complex syndicates involving Zambian nationals and local accomplices who stay in Binga are some of the cross-border crimes that effectively lead to the loss of economic resources from the district.

Between 2001 and 2018, for instance, a total of 42 poaching cases were reported at Binga Police Station (Binga ZRP 2019). A total of 120 elephant tusks were recovered mainly in Binga in areas such as Sinakoma (Ward 5), Sinansengwe (Ward 4), Sianzyundu (Ward 9) and Siachilaba (Ward 10) (Binga ZRP 2019). The total value of these tusks is around US$600,000. An analysis of the criminal records at Binga Police Station involving big-game poaching shows that more than 50% of them are committed either by Zambian nationals or unknown culprits. These unknown culprits could either be Zimbabweans or Zambian nationals. The fact that some culprits are unknown might also indicate the presence of well-placed actors in the poaching syndicates who can easily manipulate weaknesses in the border security mechanisms to evade the law. This insinuates that even security personnel in the various security institutions in Binga District may be involved in the syndicates committing cross-border crimes including poaching. Other police stations operating in the district, such as Siabuwa, Lusulu and Kamativi police stations, have recorded poaching cases as well, although at varying rates. There is a possibility that most of the poaching cases in Binga go undetected by security apparatuses due to the porosity of the border.

According to an interviewed prison officer, these syndicates entail well-connected linkages to Harare (Zimbabwe), Lusaka (Zambia) and Kinshasa (Democratic Republic of Congo). Consequently, there are likely numerous undetected cases of big-game poaching in the district which have resulted in the growth of a sophisticated network of illicit transnational trade of wildlife products, mainly ivory, involving various nationals (Zimbabweans, Zambians and Congolese, among others), and fuelled by ineffective border management strategies in Binga District. Thus, substantial amounts of money that could be generated from wildlife proceeds, either for the national fiscus through the ZIMPARKS or the local authority through CAMPFIRE game, are lost through poaching activities in Binga. However, the lost wildlife proceeds would not directly translate necessarily into an improvement of the Tonga community's livelihoods because it is not obvious that the revenue generated would be ploughed back into the community. This is because it is the BRDC, through CAMPFIRE, that administers the game royalties on behalf of the community, while the ZIMPARKS revenue is channelled straight to the national state's coffers which use the finances as it deems necessary. Through illicit trading networks, though, the contribution of wildlife to Binga community development is adversely affected, hence undermining the country's prospects of improved economic development.

There are also high levels of poaching of *kapenta* along the Zambezi borderline in Lake Kariba. Of the 527 people arrested for entry by evasion from 2001 to 2018 (as per the records of Binga Police Station), 273 people were arrested while involved in *kapenta* fishing on the Zimbabwean side of the lake. This number translates into 51.8% of the illegal entry cases recorded at the station, showing that fish poaching is one of the main reasons why Zambians cross the border illegally into Zimbabwe. The trend at the Zimbabwean-Zambian borderline shows that it is the Zambians who encroach into Zimbabwean space more than the Zimbabweans do on the Zambian side. This is mainly due to the depletion of *kapenta* on the Zambian side of Lake Kariba over the past few years. The depletion of *kapenta* is attributed to Zambian legislation on fishing which is relatively less strict than the Zimbabwean legislation In an interview, one ZIMPARKS ranger revealed that, in Zimbabwe, there is a policy of one permit per three fishing vessels while, in the case of Zambia, one permit has no limit on the number of fishing vessels owned by the fishing permit holder. He added that:

> This situation effectively results in a lot of fishing vessels involved in fishing on the Zambian side of the Lake as compared to those operating on the Zimbabwean side of the border.

Another ZIMPARKS official also revealed that the recommended fishing nets in Zambia have smaller mesh sizes, thereby catching all *kapenta* fish sizes. He contrasted this to the recommended meshes for fishing nets in Zimbabwe, which are much larger to give leeway for smaller fish to survive. A fishing company owner further highlighted that, though Zimbabwe has breeding areas designated by the ZIMPARKS, Zambia has no designated fish breeding zones in the lake. Thus, the Zimbabwean laws governing the fishing industry are more conservative and relatively more sustainable in terms of ensuring fishing stocks, in comparison to the Zambian fishing regulations.

However, this does not exonerate the Zimbabwean fishermen from fish poaching, as they are also in the habit of fishing at undesignated and breeding areas to increase their monthly output of *kapenta*. In this sense, fish poaching is one of the means to survive in the fishing industry by fishermen from both sides of the border. Effective security-monitoring of the maritime border would help prevent fish poaching by both Zimbabweans and Zambians along the Zambezi borderline. Meanwhile, the overall result of border insecurity in Binga is that fishermen take advantage of the situation to catch fish in breeding and undesignated areas in both Zambia and Zimbabwe. The Chairman of the Binga Fisheries Association (BFA) emphasised the importance of the fishing industry in Binga, as it contributes to household income for owners of *kapenta* fishing companies and employment for the *kapenta* fishermen, as well as to the prevalence of formal and informal groceries and clothing businesses dotted around the district. This highlights that the fishing industry has a potential for transforming lives in Binga not only amongst the fishing communities but also for those involved in upstream and downstream sectors. Yet, the lack of effective border security measures to reduce *kapenta* and larger fish poaching negatively affects the production rates of the mainstream fishing industry in Binga District, with this fishing industry being central to Binga livelihoods.

Stock theft in the district results in the loss of economic resources to areas in both Zimbabwe and Zambia. The areas characterised by high rates of stock theft in the district are mainly those close to the Mlibizi and Simatelele border crossing points. These include Sianzyundu, Saba, Siachilaba, Bulawayo Kraal and Simatelele. The recorded cases at Binga Police Station (Binga ZRP 2019) show that most of the culprits for this crime are unknown. A police officer based at Binga Police Station said that the high number of cases with unknown suspects makes it very likely that the perpetrators are Zambian nationals or syndicates involving both Zimbabwean and Zambian nationals. The statistics show that 78 out of 100 (78%) of the stock theft cases reported at Binga Police Station from 2001 to 2018 had unknown culprits. By far, most stock stolen were either cattle (648) or goats (554). Of those arrested, 18 were Zimbabweans and 11 were Zambians (Binga ZRP 2019).

Most of the cattle are taken to Zambia via the Mlibizi area where the Zambezi River is narrow in comparison to the other crossing points along the Lake. The cattle are simply driven on the hoof across the river to the Zambian side of the border. The value of cattle lost in the recorded cases amounts to an average of US$16,900 per year from 2001 to 2018 (Binga ZRP 2019). Considering the importance of cattle in African culture, the loss of cattle in Tonga households – mainly due to cross-border cattle rustling – entails a hard blow to the household economies affected. Emphasising the importance of livestock in a debate in parliament, Chikanga-Dangamvura House of Assembly legislator, Prosper Chapfiwa Mutseyami noted: "You remember that in this country, the culture that we have is that livestock is part of our wealth. Livestock is part of what we use whenever we have problems" (Zimbabwe Parliamentary Debates National Assembly Hansard 2016: 31).

The cattle losses also dissuade villagers who would otherwise want to invest their savings in cattle, for they find it a risky exercise due to the threat of cattle rustling. Senator Tambudzani Mohadi expounded on the importance of cattle in rural economies during a separate Senate debate in 2016, when she said: "When you look at areas like Beitbridge which is in region five, who solemnly rely on livestock and their livestock being stolen in large quantities, you find those people will remain poor" (Zimbabwe Parliamentary Senate Hansard 2016). Binga, like Beitbridge, is also in the agro-ecological region five farming zone where crop production is deficient due to low rainfall patterns; hence there is a greater reliance on livestock production. For Tonga villagers, and others, livestock provides a coping mechanism regarding various financial shocks and stressors in rural livelihoods. The insecure character of the Zambia-Zimbabwe borderline in the district largely fuels the occurrence of cattle rustling to Zambia.

The anti-personnel zone along the Zambian-Zimbabwean border in Binga contributes to the porosity of the border especially regarding cattle rustling. The history of landmines dates to the days of the war of liberation during the 1970s in colonial Zimbabwe when the Rhodesian Army laid mines on the borders with neighbouring countries particularly Zambia and Mozambique (Zimbabwe Parliamentary Debates National Assembly Hansard 2016). The primary objective of the mine-planting exercise was to prevent incursions into the country – by the Zimbabwe National Liberation Army (ZANLA) in launching its attacks from Mozambique and Zambia and the Zimbabwe People's Revolutionary Army (ZIPRA) in the case of Zambia. The Zimbabwe-Zambia border contained key crossing points used by ZIPRA liberation war fighters to enter Rhodesia and the Rhodesian regime used landmines to protect the borders against ZIPRA incursions. The Zimbabwe Parliamentary Debates National Assembly Hansard (2016) reveals that the Victoria-Mlibizi area had been successfully de-mined and was ready for economic utilisation, but the Binga communities were still experiencing major challenges.

In an interview, one resident in the Saba community revealed that most cattle in Mlibizi and adjacent areas are lost because the local cattle owners are not able to follow the trails as they fear being harmed by antipersonnel landmines in the Mlibizi minefield, despite the area being demined. He added that the cattle rustlers, including both Zimbabwean and Zambian criminals, were able to pass across the minefields as they had mastered the particular routes that are relatively safe to drive the cattle (through to Zambia), unlike the cattle owners. As such, the cattle rustlers capitalise on the ordinary Binga people's fear of passing through the former anti-personnel minefields. While the colonial government used landmines as a border security mechanism against ZIPRA's liberation war fighters, the current effects of landmines on the household wealth of the Tonga community are detrimental due to loss of cattle – thus compromising Tonga livelihoods and economic development prospects in the district in general.

Armed robberies and theft of boat equipment, telephone copper cables and electric appliances, mainly by Zambians, are some of the other cross-border crimes that also affect the district. Consequently, along the borderline, a wide range of the district's economic resources illicitly find their way to the other side of the border due to diverse border security flaws. Thus, ineffective border security in the district leads to rampant pilfering of economic resources from Binga and Zimbabwe at large.

Ineffective Border Security Negatively Affects National Revenue Collection

The Zimbabwe-Zambia border in the district is characterised by activities that deprive revenue inflow to the national coffers due to lack of border security infrastructure and services. Apart from the pilfering of resources through smuggling out of the country, a considerable number of goods which should be taxed (via customs duty) to generate income for the national exchequer are being illicitly brought into Binga and elsewhere through the porous Zambezi River. Informal cross-border traders based in Binga and various cities and towns in Zimbabwe (including Harare, Bulawayo, Gweru and Kwekwe) are involved in smuggling goods for their informal businesses. A notable case, for example, was brought before the Binga Magistrate Court in September 2017 where a syndicate of five men were arrested by the police at Tobwe Fishing Camp (Simatelele) for smuggling assorted goods worth US$15,970.53 (Binga Magistrate Court 2018). The goods involved bales of second-hand clothing, footwear, skin lightening chemicals and sexual enhancers. In their mitigation during the court ruling, the syndicate members indicated that they had avoided using the Victoria Falls border post to evade high customs taxes charged by ZIMRA.

The tendency to avoid official border posts in Zimbabwe is a broader coping mechanism used by cross-border traders in reaction to government border legislation. In 2016, for instance, the government of Zimbabwe introduced Statutory Instrument 64 (SI 64) of 2016 aimed at reducing imports while promoting growth of local industries to boost economic growth in the country (Zimbabwe Parliamentary Senate Hansard 2016). Debating on the utility of SI 64, Senator Tambudzani Mohadi argued that, in response to the introduction of SI 64, cross-borders used undesignated border areas for smuggling instead of proper border posts despite the fact that the latter are typically quite porous (Zimbabwe Parliamentary Senate Hansard 2016). As it has several informal border crossing points, Binga is a hotspot for smuggling goods to and from Zambia.

Meanwhile, one fishing company owner highlighted that the smuggling of goods, especially bales of second-hand clothes, disrupts the fishing industry in Lake Kariba as some shrewd fishermen are hired by smugglers (informal traders) to carry contraband instead of engaging in the fishing of *kapenta*. To the informal traders, the major advantage of using fishing rigs is that they are not usually searched by the security forces, as the assumption is that the rigs will be solely engaged in *kapenta* fishing, as one cross-border trader claimed in an interview. The involvement of the fishing vessels in the smuggling business means that the main economic activity in the district (fishing) is dwarfed by illicit activities along the border. Besides affecting fishing company's output, smuggling also negatively impacts the ZIMPARKS revenue inflow as low catches of *kapenta* are usually associated with backlogs in payment of ZIMPARKS fees by fishing companies. Thus, smuggling has implications for both local fishing companies operating in the district and national revenue collection for various government departments.

The absence of a fully fledged operational border post in Binga, including with government agencies involved in revenue collection, health and security, among others, makes it impossible for Tonga villagers to use the nearby border for legally moving goods to and from Zambia. Legal cross-border trade becomes simply impossible for Binga people, thereby reducing the utility of this trade as a livelihood means for local communities.

Poorly Economically Developed Border Communities and Border Security

Binga District is characterised by low levels of economic development in terms of, for example, household livelihoods and an acute shortage of basic social service infrastructure (for health, education water and sanitation). Lack of economic development, mainly at a household level, drives Tonga people in Binga to engage in activities that compromise the border security of the country.

An analysis of the court cases recorded at Binga Magistrate Court involving poaching and smuggling, for instance, shows that most accused persons cited unemployment and lack of income-generating projects as the reasons why they took part in cross-border crimes. For example, two women who were found guilty of contravening Section 182 (1) of the Customs and Excise Act (Chapter 23: 09 "Smuggling") in March 2016 revealed that they smuggled solely for improving their livelihoods. The case involved 870 kilogrammes of mealie meal (with a total market value of US$91,50) which were bought in Zambia for resale at Mujele Fishing Camp in Luunga (Ward 1), Binga (Binga Magistrate Court Records 2018). One of the women pleaded with the court that she supported both her elderly mother and her own children through informal trade and that, should she be imprisoned, the whole family would suffer (Binga Magistrate Court Records 2018). One pastor also revealed that most local people do not report poaching cases because, even though the poachers take away the elephant tusks, the villagers are able to scramble for the elephant meat for relish for meals. This makes poaching cases at times go unnoticed by the security institutions in the district. Thus, collaboration between Tonga people and foreign poaching syndicates is made possible by the "benefits" obtained by locals from poaching activities, which means that weak household economies indirectly promote border insecurity in Binga District.

The lack of border security in Binga District also indirectly affects the development of vital infrastructure such as the road network. One resident argued that, if the district had a fully functional border post, the Binga-Siabuwa-Gokwe gravel road would be tarred by now. He further claimed that the refurbishment of the Bulawayo-Plumtree Road and the Harare-Mutare road as well as the current efforts by the government to rehabilitate the Beitbridge-Nyamapanda road can only be explained by the importance of the border posts connected to these roads. Thus, the deficient infrastructural development in the district, at least in terms of roads, interfaces with border posts in minimising the extent of local economic development. This is yet another example of the nexus between border security and economic development in Binga.

The lack of agricultural productivity in the district, mainly in areas close to the Zambezi River, can be contrasted to the more agriculturally productive borderlands in Zambia such as Sinazongwe District, and this poses challenges for both economic development and border security in Binga. An agricultural extension officer argued that the reason why agricultural productivity continues to be low in Binga, especially in Binga North constituency, is because local people do not actively take part in government initiatives to improve crop production. He added that, while the government annually provides support through free and subsidised farming inputs (namely, crop seeds and fertiliser), most people in Binga resell the inputs in Zambia as well as people from other places in Zimbabwe such as Chinhoyi and Harare. The smuggling of fertiliser to Zambia has been characteristic of the district over many years, thereby negatively affecting agriculture amongst the Tonga.

Conclusion

The Zimbabwe-Zambia borderline in Binga District is a typical African border that is characterised by rampant illegal cross-border activities which have dramatic implications for both local communities and the national economy at large. Poaching, entry by evasion, smuggling and cattle rustling are some of the cross-border crimes that are found in the district, involving wide syndicates comprising ordinary people, criminals and security personnel from both sides of the border. Lack of border security infrastructure and services fuel the spread of most of these border crimes in Binga. Overall, the flaws in border security in the district negatively impact the Tonga's borderland community livelihoods and economic development. Clearly, the border security-economic development nexus in Binga District is quite dynamic in how it affects Tonga community livelihoods. By showing how cross-border crimes such as entry and exit by poachers and cattle rustlers are shaped by, and shape, the low level of economic development in Binga

District, it becomes evident that ineffective border security management strategies in Binga are both a cause and a product of the lack of economic development. Thus, in general, effective border security enhances economic development in the borderland communities and the country in general, while sound economic development of a borderland community is key to the implementation of border security mechanisms by the state.

References

Alexander, J. and McGregor, J. (2000). Wildlife and politics: CAMPFIRE in Zimbabwe. *Development Change*, Vol. 31: 605–627.

Asiwaju, A. I. (1984). *Artificial boundaries*. Lagos: Lagos University Press.

Babatola, J. E. T. (2015). *Challenges on Nigeria Borders and Frontiers Security, 1960–2014*. Ekiti: Ekiti State University.

Binga Magistrate Court Records (2018).

Binga Rural District Council (BRDC), BRDC Records (2019).

Binga ZIMPARKs, Fishing Permits Records (2019).

Binga ZRP, Criminal Records (2019).

Chipere-Ngazimbi, M. (2020). Invisible – visible borders between Zambia and Zimbabwe along the Zambezi Valley: Tonga fishermen, cross-border livelihoods and monetary practices. In C. C. Nshimbi and I. Moyo (eds), *Borders, mobility, regional integration and development: issues, dynamics and perspectives in West, Eastern and Southern Africa*. Chan: Springer. https://doi.org.10.1007/978-3-3-030-42890-7-8

Coplan, D. (2010). Introduction: from empiricism to theory in African border studies. *Journal of Borderlands Studies*, Vol. 25(2): 1–5, doi: 10.1080/08865655.2010.9695757

Daimon, A. (2016). Commuter migration across artificial frontiers: the case of partitioned communities along Zimbabwe-Mozambique border. *Journal of Borderland Studies*, Vol. 31(4): 463–479.

Englebert, P., Tarango, S. and Carter, M. (2002). Dismemberment and suffocation: a contribution to the debate on African boundaries. *Comparative Political Studies*, Vol. 35(10): 1093–1118.

Flynn, D. K. (1997). "We are the border": identity, exchange and the state along the Benin-Nigeria border. *American Ethnologist*, Vol. 24(2): 311–330.

Frost, P. G. H. and Bond, I. (2006). *CAMPFIRE and payments for environmental services*. London: International Institute for Environment and Development.

Ikome, F. N. (2012). Africa's International Borders as Potential Sources of Conflict and Future Threats to Peace and Security. Institute of Security Studies Paper No. 233.

Jackson, S. (2006). Borderlands and transformation of war economies: lessons from DR Congo. *Conflict, Security and Development*, Vol. 6(30): 425–447.

Le Febvre, R. K. (2014). Interests and identities in peace negotiations: Nigeria, Cameroon and the Bakassi Peninsula. *African Social Science Review*, Vol. 6(1): 83–94.

Manyena, B. S., Collins, A. E., Mudimba, F. and Mudimba, D. (2013). "Are you serious to ask me about who owns wildlife?" Politics of autonomy over wildlife resources in the Zambezi Valley, Zimbabwe. *Forum for Development Studies*, Vol. 40(1): 87–109.

Manyena, B. S., Collins, A. E., Mudimba, F. and Mudimba, D. (2016). Reducing marginalisation of fisherman through participatory action research in the Zambezi Valley, Zimbabwe. *International Journal of African Development*, Vol. 3(2): 5–22.

Marowa, I., Matanzima, J. and Nhiwatiwa, T. (2021). Interactions between humans, crocodiles, and hippos at Lake Kariba, Zimbabwe. *Human-Wildlife Interactions*, Vol. 15(1): 212–227.
Mashingaidze, T. M. (2013). Beyond the Kariba Dam induced displacements: the Zimbabwean Tonga's struggles for restitution, 1990s–2000s. *International Journal on Minority and Group Rights*, Vol. 20: 381–404.
Mashingaidze, T. M. (2020). The Kariba Dam: discursive displacements and the politics of appropriating a waterscape in Zimbabwe, 1950s–2017. *Limina Journal of Historical and Cultural Studies*, Vol. 25(1): 1–15.
Matanzima, J. (2021). Lived experiences of cross – border traders: the case of Kariba. In K. Helliker, S. Bhatasara and M. K. Chiweshe (eds), *Everyday crisis – living in contemporary Zimbabwe*. New York: Routledge, pp. 143–154.
Matanzima, J. and Saidi, U. (2020). Religious rituals and socio-economic change: the impact of the Zimbabwe "cash crisis" on the BaTonga masabe (alien spirits) ceremony. African Identities. doi: 10.1080/14725843.2020.1811673
Mutale, M. (2018). Challenges and opportunities of information and communication technologies (ICTs) in Binga District, Zimbabwe. *African Journal of Social Work*, Vol. 8(2): 55–62.
Muwati, I. (2015). Negotiating space, voice and recognition: an analysis of the "district song" of the Tonga people of Binga, Zimbabwe. *Muziki, Journal of Music Research in Africa*, Vol. 12(2): 22–36.
Pophiwa, N. (2010). Mobile livelihoods – the players involved in smuggling of commodities across the Zimbabwe-Mozambique border. *Journal of Borderlands Studies*, Vol. 25(2): 65–76.
Yoon, M. (2014). Colonialism and border disputes in Africa: the case of the Tanzania-Malawi dispute over Lake Malawi/Nyasa. *The Journal of Territorial and Maritime Studies*, Vol. 1(1): 75–89.
Zeller, W. (2015). *What makes borders real in the Namibian – Zambia and Uganda – South Sudan borderlands*. Helsinki: Department of Political and Economic Studies.
Zimbabwe National Statistics Agency (2012). Zimbabwe Census National Report.
Zimbabwe National Statistics Agency (2020). Matabeleland North Province District Population Projections Report.
Zimbabwe Parliamentary Debates National Assembly Hansard (2016). The National Assembly, Vol. 42, No. 35, Motion on the Report of the Portfolio Committee on Defence, Home Affairs and Security Service Report on Landmine situation in Zimbabwe, Tuesday 16 February 2016.
Zimbabwe Parliamentary Senate Hansard (2016). Motion on the Report of the Thematic Committee on Peace and Security on the State of the Country's Borders, 20 July 2016.

INDEX

For Product Safety Concerns and Information please contact our EU
representative GPSR@taylorandfrancis.com
Taylor & Francis Verlag GmbH, Kaufingerstraße 24, 80331 München, Germany

www.ingramcontent.com/pod-product-compliance
Ingram Content Group UK Ltd.
Pitfield, Milton Keynes, MK11 3LW, UK
UKHW020202200926
475702UK00004B/580

* 9 7 8 1 0 3 2 2 4 4 3 2 7 *